Warpath and Council Fire

CHEYENNE WARRIOR ROMAN NOSE AND SIOUX CHIEFS

Left to right: Spotted Tail, Roman Nose, Old-Man-Afraid-of-His-Horses, Lone Horn, Whistling Elk, Pipe, Unknown. Taken at Fort Laramie shortly before the death of Roman Nose. This picture, (probably the only one of Roman Nose) so far as is known, has never appeared before.   (See Chapter 12, Page 129.)

Warpath and Council Fire

The Plains Indians' Struggle for
Survival in War and in Diplomacy

1851-1891

By Stanley Vestal

RANDOM HOUSE · *New York*

TO

MY COUSIN

JAMES D. MCCOID

COMPANION IN

MY RESEARCH AMONG

PLAINS INDIAN

WARRIORS

Table of Contents

Contents

Illustrations

Maps

PREFACE

THE LAST bloody battle of the Indian Wars was yet to come when, after a world-wide inspection tour in the late 1880's, Lord Wolseley, then Commander-in-Chief of the British Army, declared in no uncertain terms that, man for man, the little United States Army was the best in the world. That Army had been whipped into shape by nearly forty years of fighting Plains Indians.

Three times in our history an American military force has been utterly wiped out by its enemies. Every time, those enemies were Sioux. Other Plains tribes fought quite as well, and the officers who faced them through the campaigns of forty years have testified abundantly to the Red Men's superlative soldiership. Custer praised their "individual daring," their tactics, and their horsemanship as the best in the world. Major Walsh of the Royal Northwest Mounted Police declared them "superior to the best English regiments." One of General Crook's staff officers described them as "the finest light cavalry in the world." General Charles King rated them "foemen far more to be dreaded than any European cavalry." Colonel Ford called them "the finest skirmishers." Major Anson Mills declared, "Their like will never be seen again." General Frederick W. Benteen summed it all up in the words, "good shots, good riders, and the best fighters the sun ever shone on."

These officers all heartily agreed with George Washington's statement in his official report after Braddock's defeat: "Indians are the only match for Indians." No wonder that the troops which finally—with Indian assistance—subdued such warriors were recognized as "the best in the world."

The Plains Indians put up a great fight, inflicting five casualties on the troops for every one they suffered, and winning most of the battles, though they lost the war—forced to surrender at last by the destruction of their commissary, the buffalo herds. And the best of them were also no mean diplomats. This book is the story of their struggle, in war and in diplomacy, to keep their country from the whites.

Probably no American now wishes to give the Plains back to the Indian, though many have an uneasy feeling that the Indian has received a raw deal. Yet it may be argued: (1) that we legally acquired the Plains country by purchase from the French and by cession from the Mexicans; (2) that, at the time of the Louisiana Purchase (1803), many of the Plains tribes had not yet occupied the lands which we afterward paid them for; (3) that the Indians themselves had acquired their lands on the Plains by the recent conquest of weaker tribes; (4) that the Indians had acknowledged our supremacy in repeated treaties and afterward rebelled against it; (5) that in spite of having acquired title to the Indian lands from powers which had previously held them, our government also paid the Indians for the lands it took and has since spent huge sums for Indian relief, free education, medical care and other benefits; and (6) that the result has been a loyalty to the United States on the part of our Indians far more complete even than that of the Filipinos.

When World War II began, the Sioux thronged the recruiting stations. They regarded conscription as an insult. "Since when," they demanded, "has it been necessary to draft a Sioux to fight?" It is the boast of the Southern Cheyennes that not a man of them was drafted; every Cheyenne in war service was a volunteer. So with other tribes. The Plains Indians understand war. They know all about teamwork for victory. In the old days they listened skeptically to white men who called them "Brothers," and the wars dragged on. But once the white man invited them to fight in his Army, peace was soon established. To the Plains Indians the word "Brother" had no meaning until it meant "Brother-in-Arms." The history of their struggle on the warpath and in council is a great American story.

But there is another reason why we today should find that story gripping. It is a little mirror of ourselves and of our government at work in international affairs. We can learn much from looking into it. For there, in a small frame, are all our typical virtues and follies, our failures and triumphs, our successes and mistakes. From that mirror we can learn what to expect and hope for, what we must fear and avoid in future international relations.

Three times (1865, 1918, 1945) the United States has emerged from a major war as a first-rate power. Every time we have behaved after the war like a third-rate nation, bringing difficulty or disaster upon all within reach of our influence.

After the Civil War, in which both sides can feel a solemn pride, we stooped to Reconstruction in the South, and all the needless horrors of the Indian Wars. After World War I, a struggle until then unequaled in heroism, we permitted the festering mess in Europe, the collapse of the League of Nations, a world-wide depression, and the rise of totalitarian tyranny. After unparalleled achievement in production and global combat in World War II, we again squandered our strength by reckless demobilization, plunged greedily into inflation, appeased our avowed enemies, and neglected our responsibilities to a world sunk in famine and despair.

Hitler thought us a peaceful people who could not make war. History shows us a business-like people who cannot make peace. Will Rogers put it aptly: "The United States never lost a war or won a conference."

The day has gone by when we can afford to behave like that. It is high time we took stock of our follies and failures, and brought our methods, as well as our purposes, up to a standard on a level with our destiny. A look at the handling of the Plains tribes during their forty years' war may do us that service and so spare us many a headache in the future. For, though we are now so powerful and so rich, we belong on this globe to a minority. We had better be watching our step. The next time we have war within our borders, we shall not be fighting a handful of redskins armed with bows and arrows. Though, few as they were, they put up a terrible scrap!

STANLEY VESTAL

Warpath and Council Fire

I

WAR ON THE PLAINS

Warpath and Council Fire

It was late summer on the Great Plains. All the principal tribes living between the Yellowstone and Arkansas Rivers, between the Missouri River and the Rocky Mountains, were gathering at Fort Laramie for the great treaty council of 1851. The whole valley between the Fort and the encampment of the United States Dragoons was thickly studded with vast, smoke-browned tipis, lodges sheltering thousands of warriors and their families.

Fort Laramie stood in the midst of the hunting grounds of the allied Sioux, Cheyenne, and Arapaho, who were present in great numbers. But there were also large bands of the Assiniboine, Crow, Mandan, Hidatsa, and Arikara. That these camps filled the valley, their countless ponies covered the hills around. It was the largest assemblage of Indians in the history of the Plains.

Their chiefs had pledged a truce for the duration of the encampment. But the Dragoons and Mounted Rifles—less than three hundred in number—knew themselves helpless to keep the truce among those warlike thousands. In fact, they knew that they could not even hope—if attacked—to save themselves. The Commissioners were eager to get the council over and the treaty signed. But nothing could be done until long

1

WAR ON THE PLAINS

It was late summer on the Great Plains. All the principal tribes living between the Yellowstone and Arkansas Rivers, between the Missouri River and the Rocky Mountains, were gathering at Fort Laramie for the great treaty council of 1851. The whole valley between the Fort and the encampment of the United States Dragoons was thickly studded with rakish, smoke-browned tipis, lodges sheltering thousands of warriors and their families.

Fort Laramie stood in the midst of the hunting grounds of the allied Sioux, Cheyenne, and Arapaho, who were present in great numbers. But there were also large bands of the Assiniboine, Crow, Mandan, Hidatsa, and Arikara. Their thronging camps filled the valley; their countless ponies covered the hills around. It was the largest assemblage of Indians in the history of the Plains.

Their chiefs had pledged a truce for the duration of the encampment. But the Dragoons and Mounted Rifles—less than three hundred in number—knew themselves helpless to keep the truce among those warlike thousands. In fact, they knew that they could not even hope—if attacked—to save themselves. The Commissioners were eager to get the council over and the treaty signed. But nothing could be done until long-

3

delayed wagons, bringing presents and provisions for the Indians, rolled up the Platte into sight.

One bright day about noon, the Dragoons, looking west from their camp toward Laramie Peak, saw a long line of dust rising from the overgrazed hills beyond the river. "Boots and Saddles" sounded, and by the time the troops were mounted, they could see on that high prairie a long line of warriors moving slowly forward in battle array, and behind that a compact ruck of pack horses and travois, women and children bringing up the rear, well guarded. Chief Washakie rode a short distance in advance, and behind him the broad line of his mounted warriors, dressed in their colorful war costumes, chanting their martial song, rode fine war horses, making a grandly savage appearance.

Every man of those Snakes or Shoshones had a good rifle. They came boldly on toward the camp of their enemies, where the Sioux alone outnumbered them five to one.

By the time the Snakes reached the brow of the hill overlooking Laramie River, not a mile away, all the Indians in camp had swarmed out of their lodges to watch. Here and there some Sioux or Cheyenne woman wept and howled in anguish for relatives killed in battle by the warlike Snakes. Whatever their chiefs might say, it was hard for those Sioux warriors to hear the wailing of their women and still keep their hands off the arrows in the quivers on their backs. One Sioux was unequal to the strain.

The Snake chief began to ride slowly down the hill. Just then that Sioux warrior recognized him as the very enemy who had killed his father. Heedless of danger, the vengeful Sioux jumped on his horse, bow in hand, and sped away to attack.

As one man the Snakes halted and set up a wild shout of defiance. Their chief rode forward still, deliberately raising and cocking his gun, ready to fire. After that one shout, the self-reliant Snakes stood their ground, firm and silent, not even the women and children making any stir or outcry.

The troops were too far off to interfere. It seemed certain that rash hothead would attack, be killed, and so bring on a general war, ending all hopes of a treaty.

But one of the interpreters, a Frenchman, expecting trouble, had kept his eye on the Sioux. Now he too was in the saddle, lashing his horse, racing in pursuit. Slowly he gained on the trouble-maker. Already the Snake chief was taking aim at that reckless Sioux. But before his finger pressed the trigger, the Frenchman overtook the hothead, grabbed him by the shoulder, jerked him from his horse, and, as he staggered to his feet, knocked the bow from his hand and stood over him.

The Snakes held their ground. The angry Sioux was led back to camp.

Jim Bridger, trader and interpreter for the Snakes, saw it all. He declared the brave Frenchman had saved that Sioux "from hell. My chief would 'er killed him quick, and then the fool Sioux would 'er got their backs up, and there wouldn't have been room to camp 'round here for dead Sioux. You Dragoons acted nice, but you wouldn't have had no show if the fight had commenced—no making peace then. And I tell you another thing: the Sioux ain't goin' to try it again. They see how the Snakes are armed. I got them guns for 'em, and they are good ones. . . ."

Not one out of a hundred Sioux had guns.[1]

That threatening incident is a parable of what followed— the eternal enmity between the warlike tribes on the Plains, the inadequacy of the white men's forces, the inability of chiefs to control trouble-makers—and the truce which immediately followed the discovery by the hostiles of the superior armament of their enemies.

The real concern of Uncle Sam in 1851 was to keep Indians from attacking white men passing through their country—"to keep the road open" to Oregon, Salt Lake, and California. To do this meant maintaining an effective control over every tribe through whose domain the road passed. Such control could be assured only by vigorously supporting in good faith, and with a show of ample force, those chiefs and tribes who were friendly to the whites.

For war was the mainspring of Plains Indian civilization. To have any property, authority, safety, prestige or following —even to marry—a Plains Indian had first to distinguish himself on the warpath. Personal vengeance was a religious duty and a social obligation. Moreover, war was the Indian's only way of getting something for nothing.

Hunting was his business, a drudgery which he never engaged in for fun; war was his principal amusement, sport, and speculation. Moreover, for him the change from peace to war was only the work of an instant. He had no problems of reconversion. The tools with which he earned his living were the weapons he used in his wars. Any Indian, when affronted, was likely to change from a killer of buffalo to a killer of men at a moment's notice. To prevent such men from fighting was then as difficult, under their laws and customs, as it would be in our time to keep Americans from trying to make money— or Russians from forming conspiracies. Already most of these tribes had had trouble with white men, and were chronically at war with each other.

The first article of the proposed treaty provided that the Indians should agree to abstain in future from all hostilities against each other, to maintain good faith and friendship in their mutual intercourse, to make an effective and lasting peace among themselves. Eastern humanitarians and pacifists may have hoped that the redskins would not break this pledge, but surely few who knew the Plains and the warlike character of the Indians there could have had any firm expectation that it would be kept.[2]

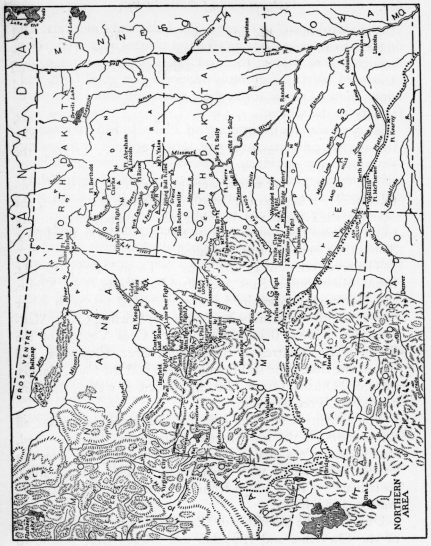

RANGE OF THE NORTHERN PLAINS INDIANS
AND ADJACENT AREAS
Present state boundary lines are shown for the convenience of
the reader.

For generations the implacable, aggressive Blackfeet and their only allies, the thieving Atsina or Big Bellies (Gros Ventres of the Prairie) had been fighting the Cree, Assiniboine, Sioux, Crow, Flathead, Nez Percé, and Kutenai tribes—and such hapless white men as came among them.

Their neighbors, the feckless Assiniboine or Stone Boilers, though few in number and friendly with the Cree, continually had to defend themselves against the Sioux or Dakota, the Blackfeet, and the Cheyenne.

The Crow, farther south, were good fighters, expert horsethieves. They had no consistent friends but the Kiowa, the Mandan, the Hidatsa and the white men—and not infrequently robbed them. They were forever fighting with the Blackfoot, Sioux, the Cheyenne and Arapaho.

The seven tribes of Prairie Sioux or Teton Dakota (Oglala, Brûlé, Minniconjou, Sans Arc, Blackfoot Sioux, Two Kettle, and Hunkpapa) maintained almost perpetual war with white men and with the Assiniboine, Shoshone, Pawnee, Crow, Mandan, Ree, Kiowa, Blackfeet, Flathead, Gros Ventres of the Prairie, Gros Ventres of the Village, Cree, Chippewa, and Comanche tribes, and still found time to raid the Iowa, Kansas, Missouri, Omaha, Osage, Oto, and Ponca, as well as the Bannock, Nez Percé, and Ute.

The haughty Cheyenne tribe habitually fought against all the enemies of the testy Sioux, against the Mexicans—and, after the early '60s, against the whites. The easygoing Arapaho usually went along with their Sioux and Cheyenne allies, though taking most scalps from the Shoshone, Ute, Pawnee, Navajo, and whites.

Until 1840 the bloodthirsty Kiowa had been mortal enemies of the Cheyenne and Arapaho, and always were hostile to the Sioux. They were forever raiding southward into Old and New Mexico, killing more white men in proportion to their small numbers than any other tribe.

Their allies, the Kiowa-Apache, called Bad Hearts or Thieves, were so few they inclined to peace, but perforce joined the Kiowa in their sanguinary wars.

The predatory Comanche were allied with their relatives, the Ute and the Shoshone, and friendly with the Kiowa. They were long hostile to, but after 1840 friendly with, the Cheyenne and Arapaho. But for 200 years they had regularly raided far to the south of their home range, killing and robbing Spaniards, Mexicans, and Texans with complete impartiality.

All this, also taking account of inveterate feuds between minor tribes, totals almost 100 chronic intertribal wars. And, of course, when known enemies were not available for scalping, any passing stranger might serve to supply the hair.

In the face of such an array of bitter tribal enmities, many of them centuries old, it was hardly to be expected that peace would come to the Plains through the mere flourish of a pen.

Even so, the balance of power on the Plains might have remained fairly steady but for the coming of the white man with his deadlier weapons, his wagons, his liquor, his diseases, his greed—and his good intentions.

Emigrants heading for Oregon and Salt Lake had disturbed the tribes along the trails and had given them a bad name in the States. Epidemics of smallpox and cholera had already destroyed fully half the Indians on the Plains. The Forty-Niners, one hundred thousand strong, pouring through the buffalo pastures, had cut down the scanty timber, burned off the grass, and swept the game away, turning that great hunting ground along the Platte into an empty desert. Everyone saw that the government must take a hand, and in 1849 Fort Laramie had been purchased and garrisoned.

To make this treaty, the government had enlisted the services of the most influential white men on the Plains. And so the Indians, little as they cared for peace, had followed the advice of the beloved Black Robe, Father De Smet, of Jim Bridger, and of many another trader and official, and had gathered at Laramie to hear the words of the Great Father.

"The Indian Department had become a great branch of the political machine, large amounts of money were appropriated, growing larger annually, and it must be spent. There were many beneficiaries interested—manufacturers of Indian goods, merchants, freighters, officials and hangers-on in large numbers. Whether it led to tragedy or ended in a farce, here was a well-laid plan, with the largest assemblage of Indians ever gathered at one council or on one treaty ground." [3]

But, as old warriors put it now, with a nostalgic smile, "Plains Indians will always be fighting; they are like two mean dogs. If you catch them fighting, you can drag them apart; but as soon as you turn them loose, they will go right back to fighting again."

Still the wagons did not come. All the grass for miles around Fort Laramie had been grazed and trampled to dust by Indian ponies. The bulging parfleches of dried meat in the lodges grew flat and empty, and dogs by the hundred went into the kettles of the hungry Indians. The Commissioners decided to move Indians and troops to a better camping ground, thirty-four miles down the North Platte, where Horse Creek comes in from the southwest.

There they could put the troops and the Snakes on one side of Horse Creek and the Sioux on the other. There everyone could camp within easy reach of water and plentiful grass.

So they all packed up and marched downriver to the treaty ground.

There in September, 1851, our wars with the Plains Indians began with a great Peace Conference, full of warm good will and excellent intentions: they ended not far off—after nearly forty years of bitter fighting—with the massacre at Wounded Knee.

2

PAPER PEACE

WHEN the signal cannon roared next morning, the chiefs
assembled at the council house, followed by their delegations.
There an ominous thing happened.

A prolonged discussion took place as to the precedence and
seating of the various nations. The Sioux, being most numerous, insisted upon having the place of honor. The Cheyennes,
basing their claim on deeds of valor, would not yield. And the
other nations all put in bids for the chief place. At last, in
despair, the Commissioner arbitrarily settled the matter, and
indicated the section to be occupied by each nation.

Immediately a new wrangle began, for in each nation were
several tribes and bands, all of which had some claim to consideration, and all of which desired the first rank. The Commissioner settled this dispute in the same manner, arbitrarily.

But then began a third palaver as to the relative rank and
merits of individual chiefs and braves within each tribe or
band. This was a thorny problem, bristling with personalities.
Two men might have the same number of *coups*, but were
they first *coups*, or seconds, or mere fourths? Was a wound
more creditable than a captured weapon, or a rescue better
than a stolen horse? It began to look as though the council
could never be seated. But at last the Commissioner intervened
a third time and seated them all without regard to rank.

I I

That little comedy was portentous. But the Commissioners ignored it.

Only the head men of the Indian nations entered the circle of shelters erected for the council. The Sioux, Cheyennes, Assiniboines, Shoshones, Arikaras, Gros Ventres, Mandans, and Arapahoes seated themselves in that order about the central arbor. In it Colonel D. D. Mitchell, Superintendent of Indian Affairs, and Major Thomas "White Head" Fitzpatrick, Indian Agent, the two Commissioners, presided. Along with them sat Father Pierre-Jean De Smet, military officers, sub-agents, journalists, traders, and interpreters. These were joined by the wife of Lieutenant Elliott of the Mounted Rifles, the only white woman in the encampment. Everything was conducted with the gravity and decorum characteristic of old-time chiefs in council.

After smoking together, proceedings began with a speech from Colonel Mitchell. He said he spoke for the Great Father at Washington: "We do not come to you as traders; we have nothing to sell you, and do not want to buy anything from you. *We do not want your lands*, horses, robes nor anything you have; but we come to advise you, and make a treaty with you for your own good. . . ."

Mitchell promised compensation for the losses of the Indians caused by emigrants passing through, but insisted on the right to establish military posts and such other posts as the Great Father might deem necessary. He also wished to establish the boundaries of the various tribal domains, though "in doing this it is not intended to take any of your lands away from you, or to destroy your rights to hunt, or fish, or pass over the country, as heretofore. But it will be expected that each nation will be held responsible for depredations committed within its territory, unless it can be clearly shown that the people of some other nation committed them, and then that nation will be held responsible. . . . The nation will be held responsible for the acts of its people."

Mitchell went on to explain the terms of the proposed treaty and ended by assuring the Indians that their presents and provisions, long delayed, were soon to be expected. He gave them one day to think the matter over.

The council was concluded after one of the chiefs, having promised to do his best to satisfy the Grandfather in Washington, rather touchingly expressed the hope that "he will send us more buffalo."

It was a hard task the Colonel had assigned those chiefs. Heretofore, some of the tribes had had no chiefs, and had been ruled by the Warrior Societies—as, in fact, were those who had long had chiefs. And now these figureheads found themselves expected to assume an authority and responsibility such as no Indian chief had ever dreamed of.

The chiefs sincerely wished for peace; they were too old for the rigors of the warpath. How pleasant to sleep soundly, never to worry over the safety of women and children, nor to have to watch the horses in the night! They wanted trade with the whites and other tribes. If some way could be found to keep other Indian tribes out of their hunting grounds, they were quite willing to be friends with them. But, as one chief put it, "War is indispensable. Of course, we lose a few men every year, but so do our enemies. If we smoke with them, they will crowd into our hunting grounds, and we shall starve. Anyhow, I don't believe that our old enemies will keep the peace, if we make it. They cannot be trusted, and then we shall be blamed for fighting. . . ."

However, the Indians agreed to make the best of that.

The second point—the white men's demand to be allowed to build roads and forts in Sioux country—was a great difficulty. That was hard to grant. Roads meant more trouble, more hunger for the Indian. In fact, it was a road—the Oregon

Trail—that had caused all the trouble which made *this* treaty necessary, and now—instead of closing that road—the Grandfather asked them to let him make certain others. That might mean starvation. Yet the Sioux were eager for peace; they had confidence that the Grandfather would not let them down. They conceded the point.

The payment of damages to Indians for white depredations was all very well, but how catch the criminals? And as for turning over Sioux criminals to the white men—that *was* a problem. What chief would dare do it? It was contrary to custom. No chief had ever turned over a Sioux to another nation. If he did, the man's relatives would probably kill the chief. Yet this might never happen; they risked this point, also.

Boundaries of the various nations were readily settled. Their boundaries were clearly marked—by the graves of their young men.

But the great crux came when they considered the demand of the Commissioner that they should elect one chief for the whole nation. That was staggering! One chief who would be responsible to the Grandfather at Washington, one chief whom all the Sioux would obey! That was a glittering ambition, indeed, a dream, an impossibility—like the United States of Europe, the League of Nations, the Federation of the World!

The Sioux government really existed only for the duration of some emergency, and as soon as that emergency was ended, it automatically ceased to be. And it was local government, intensely so. What a problem the Commissioner had set those new-fledged chieftains!

If all the Sioux could have agreed upon a chief, he could not have enforced his sway over that great, far-flung people.

The organization of the Sioux nation reminds one irresistibly of the man who was going to St. Ives. Seven (or more—usually many more) family tents made one band; seven bands made one tribe; seven tribes made one grand council fire;

seven grand council fires made up the Sioux nation. The area occupied by all these scattered groups, each with its own local and independent government, was about that of the State of Texas. How could such a population (each unit entirely self-supporting)—speaking three different dialects, part Christian, part pagan, part tame, part wild—agree upon one man to lead them? How could such a man, if chosen, manage to enforce the treaty clauses upon bands which had only a distant rumor of his name? There was no machinery for such enforcement, even had the chief been acknowledged.

From the beginning the white men consistently confused the hereditary chieftaincies of the American Indian with the monarchies of Europe. They called chiefs "kings"—King Philip, King Massasoit—and held them responsible for matters over which they had no control whatever. No chief ever held more than a personal authority, a personal prestige, and this was endangered every time he failed in an enterprise or disregarded the wishes of his people. He could not tax, or imprison, or punish his people. Such discipline as there was lasted only while a ceremony or a hunt, or some other public business, was going on. And the chief's duty was that of a mouthpiece, a spokesman, an arbitrator. He was supposed to keep the peace, adjust disputes, and provide for the common defense. He was supposed to see that the people had enough to eat. He was helpless to cross public opinion. The Indians obeyed literally the scriptural injunction: *If any man be great among you, let him be your servant.*

The real power of the Prairie nations lay in the Warrior Societies, and a chief could do nothing with them when their blood was up. They had magnificent *esprit de corps*, and on occasion they even fell upon their chiefs and flogged them severely, as happened to the Keeper of the Cheyenne Medicine Arrows, in 1838.

The Sioux had been doing as they liked for too many generations to submit readily to dictation. They could never act together in large numbers. They were as touchy as so many Irishmen, and had a perfect genius for disintegration. By 1851, the Sioux nation had already sloughed off the Oto, Osage, Ponca, Iowa, Winnebago, Omaha, Quapaw, Crow, Hidatsa, Kaw, and Assiniboine tribes, not to mention long-lost relatives in North and South Carolina and in Mississippi. Already the Western (Teton) Sioux felt themselves almost a distinct nation, and looked with contempt upon the Santee Sioux and other groups to the east of the Missouri River, who had knuckled under to the white man, and had even adopted some of the customs of their bitter enemies, the Chippewa.

And so it was with other tribes.

Therefore, the Commissioner was asking an impossibility. Chief Red Horn expressed his misgivings in these words: "All our people are not here. Some of them are out west hunting in the mountains. There is no use trying to do anything until they all come back."

What wonder that, when the council met again, the spokesman of the Sioux declared, "We have decided differently from you, Father, about this chief for the nation. We want a chief for each band, and if you will make one or two chiefs for each band, it will be much better for you and the whites. Then we will make soldiers of our young men, and we will make them good to the whites and other Indians. But Father, *we cannot make one chief.*"

That treaty of 1851 was probably the fairest ever made with the Prairie Sioux. Everyone present was full of good will, and no shady tricks (which later became so common) were used in order to induce the chiefs to sign. Yet their spokesman insisted, *"Father, we cannot make one chief."*

There were too many candidates.

But the Commissioner would not be balked. He named a chief himself, Mato-wa-yuhe, Stirring Bear, or Bear that

Scatters, translated in the newspapers of the time as Frightening Bear. Then he railroaded through a unanimous vote from a constituent assembly, organized like an American legislature, each member representing a certain number of lodges.

Stirring Bear was overwhelmed. "His nomination was wholly unexpected, and came upon him like a clap of thunder from a clear sky." The new chief declared that he had no wish to be chief of the nation, that he had not been attending councils, that there were older and wiser men than himself, men who knew the whites better. He said he was just a buffalo hunter, and that—if he had known they intended to make *him* chief—he would never have come to the treaty council.

He foresaw what would happen to the man who assumed such sway over his people: "Father, I am not afraid to die, but to be chief of *all* the nation, I must be a *big chief*, or in a few moons I shall be sleeping [dead] on the prairie. I have a wife and children I do not wish to leave. If I am not a *powerful chief*, my enemies will be on my trail all the time."

Then, in a more manly tone, he went on: "I do not fear them. I have to die sometime, and I don't care when. If you and the Grandfather insist that I become chief I will take this office. I will try to do right to the whites, and hope they will do so to my people. . . . I know the Great Spirit will protect me, and give many spirits of my enemies to accompany me, if I have to die for doing what you and the Grandfather ask."

The electors representing the various tribes and bands were even more reluctant to vote for Colonel Mitchell's dark horse than the chief himself was to accept the post. They palavered with their constituents for well over an hour. Colonel Mitchell had told them that, if they did not like the man nominated, he himself would choose another; if they did not wish to vote for the Colonel's nominee, they might keep their ballot-sticks or give them back. Finally two of the electors, a Sioux and a Snake, walked over and gave the candidate their ballot-sticks.

Reluctantly the others did the same. Stirring Bear was elected.

The band to which this chief belonged was the last to vote for him. He himself threw away his ballot-stick, and refused to accept anything from the presents distributed in the assembly, not even allowing his relatives to partake.

The Commissioner was highly pleased with this arbitrary arrangement. But without an army behind him, no man could be arbitrary with the Sioux and get away with it. The Indians knew very well that this paper chief could not stand, and nobody knew it better than the man himself. In a short three-minute speech he referred to his approaching death no less than six times.

Perhaps he thought the unexampled dignity of being named chief of *all* the Sioux was compensation enough for martyrdom. Earthly glory could no further go. . . .

Between councils, Colonel Mitchell and one of the newsmen visited the Sioux village and witnessed a sham battle staged by a hundred Cheyennes, members of a Warrior Society. The reporter gave considerable space to their organization: "These Soldiers are the young men of the nation . . . formed into companies with a head or principal leader and other subordinate officers. . . . When with the nation, travelling or hunting, they constitute the guard, scouts. . . . They form the war parties, and often go to war upon their own hook, sometimes without the knowledge or consent of the chiefs. They are so numerous, and so well banded together, that *the chiefs can do nothing with them.*"

An accurate observation, which nevertheless seems to have had no influence upon the plans of the Commissioners.

One chief addressed them in derision: "Father, this is the third time I have met the whites. We don't understand their manners, nor their words. We know it is all very good, and for our good, but we don't understand it all. We suppose the half-breeds understand it, and we leave them to speak for us."

An agreement without understanding is only an agreement to disagree.

But the misunderstanding was not all on one side, as is shown by Colonel Mitchell's report on the council: "Fifty thousand dollars for a limited period of years is a small amount to be distributed among at least fifty thousand Indians, especially when we consider that we have taken, or are rapidly taking, away from them *all* means of support, by what may be considered a *partial* occupancy of their soil. On the score of economy, to say nothing of justice or humanity, I believe that amount would be well expended . . . it will in all probability save the country from the ruinous and useless expenses of a war against the Prairie tribes, which would cost many millions, and be productive of nothing but increased feelings of hostility on the part of the Indians, and annoyance and vexation to the Government. . . . Viewing the treaty in *all* its provisions, I am clearly of opinion that it is the best that could have been made for both parties. I am moreover of the opinion that it will be as faithfully observed, and carried out in as good faith on the part of the Indians, as it will on the part of the United States, and the *white* people thereof. . . . Nothing but bad management or some untoward misfortune can ever break it."

But at last the treaty was signed, and the long-delayed wagon train corralled on the dusty, wind-swept plain, while the Indians gathered to receive their presents. Twenty-seven wagons were unloaded, the property stacked in one place. The cannon roared, the Stars and Stripes waved on high, and everybody turned out dressed in his best, to take his place in the immense circle surrounding the goods, the women leading pack mules or horses dragging travois.

First of all, uniforms and swords were given to the chiefs, who struggled into pantaloons for the first time in their lives, and strutted around proud as peacocks, with their long hair floating over the high collars of the new uniforms, and swords banging against their shins. Then the chiefs proceeded to distribute the presents to their people. All went forward without impatience, without apparent jealousy or haste, in decorous silence.

They ate the beef because they were starving. The bacon they burned. The soda and flour they threw away for the sake of the containers. The coffee beans they could use—some of them—but bedticking, thread, and flimsy cotton cloth were of no interest. However, there were plenty of knives, kettles, awls, paints, brass buttons, rings, beads, blankets, and twists of tobacco. The women had so many kettles that nests of them were left behind when the camps pulled out for the forks of the Platte, where fat buffalo were said to be numerous. Packing mules was no pastime, and copper kettles were heavy plunder for a long jaunt. Enough is plenty. And three hundred pounds was about all one travois could carry.

Thus ended the great Peace Conference of the Plains.

From the Indian point of view, the trouble with that treaty at Laramie was the excessive good will exhibited by both parties to the contract. At that time the Indians had not had much experience in dealing with Uncle Sam's Commissioners, and so followed the trail of the idealistic Father De Smet—at that time almost the only white man on the Plains for whom they had any deep affection or respect. Then too, Tom Fitzpatrick was an old mountain man, and with him and Jim Bridger to help, it was not difficult for Colonel Mitchell to talk the Indians into agreements which they would afterward surely regret and feel compelled to repudiate.

The Indians had an uneasy feeling that the council had not been conducted properly. They themselves never went at a treaty in any such way. What, they felt, was more ridiculous than benevolence when driving a bargain?

A bargain that is not fair to all concerned is a swindle. And so any treaty which does not take fully into account the powers which are factors in it and the interests which are at stake is a travesty, a fraud, and a scrap of paper. Bargaining must be realistic.

Peace cannot be imposed by paper agreements on men whose interests are in conflict. Peace between nations can exist only when there is a community of interest, or—what is more often the case—when those who want peace are stronger and better armed than those who want war. A community of interest will produce order, peace and co-operation which may or may not be put into written agreements. But a written agreement can never produce peace, order or co-operation unless a community of interests already exists. Understanding does not necessarily imply good will.

The Plains Indians understood this perfectly. When two tribes met to make peace with each other, they spent the time bragging on themselves and insulting the other party for all they were worth. This served the triple purpose of letting off the steam of ancient grudges, satisfying the ego of the boasters, and testing the seriousness of those who sought peace. The old men say, "We knew that if our enemies did not want peace bad enough to put up with our insults for even one day, the peace would never stick."

FIRST BLOOD

Peace on the Platte did not last long.

In June, 1853, the Indians gathered about Fort Laramie to await the arrival of their agent, Tom Fitzpatrick, and their annuities. There was a large camp of Oglala Sioux and another of the Brûlé tribe, in which were camped some forty lodges of visiting Minniconjou, a total of some 600 lodges, more than 1000 warriors. Fort Laramie was manned by a company of the Sixth Infantry, about fifty men, under a first lieutenant. In those days there was no briefing of a force sent into unfamiliar country, and probably not a man on the post knew anything about Indians and their ways.

The soldiers had a skiff on the river, which they used as a ferry, and this strange craft fascinated the Indians.

One day a visiting Minniconjou Sioux wished to cross the stream with the soldier who was using the boat. Neither knew the other's language, and when the Indian tried to get into the boat, the soldier roughly repulsed him. Knowing nothing of Indian ideas of personal dignity, he may even have laid hands on the insistent warrior before he shoved off.

At any rate, as the foolhardy soldier gained the opposite bank, the Indian fired at him.

It was a purely personal quarrel, and the soldier was unhurt.

Moreover, the treaty (Article 4) expressly provided that the Indians themselves were to "make restitution for any wrongs committed by any band or individual of their people" and (Article 6) that "all national business will hereafter be conducted" through the "head chiefs," and bound the United States government "to sustain said chiefs and their successors during good behavior." There was no provision in the treaty which could authorize an officer to arrest or punish an Indian.

But the commanding officer had issued an order that no one should fire a gun near the post "lest alarm be created among passing emigrants." Accordingly, Lieutenant H. B. Fleming took a small detail into the camp of the local Oglala Sioux, and demanded the man who had fired the gun. Of course, he had skipped, and the local Indians could not produce him. An Indian gun popped off.

Thereupon the Lieutenant, forgetting all about the alarm he might create among passing emigrants, ordered his men to fire into the camp. Most of the Oglala men were away, but the few that were left ran, covering the retreat of their women and children by firing at the troops. Several Indians were killed, but no soldiers. Nevertheless, no immediate hostilities followed. The Oglala rightly supposed that the officer was a foolish young man, and that the Grandfather at Washington was not to blame. They were frightened, of course, and complained that the soldiers who had been sent into their country to keep the peace had been the first to make the ground bloody.

Some Cheyennes, however, who hated the post trader, made this affair an excuse for running off his horses. And so there was ill feeling on both sides.

The treaty of 1851 had never been ratified, and Fitzpatrick had brought along some proposed amendments in order to get the Sioux to sign. But this time he found the Sioux in an ugly mood. Fitzpatrick, who had not been a mountain man for thirty years for nothing, saw that he must have strong backing. He asked the commander of some Mounted Rifles, then passing the fort, to stay in camp until his council was over. But even with Mounted Rifles at his back, Fitzpatrick could not persuade the chiefs to sign "another lying paper." Spurred by the anger of the relatives of the five slain Indians, the chiefs demanded that the troops be withdrawn. In his report Fitzpatrick pointed out the great folly of putting a handful of foot soldiers, under green officers, in the middle of thousands of seasoned, resentful, mounted warriors. It was like setting half a dozen turtles to watch a thousand hares.

Still, the Sioux chiefs were anxious to keep the peace. And so, in the summer of '54, when an Indian shot a worn-out, abandoned cow, to get a piece of rawhide which he needed, the Brûlé Sioux chief, Stirring Bear, immediately reported the matter to the post commandant, and asked for soldiers (according to the treaty) to go with him and arrest the guilty man. Hearing of this, the emigrant who had abandoned the cow returned to the post and put in a claim, hoping to get a little cash from the government. As before, the offending Indian was a visiting Minniconjou, not a member of the local camp. But the commandant rightly estimated that the cow was worthless, and paid small attention to the matter.

One of the officers at the post, however, took a very different view. He was a young second lieutenant named J. L. Grattan, just out of West Point, of Irish ancestry, chock-full of fight, wholly ignorant of Indians and of Indian warfare, but bursting with eagerness to show his mettle. He had come West to kill Injuns, and often threatened those about the post; he also made fun of emigrants who feared the redskins.

When some Cheyennes ran off a bunch of the post interpreter's ponies, a civilian party pursued them but gave up when the Cheyennes stopped to stand them off. Grattan ridiculed the citizens. "He declared that all Indians were cowards, and that with ten soldiers he could whip the entire Cheyenne nation, while with thirty he would make all the tribes of the Plains run." [1]

Grattan begged so hard to be allowed to go after the man who had killed the cow that Lieutenant Fleming, then in command of the post, reluctantly consented.

Grattan's orders were strictly limited and directed that the Indian was to be arrested only "if practicable and without unnecessary risk." But no sooner had he got his orders than he seemed to lose his head. He called for volunteers "for dangerous service," took ten more men than he was authorized to take, and two howitzers, and headed for the Brûlé camp, nine miles upriver. He told the men at the fort that he was going "to conquer or die" and marched away, evidently believing a dead cow sufficient excuse for launching an Indian war.

At the camp, he talked for some time with the chiefs, Stirring Bear and Man-Afraid-of-His-Horses, who could not produce the Minniconjou at the moment, and begged him to wait until their agent could come and settle the matter. Stirring Bear offered good horses in payment for the worn-out cow and promised to make all amends possible. Man-Afraid-of-His-Horses offered the Lieutenant a mule if he would only wait until Fitzpatrick showed up.

The drunken half-breed acting as Grattan's interpreter continually abused and threatened the Sioux, so that many were frightened and believed that Grattan was determined on a fight. The Minniconjou who had killed the cow was in the Minniconjou camp, and though unwilling to give himself up to unknown punishment, declared he was willing to die where he stood. He told the chiefs to take the other Indians away and leave him to face the music alone.

All the chiefs asked was to postpone the matter. But Lieutenant Grattan would not listen. He went back to his thirty men. They fired into the camp and shot down Stirring Bear, the very chief who had first reported the killing of the cow.

That was a little more than the Brûlé were prepared to stand. They immediately attacked Grattan's force, which retreated and ran into the Oglala, who were coming to join the fray. In a few minutes, Grattan and his thirty men were all dead. Not a single man escaped the Sioux arrows.

Afterward, the Indians began to loot the store of the unpopular trader, but made no attack upon the Army post. Stirring Bear, badly wounded though he was, stopped the looting and posted a guard of warriors to protect the trader's goods.

The officers of the post later testified that Grattan had exceeded his authority and was responsible for the tragedy. But the newspapers in the East had by that time inflamed public opinion. Misled by the false stories in the newspapers, the public demanded reprisals. Meanwhile, Stirring Bear died of his wounds.

The Indians, of course, had no newspapers. Had they been wiser, they would not have accepted annuities when they "touched the pen." A controlling interest in the New York *Herald* would have been far more valuable to them.

Had they had it, they might have published their own story of the "Grattan Massacre," a story which is in substantial agreement with the findings of the War Department—after the mischief was done.

Until March 3, 1849, when Congress created the Department of the Interior (or "Home" Department, as it was called at first), the Army had handled Indian affairs. Not without reason, it was proud of its record for honesty, efficiency, and for promptness in putting down Indian uprisings. Naturally enough, the War Department resented the transfer of the Indian Office to civilian hands and was eager to put its own finger back into the pie.

Colonel William S. Harney was sent to "punish" the Sioux. When he arrived on the Platte, he repeated the conduct of

Fleming and Grattan, but with better luck. Not being able to find the "murderers" of Grattan, he pitched into the first Sioux he could find (and, of course, only friendly Indians would ever allow themselves to be found), killed a lot of innocent people, destroyed their camp, and carried off seventy women and children. Harney himself, in his own report, admits that these people at Ash Hollow were blameless, and says, "If it had been any other band it would have been the same." He was no hair-splitter when it came to killing Indians: he killed them quite impartially. Ignoring the provisions of the treaty of 1851, which provided for damages for depredations, he declared to the chiefs in council, "We will have blood." Whose blood hardly mattered.

This sort of thing was repeated with tiresome regularity on the Plains. It was nearly always impossible for the troops to find the hostiles, and always easy to reach friendly bands. It happened, as we have seen, twice at Fort Laramie; again when Harney attacked Little Thunder's band at Ash Hollow, 1855; at Sand Creek, 1864; in the Baker fight on the Marias River, 1870; and on Powder River, March 17, 1876. Indians have been much criticized for taking vengeance on innocent parties, but the troops consistently did the same thing.

When the Hunkpapa Sioux, away to the north on Grand (Ree) River, heard what had been happening on the Platte, they made up their minds that the soldiers could not be trusted, and that any Sioux who would voluntarily go and camp in their neighborhood was a fool.

They themselves, now that the white men had broken the treaty, committed a few depredations around Fort Clark, and finding a trader's wagon with some Rees whom they were after, broke it to pieces. But they were much too busy with their old tribal wars to give more than a passing thought to the Long Knives at that time.

Colonel Harney's attack on Little Thunder's camp struck

terror into the Southern Sioux. Therefore, when "White Beard," as they called him, demanded the "murderers" of Grattan, five young men rode into Fort Laramie, dressed in their war clothes for burial, singing death songs. Two of them, Red Leaf and Long Chin, were brothers of the dead chief Stirring Bear, whom Grattan's men had killed. Stirring Bear had met the fate he foresaw when appointed head chief of all the Sioux at the treaty council of 1851. Two others of the five young men, Red Plume and Spotted Elk, offered themselves in place of the two who could not come in. The fifth was Spotted Tail, afterward the well-known chief and ally of the white men, who, as a friend, was to be murdered in his turn.

But "White Beard" was not content. He sent out runners asking the chiefs of all the Tetons to a council at Fort Pierre, at the mouth of the Bad (Teton) River on the Missouri. Little Thunder was anxious to recover his captured women and children, and urged the chiefs to attend. The council was held in March, 1856. In Colonel Harney's verbatim report of the proceedings will be found a complete statement of the views of both parties to the proposed agreement. It gives a very clear picture of conditions at the time.

"White Beard" was a man of impressive bulk, strong character, and intelligence. He held an iron rod over the Sioux, and he knew it very well. They were humble, ready to do what they could to make amends, honestly anxious to keep the peace. "White Beard" began by threatening them with dire penalties. But before he got through he was so impressed by the character and good will of the chiefs that he actually apologized for having attacked Little Thunder's camp!

Yet he began by threatening them. He demanded "the man who killed the cow," the return of the captured horses. He said there must be no more payments to traders to "cover dead white men," swore he would "have blood for blood," and declared, with terrifying emphasis, "Big Head's band shall not live upon the face of the earth!" Vain threat!

Harney was furious with the traders at Fort Clark, who had brought ammunition up the river and afterward brought pressure to bear on the Indians to compel their agent to let them buy it. This, after such trade had been forbidden by the Superintendent of Indian Affairs. He accused Peter Sarpy, a trader, of persuading the Ponca to go to war. He proposed that thereafter all traders must remain near military posts, so that they could no longer act as "fences" for property stolen by the Indians, sell liquor or ammunition, or foment intertribal wars. He proposed to settle the Indians on reservations, put them to farming, give them annuities in payment for their lands.

But his most original proposition was to appoint chiefs for every band, who should command organized companies of Indian policemen, with uniforms and arms issued by the United States. These chiefs and these police he proposed to back up with the authority of the Army, which was also to supervise the issue of annuities. The Sioux themselves had proposed this very plan during the treaty council at Laramie in 1851.

A good plan—if it could have been carried out. But the United States government, having been created in fear of tyranny, was too full of checks and balances to permit any one department to manage the Indians. The War Department was balked by the Indian Bureau, which in those days filled its posts with political appointees, who went to the Indian country determined, as a rule, to enrich themselves from the Indians' annuities. For many years it was a tug of war between the Army, with its talk of "wars of extermination," "nits make lice," "the only good Indian is a dead Indian," and the Indian Bureau, with its humbug of "progress" and "humanity," concealing a long and almost uninterrupted series of frauds. From the point of view of the Indians, it was generally a toss-up as to whether the Army was to kill them, or the Indian Bureau was to rob and starve them. However, an impartial compromise was effected, so that these enterprises were attempted alternately and in rotation. No real attempt was ever made to put Colonel (later General) Harney's scheme into operation.

The chiefs also had their grievances, and felt that "White Beard's" demands were too hard. They had tried to keep peace. The Yankton chief, Struck-by-the-Ree, explained that when one of his young men had killed a white man, he himself had killed the offender. Long Mandan had done the same in two instances, in punishing mere insults. And Bear Ribs I, the Hunkpapa chief, who spoke for the delegation, mildly rebuked Colonel Harney for his bloodthirstiness, reminding him that when the whites killed Bear Ribs' brother, he had let it pass. That put Harney in a corner: he had to confess that he was not as great a chief as Bear Ribs, for *he* could not forgive wrongs done to the Grandfather at Washington.

The chiefs complained that the white soldiers had not protected the "good" Indians, as promised in 1851; that they were starving; that their agents stole everything, and that their traders had been taken away. To his proposals that they assist him in rounding up the Sioux criminals, they replied, "All of us here don't wish and don't pretend to fight our brothers." It was impossible for Sioux to fight Sioux. But Harney insisted that the chiefs control their young men, and that—if their enemies would not keep the peace—they must fight them. Another war to end war!

The chiefs' cry was, *"Help us to do what you want us to do!"* Said one, "I was so hungry that when I saw your cattle I could not help eat them, and that's what kept me alive." Said another, "I am a man, and I am not going to beg for my life." Another—with regard to the Indian agents sent out from Washington: "You pick out the poorest man you have and send him up here to give us our goods. When an agent comes here he is poor, but he gets rich; and after he gets rich he goes away, and another poor one comes." Another: "You came here and whipped me, and after that you starved me." And Smutty Bear had a laugh at the expense of the elaborate pretenses of the Indian Bureau. Said he, "The chief on the Platte told me I would be like a white man; but he told me a lie, for I am not like a white man yet."

The Colonel's most startling proposal was that the Sioux aid him by catching deserters from the Army. He offered a reward for each deserter brought in. And when a chief suggested that the deserter might shoot him if he tried to make the arrest, Harney replied, "You must shoot him first, and if you kill him, you shall have the reward by telling me where he lies."

Colonel Harney saw clearly that what was needed in the Sioux country was a strong, organized government, with the backing of the United States Army. For a long time the Sioux nation had been falling to pieces of its own weight and size, and this had been hastened by the conflict of authority. Every trader had some reliable warrior in his pay to protect his wares, and this warrior was given a medal and a paper stating that he was a chief. The Indian agents, in order to protect themselves, also gave medals and commissions. The military officers at the various posts were accustomed to do the same thing. And even missionaries played politics sometimes, for reasons best known to themselves. In every tribe there was therefore a considerable number of men who claimed to be chiefs, but had not been elected by the nation itself. What wonder that there was confusion!

Harney proposed to remedy this condition by naming more chiefs—of his own! But, like the traders, the agents, and the missionaries, he named as chiefs not those who were actually powerful and rightful chiefs, but such as were obedient to his suggestions. And then, to make these paper chiefs weaker than they already were, he demanded that they cast out of their bands all who would not obey them, thus breaking in two the very authority he was trying to create!

In fact, some of the sub-chiefs of each band were really much bigger chiefs than the ones he named as their superiors. Thus, Bear Ribs was made head chief of the Hunkpapa, though Four Horns and three others (not present) were all more important. Fire Heart, named head chief of the Blackfoot Sioux, was certainly less influential than Used-as-a-Shield, the father of the celebrated John Grass, or than High Eagle. However, a great number of the most important men of the Teton Sioux were present, they were under "White Beard's" heavy club, and for the time all went smoothly.

For all that, the Sioux is tough-minded, with an overwhelming sense of reality. Only facts impinge upon his mind. White men might attach great importance to a piece of paper saying that a man was a chief; but unless the Sioux could see that the man *was* a chief, the paper meant nothing.

Probably young Sitting Bull found much food for thought in the deliberations of the chiefs at Fort Pierre. Only one remark of his made at that time has come down to us. After hearing of the frauds of the Indian agents, he said, "I would have more confidence in the Grandfather at Washington if there were not so many bald-headed thieves working for him."

Colonel Harney's council at Fort Pierre in 1856 is well remembered by the Sioux. They respected his common sense and straightforward methods, and more than one old man has told me that "White Beard" (as they call Harney) was the only white man they had ever met who could talk sense or tell the truth, with the exception of Father De Smet. The thing which convinced them of his intellectual powers is a remark he made at that council—a remark not found in the official minutes. (Generally speaking, the most important statements made at Indian councils were usually left unrecorded, it appears!) Harney prophesied that within ten years the Sioux and the whites would be fighting again. Killdeer Mountain and Red Cloud's War were the fulfillment of this prophecy, and old Indians remember it as a true saying. Therefore, of all the soldiers who fought and talked with the Sioux, William S. Harney stands pre-eminent in their memories as a wise man and a soldier.

But the only result of all that talk and fighting was a lot of dead men. Of them all, we may perhaps remember Chief Stirring Bear with most respect and admiration, as one who—for the sake of his people and his own honor—went open-eyed to his death in the endeavor to perform an impossible task. Betrayed by the whites who had promised to back him up, he became a warning to the Sioux who might otherwise have followed his peaceful trail.

But that trail led only to the Indian's grave. Stirring Bear, Bear Ribs, Crazy Horse, Spotted Tail, Sitting Bull, Big Foot, Dull Knife, White Antelope, Yellow Wolf, Black Kettle— they all met violent ends as a result of their making friends with the white man. The white man was more deadly to his friends than to his enemies.

And among the Sioux he had plenty of both.

4

SITTING BULL AND BEAR RIBS

Sitting Bull, though a young man, was already making himself felt as a leader of what we may call the National Party among the Sioux west of the Missouri River. And in the summer of 1857 something happened which gave him an opportunity to take a prominent part in international affairs. He made his first notable speech at this time, a speech which sums up the policy of his faction among the Teton Sioux with admirable clarity.

Colonel "White Beard" Harney had made his treaty with the Sioux only the year before at Fort Pierre, following his victory over them at Ash Hollow in 1855, and had named a number of chiefs of his own selection. Sitting Bull was not one of these, for Harney naturally named men who were most pliant and friendly toward the white man, and Sitting Bull was not the man to serve two masters.

In 1857 Harney was in command of the United States forces sent against the Mormons. His topographical engineer, Lieutenant G. K. Warren, was detached and sent into the Black Hills from Fort Laramie to make a survey of that lovely, and as yet officially unexplored, region. Warren was a man of unusual character and intelligence, a fine type of the scholar-soldier, and was later a general during the Civil War. He and his handful of men ran into a camp of forty Minniconjou Sioux lodges near Inyan Kara Peak.

Those who are acquainted with the peculiar charm of the Black Hills will not wonder that they were the most precious part of the Sioux domain, a region so dear as to be considered sacred, where generations of seers and shamans had climbed the peaks to pray, where game abounded, clear streams slid down between hills clad with white aspens and dark pines, a region believed to be the capital and metropolis of all the Animal People. Nowhere in all the Sioux country are there lovelier pastoral valleys, or peaks which—though imposing—lack so completely the harsh ruggedness and fatiguing scale of the great Rockies farther west. The highest range east of the Rockies, and the most individual, the Black Hills have a feeling all their own, a friendly, homelike feeling, offering rest and comfort. The Eastern ranges of North America, what are they but old men, gracious—but bald? The Western ranges, crude and vigorous in their lusty youth, have not yet shaken down into their mellow maturity. But the Black Hills range has something lacking to them both: of all the ranges in America it is unique—having a quality as of some charming woman, midway between youth and age.

There the Minniconjou were encamped, looking after the great herds of buffalo in the neighborhood, waiting for the animals' pelts to reach their prime condition. Then they intended to make a series of surrounds, kill each herd without alarming the others, and so provide themselves with shelter, clothing, and food for the coming winter. They were, as Warren put it, "actually herding the animals." In former days such methods had not been necessary, but now the buffalo were becoming scarce, and the Southern Sioux had to be careful. If the herds were stampeded, they might run into enemy country, where the Sioux would have to hunt at the risk of their lives. Indian "soldiers" had been put in command of the camp, and had forbidden any Indian to hunt on pain of death, until the tribal hunts were ended. The "soldiers" told Warren that he could not proceed.

Their lives depended upon those bison, and Warren frankly admits that "their feelings towards us under the circumstances were not unlike what we should feel towards a person who should insist upon setting fire to our barns." The Minniconjou could not put up with such sabotage. White men did not understand buffalo, or buffalo hunting; they were careless, wasteful, and stampeded the animals senselessly. Indeed, it was believed that buffalo would never return to a spot where their nostrils had been offended by the smell of a white man. Some of the Minniconjou threatened to kill Warren's men, if he went on. But when Warren reminded them of what Harney had done to Little Thunder's band in 1855, they begged him to take pity on their children. Warren goes on to say, in his report, "it was almost [sic] cruelty to the Indians to drive them to commit a desperate act which would call for chastisement by the government." Few military men in those days were troubled by such humane scruples.

But Warren was a reasonable man, and agreed to wait three days, until Chief Bear Ribs (the head chief appointed by Harney in '56) could get there and talk it over. Meanwhile Warren's Sioux guide became so alarmed that he deserted and camped with his own people. But that was not the most trying thing. Suddenly Chief Four Horns and his Hunkpapa Sioux came dragging into camp—tipis, dogs, kettles, pack mules, and all—and with them a lot of Blackfoot Sioux. Sitting Bull rode with his uncle, Four Horns.

At once the Sioux tone became firmer. The Hunkpapa dominated the council, because they outnumbered the men of other bands. Their Strong Hearts erected a big double lodge in the middle of the encampment, and sat in council. At such a time—as at all times when the Strong Hearts appeared determined—the chiefs were glad to let them decide upon the course to be taken. Afterward, the chiefs would present the consensus to Warren.

At this time Sitting Bull was twenty-six years old and on the verge of being made head man of the Hunkpapa chapter of the Strong Heart Society. While the sleet pelted upon the taut lodge-skins and the long pipe was passed from hand to hand around the circle, he made his first important speech: a declaration of policy which stands as one of the most significant of his public utterances. It may not have been his maiden speech, but it is the first that has come down to us.

He stood up, a stocky figure with a single eagle feather upright in his hair, and with that peculiarly individual combination of force and graciousness which he always showed to his own people, summed up his views. The question before the house was, "Shall Warren be allowed to go on with his survey?"

"Friends! The Black Hills belong to me!

"Look at me, and look at the earth. Which is the oldest, do you think? The earth, and I was born on it. How old is it? I do not know. I will tell you what I think: it is far older than we are. It does not belong to us alone: it was our fathers', and should be our children's after us. When I received it, it was all in one piece, and so I hold it. If the white men take my country, where can I go? I have nowhere to go. I cannot spare it, and I love it very much.

"Let us alone. That is what they promised in their treaty—to let us alone.

"What is this white soldier doing here? What did he come for? To spy out the land, and to find a good place for a fort and a road, and to dig out gold. He is thinking about the next war, after telling us to make peace with all nations and go to war no more. The white men tell us to make peace, but our enemies will not keep the peace. We have to make war, and besides, it is our pastime."

"Hau! Hau!" came the hearty applause of the Strong Hearts. Sitting Bull went on:

"This white soldier chief, this White Beard [Harney] came out here and told us to make peace, to shake all nations by the hand and smoke together. But after he left here, he went to war himself, first in the South [Florida], and now against the Mormons. He says one thing, and does another.

"Friends, the Black Hills belong to me. This white man must stop here. He must go back."

These remarks were reported to Warren, and as Bear Ribs did not come at the end of three days, the officer wisely took his detail and went back toward Fort Laramie. Later he turned aside to the east, and explored the southern valleys of these mountains. And there Bear Ribs found him, bringing another Indian along.

Bear Ribs repeated all that the Hunkpapa had told Warren, and added that his own faction was in a hopeless minority among the Tetons, and that—if Warren persisted in going through the Hills—the chief was powerless to protect him. Yet Bear Ribs was trying hard to be friends with the whites, who had given him such importance as he possessed, had made him chief. He said he would try to get the Sioux to leave Warren alone, upon certain conditions.

"Tell the Grandfather at Washington," he said, "not to let white men come into our country. That is what they promised in their treaty—that white men would only come up the Missouri River in boats, or follow the White River between Fort Laramie and Fort Pierre. If you think you are buying the right to go through our country with your annuities, keep them, we do not want them. What good are they, anyway? They are not worth making a special trip to get. If we cannot get them when we visit the posts to trade, you may as well keep them.

One more thing: I hear that the Yankton Sioux are going to sell you their lands. If they do, tell them not to come to *us* and ask for land. Let them live with the white men; we will not take them in. Those lands belong to *all* the Sioux. Why should the Yanktons steal and sell our lands, and then ask us to feed them?"

Warren accepted these terms, and went on his way to Bear Butte. Bear Ribs rode away and persuaded the Sitting Bull faction not to harm Warren, as he was now well away from the precious buffalo herds.

But for all that, Sitting Bull's determined stand did the Sioux little good. That year there was a panic in the East, the bottom dropped out of the fur market. Furs, of course, have no intrinsic value; their price depends upon the whims of fashion. And as will be readily imagined, the traders had a hard time explaining this to the Indians who came laden with shaggy robes, expecting the usual rate of exchange in goods. There was much ill feeling, some threats. One hothead of the Hunkpapa killed a half-breed, Le Clare. But there were no hostilities against "the white nation."

"All we ask is to be let alone," Sitting Bull kept saying. "If the Grandfather can control his young men, we shall have peace." [1]

Yet "to be let alone" was not quite all that the Sioux demanded.

Contrary to their pledge made in the treaty of 1851, they were now again at war with the Crow. Moreover, Bear Ribs made it quite clear to Warren that they intended to continue fighting with their Indian enemies. Bear Ribs said that if the white men intended annuities as a bribe to the Sioux to keep peace with the Crow, the whites could keep them. He would never accept annuities on any such terms. The white men, he said, after talking universal peace, were now waging civil war amongst themselves; therefore he saw no reason why the Sioux should not fight the Crow in like manner. Men should practice what they preach.

The Prairie Sioux were not ignorant of the great inrush of white populations all up and down the Missouri. They had heard the talk of moving all tribes to the Indian Territory (now Oklahoma) and they knew well enough how badly the Kaw and Pawnee and other friendly border tribes were being treated, cooped up and starving on reservations in violation of their right (guaranteed by treaty) to hunt buffalo elsewhere. The Sioux were not blind; they had come to the point where they would budge no further. They not only asked to be let alone; they were determined to be let alone or fight.

Few white men on the frontier dreamed of respecting the paper "rights" of an Indian. Few white men anywhere were troubled by the violation of those rights. The Indian problem in the far West seemed so remote, so minor, so unreal that it was largely ignored by the American public. Most Americans had never seen a redskin.

Bear Ribs had tried hard to fulfill his obligations as a friend to the whites, but the government had never done anything to back him up. In 1862, therefore, when the Indian agent came up the Missouri by steamboat to Fort Pierre, Bear Ribs and other friendly Sioux chiefs assembled there to meet him and make an end to all existing pacts. Solemnly, though with many words of regret, they repudiated their part in the treaties already broken, formally cancelled all former agreements, and flatly refused to accept any annuities whatever.

The Indian agent saw his mission—and his job—in the balance. He kept at the chiefs, and especially Bear Ribs, insisting that they ought to take the goods.

This conference with the agent was held on the very spot where Colonel Harney had councilled with the Sioux in 1856. And it was there that Harney had so signally honored Bear Ribs in naming him head chief of the Sioux. Therefore Bear

Ribs more than the other chiefs doubtless felt an obligation to comply with the wishes of the Grandfather. Yet for a long time he stood his ground firmly with his fellows.

He was well aware of the jealousy his appointment by Harney had aroused in the hearts of other chiefs who had been passed over. And he must have realized that among such lovers of prestige as the Sioux such jealousy was cruel as the grave. In fact, when pressed, Bear Ribs declared that if he accepted the annuities, his action would not only endanger his own life but the lives of all his following. The hostility of the Sitting Bull faction to any further dealings with the government was known to all.

Therefore, when the agent pushed him, Bear Ribs felt that to refuse to take the goods would lay him open to a charge of cowardice. Accordingly, under grave protest, he yielded and took the goods allotted to his immediate band. Like Stirring Bear, he scorned to shield his life at the cost of his honor.

What happened to Bear Ribs soon after is best told in the words of an eyewitness:

Gallineaux came up to the American Fur Company's sub-post at the mouth of Cherry Creek on the Cheyenne River, where Wandel and others were in charge. He says, "We had the worst thing that ever happened at Fort Pierre; they killed all the cattle at Fort Pierre and we had to go to Sioux City to get cattle to take buffalo robes down."

I says, "What's been the matter?"

He says, "All the hostile Indians come on and they killed Bear Ribs, that was the head chief of all the Indians."

He said the way it happened, there was Chief Bear Ribs and all his tribe, the Two Kettle band and the Minniconjou was down here on the Bad River killing buffalo, and a party come into Fort Pierre from the hostile camp and reported that they was coming in on purpose to kill Bear Ribs.

One of the Indians of the Two Kettle band was at the fort

when the hostiles come in, and he reported to Bear Ribs that they had come in to kill him. Bear Ribs just laughed at him at the time, and said that he didn't think they was brave enough. Then he says, "I am going up to see them." Bear Ribs had a mule.

His son and a head man said, "We better go with you."

He says, "No, they ain't brave enough to kill me, I'll go alone."

He went up and went in and tied his mule right above their camp to a post there, and then he went in to Mr. Primeau; and Primeau had a family, and as quick as Bear Ribs come in Primeau told his wife to give him some coffee and bread. He refused it; he says, "No," he had bad news and wouldn't eat anything. While he was talking about the bad news there was a shot fired, and after that shot was fired a fellow from the camp come in and told Bear Ribs that they had shot his mule.

Then Bear Ribs says, "I'll go out and see," and he carried a double-barreled shotgun, and he went out and didn't see anybody standing around; they was all in their tipis, and the closest tipi to him was about thirty steps. He stood some twenty feet south of the southeast bastion corner of the post, where LaPlant and others were cooking coffee at a campfire.

Then Bear Ribs looked at his dead mule and he says, "This is three times that you done such tricks to me"; and he says, "This is the third time that such a thing has happened, they done that before"; he says, "This is the third time." Then a fellow in the next tipi just fired at him right then before he had it all said out.

But as quick as that shot went out, Bear Ribs put up his gun and fired and shot and killed the same one. And Bear Ribs was going to kill another one, but the bullet went through his forearm on the left side and then through his heart. The other fellow fell dead. But while Bear Ribs couldn't take good aim he shot again and hit another one and wounded him—the chief fired two shots and then he fell. Louis LaPlant and Basil Clement (Claymore) were present and standing near Bear Ribs when he was shot, LaPlant catching him as he fell.

After he fell, all the Indians rushed, and the gate was open —they rushed right into that fort, women and children, with everything they could take hold of, leaving only the buffalo robes outside. After they all was in they closed the gate and the fort was crowded with Indians and every house and piece of ground was full of hostile Indians.

While this happened one of Bear Ribs' party was at the fort; he run down to Bear Ribs' camp on Bad River and said, "Bear Ribs is killed, the hostiles killed him. It was Mouse that got shot and wounded, that killed him."

Then in about fifteen minutes afterwards every Indian had throwed blankets and robes and leggins and stockings and everything away, and all naked and went into the creek and put mud all over their hair, and took their horses, and got on their horses and went up to Fort Pierre; but it was closed, the gate was closed by the hostiles inside.

White men in there were scared to death. Those Indians down here was friendly Indians, and they went up to the gate and knocked on the gate, and said, "Open that gate." No answer, and they hollered again, "Open that gate"; but no answer, and they couldn't knock the gate through, it was so solid. Well, them Indians laid around there behind wood piles and called for Primeau to open the gate, but he dasn't do it. They wouldn't open the gate, although the outside people called them cowards and everything else.

Primeau was afraid they would burn the fort up; he says to the chiefs, "The best thing for you to do is to make it up with them; there's only one man killed on either side, and pay for it, and pay big."

Finally they agreed right away with Primeau, that they would pay for Bear Ribs. But before this happened the outside party killed every dog and every horse outside. There was an old squaw had a travois and a mule in front of it; she run up towards the hills, and they headed her off and found that there was a man sitting in there. It was old Yellow Hawk knocked the mule down and shot the man that was riding with the woman—it was Mouse—and he shot him right through the head; and his carcass laid there for years afterwards, and the mule's bones. I passed there years afterwards and see the bones.

Primeau made a speech to the rest of them in there, and they agreed to pay Bear Ribs' son in horses for his father. And only for old man Primeau there would have been no bargain made. He done the best he could to get them to make a bargain; it was dangerous for him. The fellows on the outside could have cleaned them out; they had guns and everything. They gave this hostile party just so much time to go away and skip, and they run as fast as they could, and Primeau kept Bear Ribs' band quiet, so they wouldn't follow them right away. But they followed them two hours afterwards, and the hostiles never stopped to camp anywhere for three days afterwards, they was so scared at the party behind them.

The chief's body was buried near the fort and by the authorities of the fort and numerous friendly Indians.

Claymore says of Bear Ribs' killing: "Jealousy caused it. Bear Ribs had so much influence with the whites that they were jealous of him." Claymore states that the Indians who killed Bear Ribs were Ousta, or One-That-Limps, and Tonkalla, or Mouse.[2]

The jealousy that caused the chief's murder might have been a powerful lever for peace, had Uncle Sam backed Bear Ribs up with a strong military force. But Uncle Sam had abandoned his best friend to their common enemy.

That was an object lesson to every chief on the Plains. "Make friends with white man," they said. "Then, if his soldiers do not shoot you, the hostiles will."

Under such circumstances, trying to keep peace on the Plains between white men and Indians was like trying to keep peace between a cat and a dog in a barrel.

Peace became a painful pretense; both sides could agree on one point only—that there are things worse than war.

5

WHITE MAN'S WAR

►►►►►►►►►►►◄◄◄◄◄◄◄◄◄◄◄

The Teton or Prairie Sioux were only one of the seven grand divisions or Council Fires of the Sioux Confederacy, though they far outnumbered all the rest. The Tetons, living as they did on the Great Plains west of the Missouri River, had little contact with their Sioux kinsmen in the woodlands to the east and, in fact, few ties other than a common ancestry and a common tongue.

For the Missouri River was then, as it is now, the boundary between two cultures, two ways of life. In 1862 the Tetons, powerful and warlike and roving over hunting grounds rich in buffalo and other game, were for the most part a prosperous, multiplying, and happy people. But the Santees and other Sioux east of the river had come to the end of the trail.

They had many grievances. Their game was nearly gone, their country occupied by scattered white settlers, their scanty treaty payments taken by grasping traders, all their institutions shattered. They were ripe for retaliation, and the Civil War, then in progress, may have encouraged them to break out. Various tales are told of how the spark was struck into that powder magazine of latent fury. But the desperation of these starving people was so great that once the first shot was fired, brutal massacre followed.

Their chief, Little Crow, whose Sioux name is usually given as *Cetan Wakan Mani*, literally Holy Hawk Walking (or Hawk Walking in a Sacred Manner), was a communicant of the Episcopal Church and wore the clothes of a white man except for moccasins. In fact, he attended church at the Lower Sioux Agency near Fort Ridgely on August 17, only a day before the massacre began.

This has been held to prove his treachery, but it appears that he was unaware of the war until blood had already been shed and his people came demanding that he lead them. Among the Sioux a chief was chosen for life tenure and his duty was to speak for and act for his followers. So Little Crow, against his better judgment, felt it his duty to cast his lot with those who looked to him for leadership. His reluctance is shown by the fact that at first he was not so ruthless as other chiefs; he sheltered several white captives in his own house, and even helped one to escape. But once he had supped full with horrors, he outdid all the rival chiefs in zeal and bloodshed.

Of course it is possible that he had been led to think that the South would be victorious in the Civil War. Many of the traders on the Missouri were Southern sympathizers. At any rate he urged his men "to fight and die like brave Dakotas."

At first the Sioux had everything their own way and captured, tortured, raped and murdered hundreds of people and killed more than 700 troops in battle. They nearly took Fort Ridgely and did set fire to the town of New Ulm.

One of the traders had been accustomed to laying his hand on the scale when weighing out groceries to the Indians. When they caught him, they cut off his hand and put it on the scale to see how much he had cheated them. Another trader, so the story goes, hearing the chiefs plead that their people were hungry and needed the long-withheld annuities, replied, "If they are hungry, let them eat grass." [1] When the white men found his dead body, the Indians had stuffed his mouth with grass.

But after Colonel Henry H. Sibley took the field the situation slowly changed. Sibley understood Indians, spoke Dakota, and though jeered at for his deliberation and moderation in dealing with the Sioux, finally brought the Minnesota Massacre to an end.

All the horrors and heroisms on both sides of that bitter struggle fill volumes, but since Little Crow's Sioux were not Plains Indians, they have no place in this book.

Little Crow, seeing that he was beaten, tried to get the Indians to murder all their prisoners, but other chiefs saw that the prisoners, if saved, might save their own skins. They delivered up 269 captives.

Little Crow fled. But Sibley brought in and imprisoned 1500 Sioux known to have taken part in the massacre. Three hundred ninety-two were tried by court martial, 307 sentenced to death. Hanging had a special terror for Indians, since they believed that the spirit of a man hanged could never leave his body to reach the Happy Hunting Grounds. Hanging, to them, was death absolute. But President Lincoln, with charity for all, found time even in the midst of a disastrous civil war to review the verdicts of the court and commute all but thirty-nine of these sentences. People who think the Nürnberg trials for war criminals were without precedent have short memories.

On the 28th of December the thirty-nine war criminals, all of whom were proved guilty of atrocious cruelties, were hanged together on a common gallows at Mankato.

The Minnesota Sioux scattered for safety, many of them heading west to seek refuge with their kinsmen on the plains beyond the Missouri. Little Crow, delaying to steal horses to make the trip, was shot down in a berry patch. His body was taken to a slaughterhouse and thrown into a pit with the offal.

But Inkpaduta, or Scarlet Point, who had led the Spirit Lake Massacre, skipped out with his band ahead of the troops. He remained on the plains for years after, and his tent was pitched in Sitting Bull's camp the day that Custer fell.

The Teton or Prairie Sioux had no part in the Minnesota Massacre. They seldom went east of the Missouri River, but during the drought of 1863 they crossed to hunt buffalo, and General H. H. Sibley attacked Sitting Bull's camp there in June. Soon after, to even the score, the Sioux attacked him on Apple Creek, ran off a mule or two, and then turned homeward.

The following summer of '64, the Tetons heard many soldiers were coming up the Missouri to kill all the Sioux, and so they moved back into the Killdeer Mountains. Other bands came to join them, making a village of several hundred tipis. Brings-Plenty, an Oglala, brought with him a white woman, a captive, Fanny Kelly. The Sioux heard that three young men of their nation had killed a white straggler. These young men had been killed by the soldiers on the Little Cheyenne River. The white soldiers had cut off their heads and stuck them up on three posts.

By midsummer this big Teton camp was reinforced by fugitives from the woodlands east of the Missouri—Yanktonais and Santee Sioux. Some of these had taken part in the Minnesota Massacre, and now sought refuge with their western relatives. Inkpaduta was their ringleader. He brought the war to the Tetons.

One afternoon, hunters rode in to report that soldiers were coming. The Western Sioux had only a few old-fashioned guns and hardly any powder. So, on Inkpaduta's advice, the chiefs ordered the camp moved farther back among the hills, where there was a spring and a pond near the mouth of a canyon. The country around the camp was rough and wooded.

One morning not long after, all the warriors rode out to meet the troops, and saw bluecoats advancing on foot in a long, long line, with mounted men and wagons following. Long Dog, who believed himself bulletproof, charged the soldiers and rode at a run all along their line to see whether they came in peace or not. Many of them fired at him. Then the Sioux knew that the soldiers had come to fight.

The Tetons kept charging on horseback, while the Yanktonais and Santees from the woodlands took position on foot in a little gulch to snipe at the troops. The cavalry soon made a sudden charge against these snipers and rubbed out thirty— almost the total loss of the Sioux that day. Humanitarians in the East were very bitter against General Alfred Sully for attacking Indians "none of whom had taken part in the Minnesota Massacre." But, by good luck, it was the guilty ones whom he killed.

For when the cavalry charged the Teton Sioux, those wily horsemen raced away, leading Major Brackett's men into a trap. The troopers wheeled and raced back to the command. But not all of them reached it.

Back in camp, the old men and women were hastily packing up to hit the trail. Already shells were dropping among their tipis.

"In that camp was a man called The-Man-Who-Never-Walked, a cripple from birth. His twisted, shrunken limbs had never been any good; he could not go on the warpath like other young men. But his heart was that of a bear, full of strong courage. And now, when he saw the soldiers coming right to camp, and the shells dropping among the tipis, he knew his chance had come. He told them to put him into the basket of a travois, or drag, and carry him out to the battlefield. He wished to play the part of a man, like other men, before he died.

"The Sioux about Sitting Bull were sitting on their horses on the hilltop, watching the battle, when there came a man from the camp, singing, and leading a cream-colored horse with a drag tied to its saddle. In the basket of the drag was the cripple with the heart of a bear. When the man reached the Sioux line, he stopped his song, and called out: 'This man has been a cripple all his life; he has never gone to war. Now he asks to be put into this fight and killed. He prefers to die by a bullet, since he cannot be of any use.'

"The Sioux warriors looked at the shrunken, twisted limbs huddled in the basket, and Sitting Bull spoke up: 'That is perfectly all right. Let him die in battle, if he wants to.'

"Sitting Bull's heart was full that day. He was proud of his nation. Even the helpless were eager to do battle in defense of their people.

"So they whipped up the cream-colored horse, and the cripple in the basket of the drag sped away, trying to guide the animal with long reins made of lariats. He could use his arms a little, but he had no weapons. Away went the horse, dragging that strange chariot, galloping straight toward the line of soldiers. The Sioux on the hilltop were watching.

"All at once, down went the horse, shot dead. The-Man-Who-Never-Walked was thrown from the drag, and sat facing the soldiers, singing his death-song. The song soon ended, for he could not dodge the bullets. The soldiers killed him. Later, as they advanced and came upon his body, they were astonished to find that this man who had charged them alone so bravely was only a helpless cripple. So died The-Man-Who-Never-Walked, known also as Bear's Heart, because of his dauntless courage." [2]

Such was the fighting spirit of the Sioux that day. Yet Sitting Bull and his comrades had to fall back. Inkpaduta had told them that the cavalry could not get at them in the hills. But General Sully dismounted his troopers and deployed them on foot, armed with rifles. Fanny Kelly, the captive, has told us of the terror and confusion of the Indians' flight.

They had to abandon most of their property, their winter supplies of pemmican and jerky, their buffalo robes, tanned and untanned, and many of their tents. However, the Sioux rescued all their wounded, and put up such a stubborn resistance that the troops could not advance beyond the abandoned camp. Sully burned that, shot all the dogs, and set the woods on fire. The Sioux sent a white flag forward, but the troops would have no truce.

This battle of July 28th broke up the big encampment. Inkpaduta, who had brought all this trouble to the Tetons and whose bad advice had caused them to lose their tipis, now headed east. The Tetons scattered in the other direction, stringing their camps along the Little Missouri.

There, soon after, the troops had a brush with the Indians at the ford. General Sully was heading through the Badlands to Yellowstone River. That strange labyrinth of rugged country was dry as a bone. Grasshoppers had devoured all the grass; there was little water—and that alkali. Sully's 2000 men plodded along at the mercy of the harassing Sioux, while cavalry horses and pack mules died like flies.

One afternoon warriors under Sitting Bull trapped some soldiers in a dry box canyon. Indian scouts with the troops kept calling, begging the Sioux to let them out. Sitting Bull refused and shouted back, "Why do the white men come to fight with us?"

Nobody seemed able to answer that question.

After sniping at the troops all night, the Sioux ran out of ammunition and rode back to their camp with their wounded. The Battle of the Badlands was over.

On the Northern Plains, General Sully had, as the Indians say, "set the prairie on fire." But that year of 1864 was bloody on the Southern Plains as well.

6

KIT CARSON TAKES A HAND

THE NORTHERN PLAINS INDIANS fought the whites only in their own hunting grounds. When they followed the war-path out of their own country it was to attack enemy tribes. White settlements were distant, and all the Indians asked was to be let alone.

The situation was quite different on the Southern Plains. There the Comanche had for nearly three centuries roamed within easy reach of settlements and ranches in the Spanish Possessions. On those ranches good horses were abundant and provided an irresistible lure to the horse-loving redskins. And the Kiowa, Southern Cheyenne and Southern Arapaho moved down into Comanche country soon after 1800 in order to share in the loot.

The laws of Mexico forbade its citizens to carry or own firearms, and so the Indians had things pretty much their own way until the Texas Rangers took the field. These red-skins were expert kidnappers and on nearly every raid brought home captives to be enslaved or held for ransom. In time, some of these captives married into the tribes and some of their children even became chiefs, like Quanah Parker. There was hardly a Kiowa family which had not some Mexican blood in their veins. And as settlers occupied more and more of Kansas, these Indians raided north as well as south.

For generations their looting followed a regular pattern. At one season they raided far south, sometimes as far as Durango in old Mexico, and at another season into Texas. Again, when caravans were rolling, they struck along the Santa Fe Trail. The Comanche liked to raid in bright moonlight, and a "Comanche moon" did not suggest romantic notions to the harassed settlers on the border.

Following the discovery of gold in Colorado, the gold rush to Pike's Peak in 1859 and later brought gold seekers by the thousands streaming up the trails along the Republican River and the Smoky Hill across Kansas. These trails cut straight across the best buffalo-hunting grounds of the Cheyenne. Up until that time, because of their respect for the trader, William Bent, and his partners, the tribe had been friendly to the white men, though some slight incidents had occurred.

But there was trouble in the early sixties. Ever since the Mexican War there had been continued depredations farther north. And the Minnesota Massacre, coming as it did when the Union was hard pressed by the Civil War, had hardened American hearts against all Western Indians.

Taking advantage of this situation, some men in the West made matters worse. If a herder carelessly allowed his cattle and horses to stray or stampede, he might justify himself by laying the loss at the door of the Indians. Ambitious young officers fresh from West Point sometimes fired on friendly Indians without justification. The owners of competing stage lines and freighters alike tried to swing business to their own firms and get the business of rival firms by spreading stories of outrages committed by the tribesmen. Squaw men were always ready to give advance information of Indian raids, real or imaginary. Crooked Indian agents appropriated annuities sent to the tribes they served, or conspired with licensed

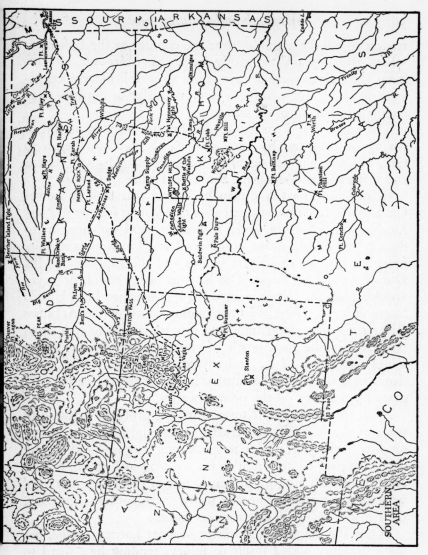

RANGE OF THE SOUTHERN PLAINS INDIANS
AND ADJACENT AREAS

Present state boundary lines are shown for the
convenience of the reader.

traders to sell the annuities over the counter to the Indians to whom they already rightfully belonged. Moreover, the Indians themselves were always ready to wreak bloody vengeance on any white man for whatever cruelty or injustice they had suffered from other whites.

The Civil War kept the troops far too busy to attend to roving Indians, and by 1863 and '64 the redskins began to raid, kill and plunder again in Texas, New Mexico, Kansas and Colorado, and along the Santa Fe Trail.

Comanches killed five men in '64 on that trail at Lower Cimarron Springs and scalped alive two young fellows in New Mexico. Chief Satanta, given to boasting and violence, impudently held a scalp dance near Fort Larned in Kansas to celebrate his murder of several whites and the capture of Mrs. Dorothy Field in Texas. The Kiowas never could, or never would, grasp the fact that since 1846 Texans had been United States citizens. They had been raiding south of the Arkansas River for a long, long time, and saw no reason to quit now, while the white men north of the river were fighting the white men south of it. And so they boldly held their scalp dance near the fort. The cavalry horses belonging to the post grazed peacefully on the prairie nearby.

After the dance two Kiowa warriors, probably wishing to trade at the sutler's store, tried to enter the fort. The sentry on duty at the gate, unable to speak their language and finding that they paid no attention to his warning in English, threatened them with his gun; promptly one of them shot him dead with two arrows. While the guard called out the garrison, the Kiowas ran off all the troopers' horses.

While the commanding officer of Fort Larned fumed, Satanta brazenly added insult to injury, sending him word to get better horses next time, as those the chief had just stolen were heap no good.

Meanwhile the Kiowas rode off to the Staked Plains and

joined the Comanches on the Canadian River. From that camp a big war party set out to raid the Texans; they brought back eleven scalps and seven captives.

At that time Uncle Sam could hardly be held responsible for what happened in Texas, but repeated raids in territory held by Union forces called for reprisals. For once, the Army had a free hand on the Plains; in wartime no sentimental civilians could interpose to make another futile treaty.

The War Department planned to send three columns against the Indians, one to Kansas, one to Colorado, and one to Texas. But the Kansas column was ordered to pursue Confederate raiders under Quantrell. In Colorado the government enlisted for one hundred days a force called the First Colorado Volunteer Cavalry.

From New Mexico General James Henry Carleton ordered Colonel Christopher "Kit" Carson into the field. Kit was an old mountain man, a seasoned Indian fighter of nearly forty years' experience. He had a great and well-deserved reputation in the West.

In January of that year Kit had invaded the Cañon de Chelly, the stronghold of the Navajo, and had tamed that tribe once and for all, rounding up some 7000 Indian prisoners. Before that he had gained a smashing victory over the fierce Apaches. Little wonder that Kit was confident he could lick the Plains tribes.

He set out on November 3, 1864, from Cimarron, New Mexico, through two feet of snow, for the Canadian River in the panhandle of Texas. His command consisted of 200 troopers, 100 infantry, two mountain howitzers, an ambulance, twenty-seven wagons, and some sixty Ute and Jicarilla Apaches who acted as scouts. In the wagons were rations for forty-five days.

All that country was perfectly familiar to Kit, since for years he had been employed by William Bent, builder of

Bent's Old Fort on the Arkansas and also of another trading post (then in ruins) called Adobe Walls. These ruins on the Canadian Kit intended to make his headquarters. There he would leave his wagons, pack his rations and ammunition on mules, and so catch up with the redskins. But his pack saddles were never used. The Kiowa and Comanche were waiting for Kit at Adobe Walls.

Captain George H. Pettis, one of Kit's officers, reports what followed:

"We arrived at Mule Spring early in the afternoon; had performed our usual camp duties, and as the sun was about setting, many of us being at supper, we were surprised to see our Indians, who were lying around the camp, some gambling, some sleeping, and others waiting for something to eat from the soldiers' mess, spring to their feet, as if one man, and gaze intently to the eastward, talking in their own language. . . . Colonel Carson . . . informed us that the two scouts that he had dispatched that morning, had found the Comanches, and were now returning to report the particulars. Although the returning scouts were at least two miles distant, and, mounted on their ponies, were hardly discernible, yet the quick, sharp eye of our Indians made them out without difficulty. . . . And what was more remarkable, they had . . . conveyed the intelligence that they had found the enemy, and that there was work to be done. . . . They reported that . . . we should have no difficulty in finding all the Indians that we desired." [1]

Kit was hardly surprised, since the night before he had dreamed of battle, and he had lived with Indians long enough to have faith in dreams. Kit made a forced night march—his wagons trailing him far behind—and at daybreak on November 24, 1864, heard a war cry across the river. He knew the Kiowas had seen him.

Hoar frost still clung to the dry grass. But the Ute and Apache scouts instantly threw off their buffalo robes and blankets and splashed naked through the river toward the enemy pony herds. Already Kit could see the Kiowas driving the Indian ponies headlong down the stream.

Kit pulled off his overcoat, tossed it away, and ordered the howitzers and troopers forward, as the Indians fell back. As soon as it was light, Kit could see—only five miles away—the thronging tipis pitched all along the stream. By that time Kit's Indian scouts came tearing back with the ponies they had captured. The cavalry were corralling their horses within the crumbling walls of the old trading post, while the infantry moved steadily forward in skirmish line.

Kit mounted a small knoll rising from the grassy river bottom to watch the action. On both sides the Indians, as usual, dashed about exhibiting superb horsemanship, displaying their courage in defiance of their enemies. By this time about 200 Kiowas and Comanches had caught up their ponies and were in the fight, all charging, says Pettis, "in the same manner, with their bodies thrown over the sides of their horses, at a full run, and shooting occasionally under their horses' necks; while gathered just beyond them twelve or fourteen hundred, with a dozen or more chiefs riding up and down their line haranguing them, seemed to be preparing for a desperate charge on our forces. Surgeon Courtright had prepared a corner of Adobe Walls for a hospital, and was busy, with his assistants, in attending to the wants of half a dozen or more wounded. Fortunately, the Adobe Walls were high enough to protect all our horses from the enemy's rifles, and afford ample protection to our wounded."

Meanwhile, Little Mountain, the old Kiowa chief, rode hell-for-leather to the farther camps to call up his reserves, and as fast as his warriors could tie up their horses' tails and uncover their shields, they raced their horses toward the sound of the guns. It was always the custom of a warrior to race his pony

before a fight in order to bring on its second wind. But this
time they had a double reason for making speed.

For Kit's men soon captured the nearest village—that of
the Kiowa-Apache—shooting down their chief, Iron Shirt, as
he came out of his lodge. But the hostiles kept Kit too busy to
let him burn their tents. Then Kit ordered Pettis to "throw
a few shell into that crowd over thar." Quickly Pettis opened
fire. At the sound of the cannon, he reports, Kiowa and Comanche "rose high in their stirrups and gazed, for a single
moment, with astonishment, then guiding their horses' heads
away from us, and giving one concerted, prolonged yell, they
started on a dead run for their village. In fact when the fourth
shot was fired there was not a single enemy within the extreme
range of the howitzers."

After that Kit's men unsaddled their horses and had breakfast. That over, the Colonel proposed to advance and destroy
the whole encampment.

But when he had got round his hardtack and coffee, he
found circumstances altered. Three miles below was another
big camp—hundreds of lodges—and from it came "at least
a thousand warriors, mounted on first-class ponies." They
charged Kit's men from all directions. Back and forth, all that
afternoon they fought. One shell made a direct hit on the
pony of a mounted Indian. The rider fell senseless, but before
Kit's scouts could run out and scalp him, two of his friends
rode up at a gallop side by side, leaned down—each catching
an arm of the wounded man—and carried him away to
safety. At first the cannon terrified the hostiles. But they soon
learned to watch the howitzers and dodge the shells.

Still Kit's men pushed slowly forward. While mounted warriors kept charging the troops, others on foot hid in the high
grass, firing steadily at the white men. Carson directed operations by having his bugler blow appropriate calls. But one of
the hostile chiefs also had a bugle and he too kept sounding

off. If Carson's bugler blew Charge, the chief sounded Retreat. All day long the redskin humorist so contradicted every order Carson gave!

From time to time Little Mountain harangued his men and joined in the fighting, old as he was, but Stumbling Bear was the active leader of the hostiles. He counted three *coups* and "made so many reckless charges that his small daughter's shawl, which he wore for good luck, was pierced by a dozen bullets." [2]

By mid-afternoon there were perhaps 3000 warriors surrounding Kit's hard-pressed command. The warriors had plenty of ammunition and good horses. Under their protection, squaws lugged away their lodges and goods from the very village Kit had taken.

By this time the Colonel was beginning to worry about his wagon train, which was coming slowly along, somewhere miles behind. If once the Indians discovered *that*, it would be all up with the teamsters, the rations, and the ammunition.

Kit's officers urged him to attack the villages below, but Kit and his scouts were not so foolhardy. The Utes had to stand by and watch the Kiowas sweep away the very ponies they themselves had captured at daybreak. Kit decided to make tracks out of there before things got any worse. He headed back toward the village he had taken earlier. The cavalry led their horses in column of fours; the infantry deployed on the flanks and in the rear. They fought well, and maintained their formation in spite of the frantic charges of the mounted Indians.

The sun had melted the frost from the tall dry grass along the river. Some of the grass was blue-stem, high as the shoulders of a man in the saddle. Hoping to break up Kit's command and rub out the white men one by one, the hostiles set fire to this grass.

But Kit was an old hand at such warfare. He fired the grass

on the trail ahead, and hurried his command out of the lush
bottoms up to a slope where the scanty grass was short. Still,
as the flames roared on, the warriors swept up behind their
smoke screen, hell-bent to count a *coup* or take a scalp. Kit
had never seen the cussed Injuns fight so bravely. But for the
howitzers he might never have got away.

Come sundown Kit got back to the village he had taken that
morning. He shelled it first, and then moved in to burn the
lodges. In them Kit found clothing of white people, army
uniforms and sabers. Every man in the command acquired a
fine tanned buffalo robe to replace his lost overcoat. Too late,
among the lodges Kit found the bodies of four Kiowas whom
his Indian scouts had killed. Two of them were women; all
were blind or crippled.

Having set the village afire, Kit marched off to meet his
wagon train, carrying his wounded on ammunition carts. That
night Kit's Utes were too exhausted, too dispirited to dance
over the scalps they had taken.

Whoever it was wrote the illiterate Kit's report on this
fight for him made it out a great victory. My old friend George
Bent, who from childhood had known Carson well, told me
that Kit himself never made any such claim. In fact, Kit declared straight out that "the Injuns licked him" at Adobe
Walls. But within a week the other expedition against the
Cheyenne was to have better luck.

7

SAND CREEK

THE CHEYENNE INDIANS, a haughty and warlike tribe, though few in numbers (about 2500) had always held their own against all comers. A legend about their beginnings tells how, after a disastrous encounter with some other tribe, they all decided they would become terrible fighters and so become great men. Ever since, they had pursued their aim with a vengeance. But, under the influence of the traders, William Bent and his partners, they had always been friendly to the whites.

In 1857 there was a little trouble, which the Cheyenne overlooked. But in 1863 and '64 a number of clashes occurred: one in which Wolf-Coming-Out and Bull-Telling-Tales, when attacked, killed a white officer; and another when troops wantonly shot down Chief Lean Bear as he rode forward alone to greet a company of Colorado Volunteers.

In those days volunteers enlisted for short periods, elected their own officers and were under no real discipline. Often they were, to all intents and purposes, simply irresponsible gangs of armed men wandering about the Plains.

Lean Bear was shot down by some man of Lieutenant Eayre's Independent Battery of Colorado Volunteer Artillery. Eayre was so far out of his district that he was—luckily for him—within a few miles of Fort Larned, in Kansas, when the killing took place. The Cheyenne chief, Black Kettle, tried to stop the fight which followed.

Lean Bear had just left Fort Larned. Shortly before, he had visited Washington. He went up to Eayre's soldiers alone, shook hands with the Lieutenant, showed him the medal he had got from the President, and stated that the Great Father, on giving him the medal, had told him to be always friendly to the whites. Then one of the soldiers shot him. The enraged Indians promptly attacked. There were several casualties on both sides, and a running fight was kept up for ten or fifteen miles. The soldiers took refuge in Fort Larned. The Cheyenne chiefs appealed to William Bent for advice.

Bent, known by courtesy since the Mexican War as Colonel Bent, was then the principal Indian trader in the Southwest, a merchant prince and a man of intelligence, good sense and strong character. He had been on the Plains and among the Indians for thirty-five years. Among his achievements was the famous Intertribal Treaty of 1840, by which the Arapaho and Cheyenne made peace with their ancient enemies the Kiowa and Comanche, at Bent's Old Fort on the Arkansas River. Bent was the husband of a Cheyenne woman, daughter of the Keeper of the Medicine Arrows, and wielded great influence in the tribe.

So now Bent went to see the chiefs on Coon Creek, having met and talked with Lieutenant Eayre on the way. Bent offered, if the chiefs would keep their young men from the warpath for twenty days, to go to Fort Leavenworth and see General S. R. Curtis, then in command of the Department. But first he decided he had better see the officers at Fort Lyon, near by.

At the fort, Bent found Colonel J. M. Chivington, an officer of the Colorado Volunteers. Bent told Chivington of his conference with the chiefs on Coon Creek, explaining that they had declared it was not their intention or wish to fight the whites, that they wished to be peaceable and friendly and keep their tribes so. Chivington replied shortly that he was "not authorized to make peace," that he was then "on the warpath."

Bent urged that there was a great risk to run in keeping up the war; that a great many government trains were traveling to New Mexico along the trails and also a great many citizens. He did not think there was sufficient military force available to protect the travel, and warned that, in the event of war, citizens and settlers of the country would have to suffer.

Chivington replied, "The citizens will have to protect themselves." Bent gave up and went home.

But toward the end of August Black Kettle and other chiefs wrote, addressing themselves to their agent, Major Colley. The letter was written in duplicate, one copy by George Bent, half-breed son of Colonel William Bent, the other by Edmond Guerrier, the half-breed son of William Guerrier. Ed Geary, as he was familiarly called, and George Bent were both well known to me and gave me their own accounts of what followed. The second letter was sent to Major Wynkoop, then in command of Fort Lyon, on the Arkansas River in Colorado.

Chiefs Black Kettle and White Antelope offered to give up their seven prisoners in exchange for Indian prisoners held in Denver by the whites. Black Kettle and other chiefs of the Cheyenne and Arapaho tribes agreed to go to Denver for a conference with the Governor.

In those days the settlers always feared that Indians would perpetrate another massacre like that in Minnesota in '62 while most of the troops were away fighting the Confederacy. They also feared that Confederates would stir up the Indians, as indeed they tried to do; and it was known that William Bent's own half-breed son George had served for a time in the Confederate Army.

But a half-breed always felt more at home with the Indians than with the whites. The blood tie among Indians was so much stronger. And so William Bent's sons joined their mother's people and were with the Cheyenne when war with the whites broke out. People in Colorado believed George Bent an enemy agent.

Moreover, some men of military age much preferred a brief enlistment in the Colorado Volunteers fighting Indians on the home front to being drafted and sent far away to fight Johnny Reb. Others were reluctant to leave their families unprotected. To such men, an Indian war seemed little short of a personal necessity.

William Bent soon received a letter from the Indian agent, Major Colley, and returned to Fort Lyon.

There Colley gave Bent a copy of Governor Evans' proclamation and a letter from the Governor directing him to send someone immediately to the tribesmen to bring in all the friendlies to Fort Lyon and Fort Larned, where they would be protected by the Government of the United States and receive rations. At that time Governor Evans was *ex officio* Superintendent of Indian Affairs.

Bent fearlessly rode off alone and located all five tribes near Fort Larned: Cheyenne, Arapaho, Kiowa, Comanche and Kiowa-Apache. In council he explained the Governor's proclamation, which the chiefs accepted. Next morning the chiefs went with Bent to Fort Larned and held council with the commanding officer. Everything was apparently settled satisfactorily to both sides. The Indians rode back to their villages on the Arkansas River, twenty-five miles from Fort Lyon.

Bent, however, could tell from the behavior of the Kiowas that *they* were up to mischief; he warned the commanding officer at Fort Larned to be on his guard.

Left Hand, the Arapaho chief, who spoke English, also
warned the commandant that the Kiowas about the post were
planning to run off his horses while the soldiers were busy
watching the Kiowa women dancing. The commandant ignored the warning, and so lost his animals. And when Left
Hand, anxious for peace, carrying a white flag, approached
the post to offer his services in recovering the horses, the
commandant ordered the troops to fire on him. This brought
the Arapaho into the war.

That summer of '64 stagecoaches between Kansas and
Denver no longer rolled. Farmers and ranchmen gathered
their families and fled to the military posts. Governor John
Evans had issued a proclamation calling on all able-bodied
citizens of Colorado to take up arms.

Meanwhile, Major Wynkoop at Fort Lyon had been trying
to persuade Black Kettle and other chiefs to keep the peace,
and took a delegation of Cheyenne chiefs to talk with Governor Evans and Colonel Chivington at Denver. Nothing very
definite was decided upon at this council, but White Antelope and Black Kettle apparently felt that things had been
straightened out. At any rate they brought their people in,
and made camp on Sand Creek in the Big South Bend, some
thirty miles northeast of Fort Lyon at the point where the
Fort Lyon-Smoky Hill Trail crossed that stream.

But at the headquarters of General S. P. Curtis, Major
Wynkoop's action was severely criticized. He had left his
post to go to Denver without permission, had issued supplies
to "hostile" Indians "in direct violation of orders," and had
even made an unauthorized treaty! Major Scott Anthony was
sent from Fort Larned to relieve Major Wynkoop, with orders to investigate and report upon his conduct. Anthony
took command there on November 2, 1864.

Finding a camp of some 600 Arapaho within a mile of the
post, he talked with them. They turned in a few head of

stolen horses and some old guns. Then Anthony, following
Wynkoop's example, issued ten days' rations to the Arapaho.
Afterward he returned their guns and advised them to go
buffalo hunting and feed themselves. Meanwhile some of the
Cheyennes on Sand Creek came in to smoke with Anthony
and make peace. Yet all this time Anthony was writing headquarters to say that if he only had more men, he would go and
attack the camp on Sand Creek.

In those days officers had no idea how much trouble the
Plains Indians could make. General Patrick E. Connor wrote
to Chivington: "Can we get a fight out of the Indians this
winter?" General Curtis urged the War Department to send
out more troops for a winter campaign.

Chivington wired Curtis that he would attack the Indians.
Already he had a regiment of men enlisted for 100 days, the
Third Colorado Cavalry. In addition the First Colorado Vol-
unteer Cavalry and some volunteers from New Mexico were
ordered to join his command. Chivington led his men from
Denver to the mouth of Huerfano Creek on the Arkansas
River, and followed down that stream to Fort Lyon. He took
great care that no one should carry the news of his advance
to Black Kettle's camp on Sand Creek. He even held up the
United States mail.

Chivington, formerly a Methodist preacher, was a man of
gigantic stature and ruthless character. On the morning of
November 29 he arrived at Fort Lyon. Major Anthony ordered out his own mounted troops and howitzers and they
set off about dark that evening across the open, rolling country covered with buffalo grass, heading for Black Kettle's
camp. Altogether Chivington commanded more than 700
men. He had as guides old Jim Beckwourth, the mulatto mountain man, teller of tall tales, and a young half-breed Cheyenne,
a son of Colonel Bent.

Naturally young Bent was reluctant to lead this treacherous

raid against his mother's people and so help to start an Indian war which his father was trying to prevent.

In his *Massacres in the Mountains*, J. P. Dunn tells what followed:

"The night was bitter cold; Jim Beckwourth, the old trapper who had been guiding them, had become so stiffened that he was unable longer to distinguish the course, and they were obliged to rely on a half-breed Indian. About one-third of the men had the appearance of soldiers who had seen service; the remainder had a diversity of arms and equipment, as well as of uniforms, and marched with the air of raw recruits. About half a mile in advance were three men, the half-breed guide and two officers, one of the latter of such gigantic proportions that the others seemed pygmies beside him. Near daybreak the half-breed turned to the white men and said: 'Wolf he howl. Injun dog he hear wolf, he howl too. Injun he hear dog and listen; hear something, and run off.' The big man tapped the butt of his revolver in an ominous way, and replied: 'Jack, I haven't had an Indian to eat for a long time. If you fool with me, and don't lead us to that camp, I'll have you for breakfast.' They found the camp."

The volunteers were out for blood. They did not care whether the Cheyennes in that camp were friendly or not. Their orders were to "take no prisoners," "to kill all, little and big." They believed the only good Indian was a dead Indian.

The camp, of about 100 lodges, stood in the bend north of the dry sandy stream bed, there about 200 yards wide and dotted with occasional pools. There was no timber or cover anywhere along the stream. Even the grass had been grazed off by the ponies. The vertical banks varied from two or three feet to eight or ten in height. West of the stream, across from the camp, the Indian ponies grazed. There were only

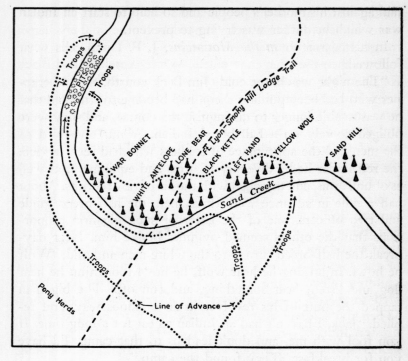

SAND CREEK MASSACRE

NOVEMBER 29, 1864

Redrawn from the map in George Bird Grinnell's *The Fighting Cheyennes* by permission of Charles Scribner's Sons, showing the attack of Colonel J. M. Chivington on a Cheyenne camp. Indian names indicate locations of lodges of different chiefs.

ten lodges of Arapahoes. Altogether the camp contained about 200 men old enough to bear arms.

It was after daybreak, cool and clear. The sun had not yet risen, but the twilight had passed. Some of the Indians heard the beat of hoofs. A woman ran out of her lodge and called aloud, "Buffalo are coming into camp!" Others ran out, looked south across the stream, and saw that her "buffalo" were soldiers on horseback. Immediately the soldiers began to fire. It was a complete surprise.

Even then the Cheyenne chiefs, White Antelope and Black Kettle, could not believe that the attack was deliberate. Wynkoop had promised them protection. Anthony had smoked with them. They had given up their prisoners, had come in and camped near the fort. In their camp that morning were several traders, including John Simpson "Blackfoot" Smith, the government interpreter, and a United States soldier, David Louderback.

Black Kettle had been given an American flag. He hastily ran this up on a lodge pole in front of his tipi, with a white flag flying beneath it, shouting to his people to be calm, that they would not be killed, that they were under the protection of the Government. A confused herd of men, women and children rallied round the flag. Only the younger men bothered to snatch up their bows and arrows, lances and guns. When the soldiers dismounted and began to fight, the half-dressed Indians ran upstream to the far end of the village, gathering about the tipi of Chief War Bonnet. A few young men ran out on the prairie and caught their ponies. Knowing that no stand could be made against such overwhelming numbers, they raced northeastward up the trail to warn their relatives camped about thirty miles away on the Smoky Hill River.

John Smith repeatedly ran out to reach the troops and stop the shooting, but was always fired on. By the time the soldiers were inside the village, Chivington saw Smith. He yelled, "Come here, Uncle John!" Terrified, Smith ran to the Colonel and, hanging on to one of the caissons, tagged along with the troops. His half-breed son Jack was also taken.

Black Kettle finally realized that there was no possibility of peace. He turned to run, calling Chief White Antelope to come with him. But White Antelope had no wish to survive the disaster which his stand for peace had caused, or else he disdained to run. He let Black Kettle go and stood calmly at the door of his tent, wrapped in his colorful Navajo blanket, with folded arms, singing his death song, until the soldiers shot him down. His blanket with the bullet hole in it may now be seen in the Laboratory of Anthropology, Santa Fe, New Mexico.

Black Kettle's wife fell as she ran with her husband up the dry creek bed. On both sides of the stream the mounted men advanced while the infantry plodded up the broad stream bed. Afoot as they were, the Indians, unable to escape the cavalry, dug in under the sandy banks of the stream above the village. It did not take long to scoop out a foxhole in that sandy soil. All morning the troops besieged them. Most of them were children or women. Not half the men bore arms, but they fought like lions.

Afterward Major Anthony reported: "I never saw more bravery displayed by any set of people on the face of the earth. . . . They would charge on the whole company singly, determined to kill someone before being killed themselves. . . . We, of course, took no prisoners."

The women in the pits soon despaired of their lives. They had been told that white men would not kill women and children. Encouraged by this story, some of them jumped out of the pits and ran toward their enemies, screaming, "We are women," and holding up their dresses to prove it, hoping in vain for mercy. The volunteers shot them down as they came on, and even massacred those who succeeded in reaching their lines.

Small groups of women and children were later found cowering in the camp, and witnesses afterward testified under oath how certain officers shot them down and scalped them, blowing out the brains of frightened children who had run back to their desolate homes fully an hour after the fight was over. These killers did not spare the little folks, justifying their cruel butchery by the saying, "Nits make lice."

A few half-breeds and Indian women married to white men were spared and eventually turned over to William Bent.

The fight went on for about four hours, almost until midday. Of the forty-six Arapaho in camp, only four survived. As the troops fell back they scalped and mutilated all the bodies. Chivington made John Smith go over the field with him to identify the dead chiefs. But Smith could not be sure, the bodies were so badly cut up. So he reported Chief Black Kettle among the dead, though Black Kettle had made his getaway.

Chivington followed down the Arkansas looking for other camps, but the Indians, apparently forewarned of his coming, had cleared out, and he finally turned back, unsuccessful. The ponies taken at Sand Creek were divided "among the boys." The blood lust of the troops was not sated by the massacre. Fully twenty-four hours after that, the Volunteers shot the half-breed Jack Smith in cold blood. Charley Bent would have been murdered too, but for some friends among the New Mexican Volunteers who guarded him.

Ed Geary, realizing when the troops first began to fire that no defense could be made, had run off afoot, and after a five-mile sprint overtook an Indian woman driving several ponies. Mounting one, he carried the news to the Smoky Hill.

George Bent was not so lucky. Running to take refuge in the pits, he had been shot in the hip, but survived. Both these men described the affair to me.

When Bent arrived at the camp of his relatives, he found all the people wailing and weeping and gashing themselves in mourning for the dead.

While the few survivors, half frozen and bleeding, plodded toward the Smoky Hill, the Colorado Volunteers marched back to Denver, carrying 100 scalps and three terrified Indian children to be exhibited in the local opera house between the acts of a show.

When these atrocities were reported, Americans all over the country were appalled and horrified. The United States Government ordered an investigation.[1] Eventually it paid the Cheyenne an indemnity.

The men responsible would have been punished, but the term of their enlistment had ended. They went scot-free.

There could be no excuse for such brutality, but it is only fair to remark that most people on the frontier approved Chivington's action. Several of the white captives surrendered by Black Kettle and White Antelope soon died as a result of their treatment in the Indian camps, and there had been too many atrocities committed by Indians. And so, many of the frightened settlers believed that Sand Creek would prove a "lesson" to the savages. These citizens were new to the Plains and could not realize what the aftermath must be.

But old mountain men such as William Bent, John Smith, and Kit Carson knew better. They were vehement in denouncing these crimes.

Said Kit, "To think of that dog Chivington, and his hounds, up thar at Sand Creek! Who ever heerd of sich doings among Christians! The pore Injuns had our flag flyin' over 'em, that same old Stars and Stripes that we all love and honor, and they'd bin told down to Denver, that so long as they kept that flyin' they'd be safe. Well, then, here come along that durned Chivington and his cusses. They'd bin out several days huntin' hostile Injuns, and couldn't find none no whar, and if they had, they'd run from them, you bet! So they just pitched into these friendlies, and massa-*creed* them—yes, sir, literally massa-*creed* them—in cold blood, in spite of our flag thar— women and little children even! Why, Senator Foster told me with his own lips (and him and his committee investigated this, you know) that that thar damned miscreant and his men shot down squaws, and blew the brains out of little innocent children—even pistoled little babies in the arms of their dead mothers, and worse than this! And ye call *these* civilized men —Christians; and the Injuns savages, do ye?

"I tell ye what; I don't like a hostile Red Skin any better than you do. And when they are hostile, I've fit 'em—fout 'em—as hard as any man. But I never yit drew a bead on a squaw or papoose, and I loathe and hate the man who would. 'Tain't nateral for brave men to kill women and little children and no one but a coward or a dog would do it. Of course, when we white men do sich awful things, why, these pore ignorant critters don't know no better than to follow suit. Pore things! I've seen as much of 'em as any white man livin', and I can't help but pity 'em."

Kit Carson pitied the Cheyenne. But after Sand Creek they, for their part, no longer took pity on white people. Their chiefs promptly sent a war pipe north to the Arapaho and the Sioux, a pipe which the warriors of these tribes gladly smoked, so pledging support to their old allies. Early one morning, the first week in January, 1865, nearly a thousand warriors struck at Julesburg on the South Platte. Driving the few white men into their little stockade, the Indians looted the warehouse and drove off the cattle.

This was the first of a series of furious attacks all up and down the Platte. The hostiles raided nearly every stage station, ranch and settlement between the forks of the Platte and Denver, killing and burning and tearing down the telegraph line. They even derailed a train, which they looted, committing cruel atrocities on all whites who fell into their hands. It was the beginning of a long and bitter war.

On one raid some Cheyenne warriors on the South Platte shot down a party of nine white men traveling east. These men had been members of Chivington's command, and while going through their baggage the Indians found and recognized the scalps of two of their friends killed at Sand Creek. They cut the bodies of these nine men to pieces.

Black Kettle, however, led his band far to the south, intending to stay out of trouble until another peace could be arranged.

General Grenville M. "Long Eye" Dodge hastened to the Plains to distribute his troops along the stage lines and keep the roads open. There was one officer who knew something about Indian fighting and promptly instructed his men in tactics which he felt confident would enable them to hold their own.

"The Indians of the plains are the best skirmishers in the world. In rapidity of movements, in perfect horsemanship, sudden whirling, protecting the body by clinging to the side of the horse, and rapid movements in open and difficult ground, no trained cavalry in the world can equal them. On foot their ability to hide behind any obstruction in ravines along creeks and under creek and river banks, and in fighting in the open plains or level ground, the faculty to disappear is beyond one's belief except he has experienced it. In skulking and sharpshooting they are adepts, but troops properly instructed are a match for them on foot and never fail to drive and rout them, if they will stand and fight and never retreat except slowly with their faces to them. I have seen several times, when caught in a tight place, bands of Indians held by a few men by holding to ridges and slowly retreating, always using our rifles at every opportunity when an Indian was in range, never wasting a shot on them unless there was a probability of hitting them. The Indians have a mortal fear of such tactics.

"In a fight the Indians will select the positions and pick out quickly any vantage ground, and sometimes as high as 200 will concentrate at such a point where we could not concentrate 20 men without exposing them, and from this vantage ground they will pour a deadly fire on the troops, and we

cannot see an Indian, only puffs of smoke. By such tactics
as this they harass and defeat our troops. Many a fight occurred between Indians and soldiers both watching the smoke
to show each other's position. You can watch this kind of a
fight and never see a person unless some one is hit and exposes
himself, when it is nearly always a sure death. The Indian
character is such that he will not stand continual following,
pounding and attacking. Their life and methods are not accustomed to it, and the Indians can be driven by very inferior
forces by continually watching, attacking and following. None
of our campaigns have been successful that have not been prepared to follow the Indians day and night, attacking them at
every opportunity until they are worn out, disbanded or
forced to surrender, which is the sure result of such a
campaign." [2]

These tactics of the General's were evidently suggested to
him by his close friend, the famous scout Jim Bridger. [3]

Dodge and his troops were spurred on by the knowledge
that the hostiles had a number of white captives of both
sexes, who dropped pitiful notes along the trail and sent word
through friendlies of their terrible sufferings, begging for
rescue. Dodge called out Major Frank North and his Pawnee
Scouts, believing that now, with all the hostiles on the warpath, their camps might be easily invaded.

The Indians had called Dodge "Long Eye" when he was a
surveyor because he could see things through his transit too
far away to be visible to the naked eye of an Indian. They
pulled down the telegraph because, having seen Dodge use
his traveling instrument to send and receive messages, they
believed that he could put his ear against a telegraph pole,
listen to the humming of the wires, and interpret the message.

Dodge had learned from Jim Bridger to be just as vigilant
when no Indians were in sight as when they appeared on the
skyline. He had never lied to them, nor did he ever allow

them to enter his camp. So now he acted very promptly and effectively, though his short campaign was not remarkable for great battles or large losses on the Indian side. His troops endured great hardships in that winter weather. With "only thirteen days and nights of untiring energy on the part of the troops in a winter of unheard-of severity, California, Utah and Colorado were put in communication with the rest of the world. . . . In seventeen days," Dodge boasts, "the stages were started and overland travel was again safe, after being interrupted for two months, and by March first commercial trains were all en route to their destinations." General Winter fought for General Dodge.

Dodge reported to General Grant that the Indians would certainly be on the warpath as soon as the grass was high enough to fatten their ponies, and that, unless the hostiles were "thoroughly chastised," there was plenty of trouble ahead. Grant ordered Dodge to plan an extensive campaign—the Powder River Expedition.

8

POWDER RIVER

THE FOUNDERS OF OUR REPUBLIC wisely attempted to create a government of laws and not of men. But what we got was a government of lawyers.

Now lawyers are trained to wrangle, not to rule. Anybody who has ever seen a Congressional Investigation in progress knows to what lengths a lawyer can go when there is no judge to keep him in order. For it is the function of a lawyer to go all out for the client who pays him his fee; and so, when elected to office, he does the same for his constituents.

After a century or so of this sort of government, it is hardly surprising that we Americans are apt to think of laws in terms of privilege or deprivation. Thus the law has sometimes almost ceased to be a code by which men live and has tended to become a game by which men get a living. We make—and break—more laws than any other people. We often forget that the true function of government is to administer justice without fear or favor. At times our law seems a mere system of economic handicapping.

This state of mind is one reason why we so seldom have had any firm policy, either domestic or foreign. For, having no stable principle to which we can refer our conduct, no fixed standard of justice to which the wise and honest can repair, we are often at the mercy of our emotions and continually swing back and forth instead of standing firm. One day, when some other nation makes a friendly gesture, we congratulate ourselves on being everybody's pal and take pride in being "soft"; next morning, when some other nation snubs us, we are stung into "getting tough" and are angry because we cannot always have our own way.

Now, it is not the function of government to "be soft" or to "get tough"; it is the function of government to be *firm* and *just* and to *keep strong enough to enforce justice.*

But this principal function of government was made very difficult by the way our government was set up. The system of checks and balances and the delegation of authority to independent and rival departments of government, though a good device to prevent tyranny, sometimes defeats justice—to say nothing of prompt efficiency.

In handling the Indians, our government created the Indian Bureau to be "soft" and mother them, and laid upon the War Department the duty to "get tough" in the manner of a careful father.

The limits of such divided authority were hard to define, and officials of either department could usually hamstring the work of the other.

The organization would have created problems enough, even had it been well administered. But it was not. Under the spoils system, the Indian Bureau, intended to be the benevolent mother of the tribes committed to its care, was far too corrupt to create or maintain good will. And the frontier Army, intended to be the stern father, ready to discipline the Indians whenever necessary, was so weakened and reduced that it could rarely do anything more than start trouble which it could not finish.

In 1865, however, both the Army and the Indian Bureau had a single purpose—to keep open the roads to the gold fields. The Civil War had bankrupted the country, and everyone agreed that the precious metals of the West were "our sole reliance to liquidate the accruing interest of the national debt."

Accordingly the War Department, spurred on by the enthusiasm of General Grenville M. Dodge (then in command of the Department of the Missouri) and by the alarming number and success of Indian depredations on the frontier, made ambitious plans involving the expenditure (as they found out later) of some two million dollars a month. The War Department aimed to strike some hard blows in the heart of the Indian country.

The plan proposed—which the War Department tried again in 1876 with equally disastrous results—was to send four columns into the Powder River country, where the Sioux, Cheyenne, and Arapaho were believed to make their headquarters. One of these columns, under General Alfred Sully, was on the Missouri at Fort Rice. General P. E. Connor—a hotheaded, red-headed Irishman born in County Kerry on St. Patrick's Day—was to command the other three. He himself, with 1000 men, was to strike northwest from Fort Laramie for Powder River. Colonel Nelson Cole, with 1400 men, was to lead his column from Columbus, Nebraska, passing east and north of the Black Hills. Colonel Samuel Walker, with 600 men, was to move from Fort Laramie by way of the Black Hills. On arriving at the Wolf Mountains, all four columns were to pitch into the Indians from as many directions and put the warriors out of business. It all looked very pretty on the map.

There can be no doubt that General Connor was in deadly earnest. He issued orders to his subordinate officers "not to receive overtures of peace or submission from Indians, but . . . kill every male Indian over twelve years of age." He took with him Captain Frank North and his battalion of

Pawnee Scouts, Jim Bridger and his staff of white and mixed-blood scouts, and about 100 "Omaha" (really Winnebago) scouts, leaving Cole and Walker, who had no experience of Indian fighting, to get along as best they could with maps.

Walker's men were by no means keen on the campaign. The Civil War for which they had enlisted was over. The day of their discharge was not far off. They had no interest whatever in fighting Indians, which they felt was not in the bond. Many of them were armed only with pistols and sabers. Killing Indians was a job for Regulars, not for Volunteers, they said. When ordered out, the 16th Kansas Cavalry mutinied. Connor had to bring out his own command and threaten to attack Walker's men to get them to march. By all accounts, Cole's men were little more enthusiastic for the campaign.

As for General Sully, he remained at Fort Rice, knowing, after his campaign of the previous summer, that he had not the strength to punish the Indians. So far as he could see, his marches and battles had accomplished nothing—except to rile the Sioux. He knew they were riled, because they repeatedly came to Fort Rice and Fort Berthold to fight him. He reports, "I feel sure I could defend myself, but that is about all I could do." Dryly Sully remarked that if Connor, Cole, and Walker wanted to find Indians, there were plenty not fifty miles from his headquarters. Sully found plenty without looking for them.

While the War Department was launching columns against the Indians, the Indian Bureau was trying to negotiate a treaty with the same tribes—both with the same purpose: keeping open the road to the gold fields.

So, that summer of '65, while the troops marched to war on Powder River, Commissioners led by Governor Newton D. Edmunds went up the Missouri, fearless and unarmed, and talked with the Indians, incidentally terrifying the captain of the steamboat by inviting hordes of armed savages aboard.

Edmunds gave them presents—blankets, calico, and flour—quieting their doubts and complaints by saying, "When the Great Father sends the white brother to make peace with the red brother, he sends him unarmed; but when he sends us to war with you, he sends soldiers to fight you." The Indians had difficulty in distinguishing one "when" from the other.

Sully was scornful of such tactics. He declared that bribing Indians to make peace was simply inducing them to make war so that they could collect again when they made peace. He distrusted the officials of the Indian Bureau who, he declared, were always ready to make another treaty "for reasons best known to themselves." He had a plan of his own: "After a peace has been made next spring, I would offer a reward for every hostile Indian captured, or for his scalp." Sully thought a million dollars a head was a high price for dead Indians. Just who was to collect the scalps he did not say.

Governor Edmunds was also scornful of the extraordinary expense. He later reported that the Sioux war had cost already more than forty million dollars, and that it would be cheaper to bribe Indians to remain at peace and stop their annuities whenever they went on the warpath. This plan ignored the fact that Sitting Bull and all the wild Sioux had, ever since Bear Ribs died, steadily refused to accept government annuities, needed no defense, and were well able to support themselves. They laughed at the idea of anyone being sent to collect their scalps.

However, Edmunds did discover one fact, that "there is in each tribe a band of soldiers—the Strong Heart band—who have in tribal affairs the control of the whole tribe. The chiefs should have an opportunity to act with the advice and consent of that band." This arrangement had been proposed by the Indians themselves at Laramie in 1851, and again by General Harney in 1856. But to allow Indians to police themselves would have put the Army out of a job; the notion never caught on in Washington.

"This wrangling between officials of the Indian Bureau and the War Department went on for years with increasing bitterness. The Army men regarded the Bureau men as either 'milk and rose-water philanthropists' and dreamers, or grafters steeped in corruption, and blamed both parties for causing Indian wars which the Army had to fight. The Bureau officials, on the other hand, professed to think the Army a lot of bloodthirsty butchers, sots, and lechers, whose presence near an agency would endanger the health and soul of the noble red man, and accused the Army of fomenting Indian wars in order to keep up the military establishment and finance corrupt war contractors. Both departments kept up a constant barrage of accusations, insinuations, and charges. But as neither side was ever allowed to put its theories into practice without interference, it is impossible to say which was right.

"One thing, however, is certain: so long as the Bureau kept on making friendlies out of hostiles, and the Army persisted in making hostiles out of friendlies, neither department could possibly lack employment. Sitting Bull summed up the matter in a nutshell: 'The white men have too many chiefs.' "[1]

Guided by Jim Bridger and the Pawnee Scouts, General Connor energetically marched out of Fort Laramie at the end of July. His officers and men, in spite of Jim Bridger's cautions, regarded their expedition as a junket, riding recklessly away from the column to hunt buffalo, losing themselves, and setting the prairie afire, so that every Indian within sixty miles knew that they were coming. Bridger found plenty of Injun sign, and when a broad trail was struck, the Pawnees followed it, surprised a party of twenty-odd Cheyennes, and killed every one of them, including one squaw, at the same time recovering some branded government animals which the Cheyennes had appropriated.

On reaching the watershed between the Powder and the Tongue, late in August, Bridger pointed out the smoke of an Indian camp, and, after investigation, the Pawnees reported they had found it on Tongue River. All night General Connor and his men stumbled through the dark, following up the Tongue, and so surprised the Indians at nine in the morning. This was Black Bear's large camp of Arapaho, who—up to that time—had not been hostile to the whites.

But that did not stop Connor—if he knew it. He charged, caught the Indians packing up, and sent them scuttling into the brush and timber along Tongue River. Those on horse-back who tried to run away, he chased. The Pawnees, who doubtless knew where the Arapaho were hiding, were too busy rounding up enemy ponies to bother with fighting, while many of the soldiers—after Connor left—seem to have lost interest in the battle and turned their attention to collecting souvenirs.

This gave the Arapaho time to reorganize. Though they had lost many of their warriors through death or flight and most of their horses had been taken, the remnant rallied and put up a stiff fight. Connor burned the tipis, confiscated and destroyed all his men's souvenirs, and set out for his wagon corral, taking along his prisoners, eight squaws and thirteen papooses. As he marched away, those Arapahoes who still had horses rode circles around him, but, having no guns, contented themselves with giving exhibitions of fancy bareback riding. Connor's own men, whom he had mounted upon captured half-broken Indian ponies, also gave exhibitions—impromptu.

One of the Winnebago Army scouts was killed, and some of the wounded white men later died. Connor almost ran out of ammunition before the fight was over. This was the only victory of the Powder River Expedition.

On his way in, Connor had spent so much time building Camp Connor—afterward dubbed Fort Reno—that he was late for his rendezvous with Cole and Walker. But now, having struck the Arapaho a hard blow, he began to wonder what had become of his colleagues and sent the Pawnees to find them.

Meanwhile Cole and Walker had a bad time of it. Their troops were slack and sulky, the weather was bad, and once they got to Powder River, they were continually harassed by large numbers of Sioux and Cheyenne. The Badlands had delayed Cole's wagons. He had no guide, no experienced Indian fighters along. Everything was strange and difficult. Walker wandered around looking for Connor. Cole trailed after Walker. Afraid they would lose their horses if they let them graze, they kept them in camp on the picket line. These animals, reared on grain, would have had enough to do to keep fit on prairie grass if turned loose, and when so confined began to die off at an alarming rate. Finally the two columns met.

But as Connor had not informed them which officer was senior, the two colonels spent their time wrangling instead of working together. Their spiritless men fought only in self-defense. During the first two weeks of September they were frequently engaged with the Sioux.

Then one day on Powder River the famous Cheyenne leader of warriors, Wo-ó-hki-nih, or Roman Nose, beautifully mounted on a fast war horse and wearing his medicine war bonnet, led his tribesmen in an attack. The Cheyennes had so few guns they could not do much against the Spencer carbines of the troops. But Roman Nose showed off his power by riding along the line of troops at the dead run, within easy range, to let the soldiers shoot at him. He did this four times. Then all his warriors charged together.

The foot soldiers fired so fast that they were hidden by puffs of powder smoke which bloomed from their guns and, as it drifted away, veiled them from sight. Powder smoke may have accounted for the gross overestimate of Indian numbers—and casualties—which Cole reported. He shelled the Indians as they withdrew, but hit nobody.

By that time Cole and Walker, short of rations, were heading up Powder River toward Fort Laramie. At the mouth of the Little Powder, Sitting Bull's Sioux attacked them in force. A norther blew in that night, and their exhausted horses died by hundreds on the picket line. They had to burn their supplies, their wagons and saddlery, and even destroyed ammunition.

When the Pawnees found them, they had only 600 staggering horses, hardly one of which could stand up with a man on its back. The whole command was starving, having no rations whatever. The Pawnees fed them until Connor came up to inspect "as completely disgusted and discouraged an outfit of men as I ever saw."

They shambled back to Camp Connor, where the General learned that he had been relieved of his command and ordered back to Fort Laramie. The harsh orders he had issued to "kill all male Indians over twelve years of age" are said to have been the cause of his recall.

Neither Cole nor Walker bothered to make a report, until Connor's stinging criticism of their incompetence spurred Cole into defense and retaliation. As for Connor, though the Indians "did most of their fighting with arrows," he reported: "Harm rather than good was done, and our troops were . . . driven from their country by the Indians." Only General Dodge persisted in regarding the expedition as a success; after all, it was his baby.

In spite of the Army's failure to give the redskins a good hiding, Indian agent Leavenworth managed to arrange a treaty council with the Southern tribes, to be held in the autumn on the Little Arkansas River. The commission was led by the redoubtable General Harney. It included such formidable worthies as General J. B. Sanborn, William Bent, the Indian trader and merchant prince of the Southwest, who always referred to the Cheyenne as "my people," and last, but not least, Kit Carson. In spite of Connor's bungling, these men, long known to those Indians, commanded such high respect that they were able to win over such chiefs and warriors as attended the council—that is, Black Kettle's Cheyenne, the Southern Arapaho, some Comanche, Apache, and Kiowa. The chiefs touched the pen and agreed to accept lands set aside for them south of the Arkansas River.

Most of the Southern Cheyenne were then far north, hunting on Powder River. But when they came home in midwinter, they saw no reason to quarrel with their kinsmen who had signed the treaty.

Only the Cheyenne Dog Soldiers, then running meat in that great buffalo pasture on the Smoky Hill and Republican Rivers, where the present States of Colorado, Kansas, and Nebraska meet, flatly refused to accept a new treaty. They were not going to swap their best hunting grounds for that hot dry country down South, nor have a railroad scaring away their buffalo. It was bad enough that wagons kept rolling across the plains to Denver. Early in '66, when Major Wynkoop, their agent, asked them to touch the pen, they covered their ears and clutched their tomahawks.

9

THE FORT PHIL KEARNEY MASSACRE

WHILE the Dog Soldiers covered their ears, officials in Washington assumed an equally classic posture—that of the fellow who is about to receive something to make him wise. They opened their mouths and shut their eyes. The Civil War was at an end, and the country had gone into its usual postwar tailspin, indulging in the release of every impulse, good or bad, which had been held under control during the long struggle between the States.

It is hard to say whether a racial minority in this country suffers more from its friends or from its enemies. The United States, having emancipated the Negro slaves, now sent its armies into the South to implement that liberation. Whatever one may think of Reconstruction in the South, one fact is clear. It drew off most of the troops which might have been used to keep the Plains Indians quiet. The frontier was left largely unprotected.

For the visionaries who were trying, with hasty and ill-considered measures, to insure the rights of Negro citizens, now also assumed control of Indian affairs.

"Let Us Have Peace" was their slogan, and they imagined, as pacifists have always done, that peace could be assured by agreements neatly copied on foolscap and signed with a pen.

89

Many of them, no doubt, honestly believed that the treaties peddled by Governor Edmunds and General S. R. Curtis in 1865 had put an end to Indian wars on the Plains. Many of them, no doubt, honestly believed that white men on the frontier were to blame for everything, and that the Army there must be kept on a short leash.

Of course, the hostile Sioux, under Sitting Bull, Red Cloud, and other chiefs, who hunted along Powder River and the Yellowstone, had never signed that treaty. In fact, at this time they had no agreement whatever with the government. The Treaty of 1851, had it been ratified, was only for ten years, which had expired even before Bear Ribs and his fellow chiefs repudiated it.

If Sitting Bull and the Northern Sioux had been agreed not to allow encroachment on their hunting grounds in 1857, they were now even more bitterly determined to resist encroachment with all their might.

This fact had been obscured by the Commissioners, who skirted Sioux country signing up tame agency chiefs. They must have known, however, that the hostiles did not approve the treaty, since they could not find one man on the frontier willing to risk his skin by carrying their message of peace to the wild Sioux on Powder River.

Thus the country was kept unaware that a crisis impended and that bloody war must follow the first attempt to build roads and forts in those hunting grounds.

The treaty made in 1865 by Generals Harney and Sanborn was, on the whole, a satisfactory one—so far as Indians were concerned. It guaranteed to the Sioux, Cheyenne and Arapaho the Powder River country—all those lands lying between the Yellowstone River, the Rocky Mountains and the Black Hills, extending from the foothills of the mountains eastward to the Little Missouri. This was the best buffalo country in all the Northern Plains.

But so quickly had times changed that this treaty no longer adequately represented the interests of the white men. And as history shows, whenever an agreement no longer represents realities, paper gives way to facts. The facts were that white men had steadily been pouring into the Idaho gold fields. Some had gone in steamboats up the Missouri River—a voyage possible only for a few weeks of spring and early summer. Others had followed the Santa Fe Trail up the Arkansas River and on to Denver, or the Oregon Trail along the Platte and so over South Pass. But when the fabulous gold deposits in Montana were discovered, hordes of impatient gold-seekers demanded a shorter road, one that led directly through the Powder River country.

Before the year was out in which Powder River had been guaranteed to the Indians, the government attempted to make a new agreement with them—to open a road through those hunting grounds. The government was rapidly being pushed into a position where it would have to use force either against the Sioux or against its own citizens. Yet the public, misled by visionaries and pacifists, actually believed that the Peace Policy was working and that the road along the Powder River to Montana was a safe highway.

The apostle of the Peace Policy was Mr. E. B. Taylor of the Indian Bureau, and in 1866 he appeared at Fort Laramie. There he ignored the warnings of frontiersmen of long experience and repeatedly announced that he had been sent out there to make a peace treaty and that nothing could stop him. He obtained a lot of signatures—none of them from chiefs of the hostiles. But he brought along such lavish presents that the wild bands were enticed to come and get them. However, when Red Cloud and Man-Afraid-of-His-Horses arrived, Taylor found them a different breed of cats from the agency chiefs —men thoroughly independent, who would never touch a pen because he told them to. They wanted to know what his treaty said.

If the Indians are to be believed, Commissioner Taylor or his interpreter misrepresented the meaning of the agreement. The point at issue was, of course, the proposed road or roads along Powder River. How Taylor, if left to his own devices, would have come out of his debate with Red Cloud, we cannot know. For on June 16, in the midst of his negotiations, Colonel Henry B. Carrington marched his command into camp at Fort Laramie. He had orders, issued some months earlier, which required him to march to the Powder River country, there to build forts and guard the new road to Montana—the Bozeman Trail.

Carrington was a garrison officer, an engineer, something of a martinet, who owed his rank to political influence. At the same time, he was a man of frank and honorable character, though without experience of frontier life or Indian warfare. He was heading into the country where Connor's 3000 cavalrymen had been badly defeated only the summer before, with less than 1000 infantry, including musicians—and most of them recruits.

Whether the top military men hoped that the troops could, like wolves in sheeps' clothing, establish themselves in Indian country during the prevalent craze for peace, and so be ready to strike when war broke out, or whether Sherman and the other generals actually took the reports of the Indian Bureau at their face value and believed it safe to send such small forces into that horde of angry savages, is not very clear. Apparently everybody in Washington had fallen into a sort of trance, like that which preceded Pearl Harbor in 1941.

Afterward it seemed that any fool could see what was about to happen on Powder River, and that even a moron could have made better plans and provided better tools for the job to be done. But officials in Washington, whatever they may have known or believed, were in no mood to face the facts and their constituents at the same time.

They tried to please people in the West by promising a better road to the gold fields and to pacify the pacifists in the East by letting them pursue their treaty-making way. If any of these gentlemen in Washington had been bold, intelligent, and honest enough to see and tell the truth, he might have lost his job—to say nothing of what might have happened to his party!

And so Carrington came to Fort Laramie to get 100,000 rounds of rifle ammunition to use in the old-fashioned muzzle-loading infantry muskets with which his men were armed. There he found Taylor and the Commissioners had their hands full to keep Red Cloud, the warlike leader of the Oglala band of Bad Faces, and even the more peacefully inclined Man-Afraid-of-His-Horses from walking out on them.

Old Jim Bridger, Carrington's guide, had told the Colonel emphatically that the Sioux would never submit to having a road built and forts established spang in the middle of their best hunting grounds. And Carrington, a reasonable man, tried to have his orders changed to allow him to wait there until the treaty was concluded. But his superiors, who anticipated no trouble and had even urged his officers to take their wives along, peremptorily ordered him to march "immediately." Before he started, he drew all the ammunition he could get for his men—less than 1000 rounds!

When Carrington rode up, a suspicious chief demanded where the Little White Chief and his troops were heading. Frankly the Colonel told him.

At that Red Cloud burst out, "The Great Father sends us presents and wants a new road, but the white chief goes with soldiers to *steal* that road before the Indians say yes or no." Another chief was quite as frank as Carrington, and told him that within two moons the Colonel "would not have one hoof left." Indignantly Red Cloud and Man-Afraid gathered their

blankets around them and stalked out of the council. Their
camps and that of Crazy Horse promptly hit the trail to the
north. If white men moved into their country, there would be
war.

Our government was designed to prevent tyranny and
guarantee freedom to all. And on the frontier—as in the States
—it did just that. It left the Indians free to kill and scalp; the
Army free to invade and fight; the pioneers free to encroach
on Indian lands; the Indian Bureau free to make treaties; the
Indian Ring free to graft; the pious planners free to scheme
and propagandize; and everyone free to object and interfere.
All this freedom broke a good many heads and eggs—but pro-
duced some sizeable omelettes.

For this chaos was not due to any weakness in our form of
government, but to the fact that everything done on the
frontier by Uncle Sam was too little and too late.

And when one considers the folly, ignorance, stupidity, and
even downright dishonesty prevalent among many who called
themselves friends of the Indian in those days, one is likely to
decide that it was a mercy they never had control on the
Plains. As it was, every treaty they ever made resulted in
trouble—usually in war!

But nobody in our time needs to be reminded that tyranny
is worse than war. Abolish war, and you abolish revolution;
abolish the possibility of revolution, and you abolish liberty.
Our Constitution provides that Congress shall pass no law forbidding American citizens to own and bear arms; for, to be
free, men must have bullets as well as ballots. The friendly
tribes had neither—and were in sorry case. But the hostile
Sioux and Cheyenne, at any rate, had bullets.

Said Crazy Horse, the fighter, "*Hopo*, let's go."

At the same time, from his headquarters in Omaha, Carrington's superior, Colonel Philip St. George Cook, who had

ordered Carrington forward, wrote to him, "There must be peace."

One people can make war. It generally takes two peoples to make peace. . . .

By the middle of July Carrington, having garrisoned Fort Reno, was building his new post on Big Piney Creek. It was named Fort Phil Kearney. Carrington had hardly got into camp before the Indians made good their boast and ran off most of his horses. In the fracas that followed, several men were killed and wounded.

That same day a French trader and his employees were butchered, and from then on the ill-armed recruits had to be constantly on guard. Whoever left camp without an escort was most unlikely to come back. Yet Carrington went ahead, felled timber, built his stockade and ample quarters, shops, stables, and a corral. The new fort was one of the best in the whole West.

Both officers and men at Fort Phil Kearney were utterly ignorant of Plains Indians and of Indian warfare. In the note-book [1] of one of the men on the post you will find a list of "game killed and wounded near the fort" during his tour of duty there. The bag includes five "common Indians." Listing Indians as "game" did not seem odd to the cocksure young officers in the fort. They went around talking of "taking Red Cloud's scalp," and Colonel Fetterman declared, "With fifty men I could ride through the whole Sioux nation." That was the day Carrington had to refuse to allow him to go with such a handful to "surprise" the Sioux camps along Tongue River. These camps extended for fully twenty miles along the stream. It was hard for young and spirited officers who had served valorously in the Civil War to stay cooped up inside the stock-ade; they were boiling with confidence that each was a match for half a hundred savages.

Early in December, 1866, Colonel W. J. Fetterman took

forty men out to bring in a beleaguered wood train. He chased the attacking Indians off into the hills, lost several men, and soon found himself hemmed in. Had it not been for Lieutenant Wands, who was a crack shot and had a Henry repeating rifle, Fetterman might not have lasted until Colonel Carrington's relief party came to rescue his detail. His rookies, never having had enough ammunition to engage in target practice, could not stand off the Indians—and that day most of them carried only short-range revolvers.

In most Indian battles, in fact, all the killing was done by two or three cool crack shots armed with repeating rifles. The rest of the men in the ranks might just as well have been setting off firecrackers for all the good they did. Green, ill-trained, ill-equipped, and for the most part led by officers wholly ignorant of Indian warfare, they had only one thing in their favor—their unquestioned valor.

By this time the Indians, always slow to organize, had gathered their forces and prepared to move against Fort Phil Kearney. Each band or tribe initiated and organized its own war party in the traditional tribal way. No one chief need be given credit for starting this war—indeed it is doubtful if any one Indian chief could ever be given full credit for starting any war—for war was in the air. So, when they had all got together and made orations, and the various warrior societies had chosen new leaders, all the warriors in camp moved up Tongue River toward the fort.

First rode more than a thousand Cheyenne, Arapaho, and Minniconjou Sioux, and after them nearly as many Oglala. The warriors took it easy, each riding with a group of his friends, leading his best war horse on a lariat, with a pack of jerky and a wooden bowl and the bag containing his war clothes tied on his rawhide saddle. Most of the warriors were armed with bows and lances.

They threw eight scouts out ahead, who signaled with hand

mirrors from the hilltops. Every day at sundown they made camp in some cozy valley, each tribe in a separate circle of wickiups. Such a large war party was very unusual; the warriors, confident in their numbers, were eager for battle.

Their last camp was about ten miles northwest of the fort. Here the herald called the chiefs to council. Black Shield was principal chief of the Minniconjou, Crazy Horse of the Oglala. "The important Cheyenne men were Dull Knife, Walking Rabbit, Wolf-Lying-Down, Black Moccasin (or Iron), Painted Thunder, Walking White Man, and Wild Hog." [2] Red Cloud, chief of the Oglala Bad Faces, was not present in this war party, though the white men have put his name on the monument where the fight took place. The chiefs sat and smoked, discussing their plans.

By this time ambush had become a favorite strategy among the Plains Indians. This had come about by accident. When attacking or approaching an enemy, men with fast horses were likely to outrun their fellows on slower mounts. For every warrior was strongly competitive and eager to count as many *coups* as possible. The man who got there first came home with most of the loot and the honors.

There was little discipline among Indians, and no one dreamed of blaming a warrior who had been successful, even though he had violated orders to do it. Even when Indian soldiers were trying to restrain the other warriors by herding them forward within a hollow square, it was always possible for an ambitious man to fall out on some excuse, wait until the war party had passed on out of sight, and then circle quickly around the party and get to the enemy before them. Thus, it was almost impossible for a large party to stage a surprise attack.

Naturally, the men left behind were usually the older and less active warriors. The young men led the way.

So it came about that the older and less daring warriors contrived to turn the daring of these undisciplined youngsters to their own advantage. Deliberately they selected a number of rash young men beforehand and sent them forward to the attack. These youths, of course, being so few, would necessarily be driven back, drawing the pursuing enemy with them —and so give the older, slower warriors a chance to take part in the battle and get their share of the loot and honors.

Therefore, anyone acquainted with Plains Indians must have expected the chiefs to plan an ambush. In fact, the Sioux had done that very thing on Tongue River before they invited the Cheyenne and Arapaho to join them in attacking the fort.

Up to this time the Northern Cheyenne had been friendly toward the white men, but only a few days before, four young Cheyenne warriors had approached Fort Phil Kearney and had been fired at by the soldiers. Probably the soldiers believed them to be Sioux hostiles. Few of those tenderfeet could distinguish Indians of one tribe from those of another. But the Cheyennes naturally had resented such treatment. So they accepted the invitation to join forces with their old allies to attack the whites.

The chiefs in council had only to detail a small party to attack the wood train next morning. Such an attack, they had found, was certain to bring soldiers swarming from the fort. Once the soldiers were out of the fort, the chiefs relied upon decoys to lead them into ambush. Accordingly, they appointed ten young men to act as decoys: two Minniconjou, two Oglala, and two Hunkpapa Sioux; two Cheyennes; and two Arapahoes.

When the next day broke, the ten decoys rode off toward Fort Phil Kearney, while a small war party went to attack the wood train. By the time the sun rose, all the warriors had their ponies saddled, had mounted and were riding up frozen Peno Creek to the forks. Tight in the forks was a grassy flat, from which a long narrow ridge rose rapidly toward the southeast.

The road from the fort to Montana came down this bare, narrow ridge to the forks of the creek.

The Indians planned to divide their forces and hide on both sides of the ridge to wait until their decoys lured the troops down the road into the trap.

Since the Sioux had invited the Cheyenne to join their war party, they gave their guests choice of position. The Cheyenne and the Arapaho, and with them the Oglala, concealed themselves on the west side of the ridge along the frozen creek. Those of them who wished to fight on foot crept into the brush and tall grass near the forks. But mounted men rode on up the little stream to hide; this put them nearly a mile from the road. On the east side of the ridge, the Minniconjou and some Hunkpapa Sioux found cover somewhat nearer.

When all were in position, they stripped the white buckskin covers from their round shields, painted their faces for war, sang and prayed, and so made ready. When all that was done, they waited, standing silent, listening, holding their war horses.

While all this was going on, Chief Two Moon, with a small party of his warriors, was visiting Fort Phil Kearney. The chief came to spy on the soldiers. But Colonel Carrington wished the Indians to know his strength. He made Two Moon welcome, led his warriors into the stockade, and showed them all over the post. Two Moon saw "the big guns that shoot twice," the stacks of ammunition and rations, and the many muskets of the parading soldiers. Jim Bridger acted as interpreter.

Big Throat (as the Cheyenne called Bridger because of his goitre) plainly told Two Moon that Indians could never take that fort. After being shown over it, Two Moon never doubted that Big Throat spoke the truth. He rode straight back to the Sioux and told them what he had seen and heard.

That morning the wood train rolled out of the fort along the trail to the west on its last trip that season. If the Indians had waited one more day to set their trap, they would have been too late. But as it was, everything happened according to plan. The small war party charged the wagons of the wood train, forcing it to corral for defense; the escort fired a volley, the flags on the lookout hill wagged warning—"Many Indians." Within a few minutes the gate in the stockade opened and the bluecoats moved out under orders to rescue the wood train and *not* to go beyond Lodge Trail Ridge.

Immediately the ten decoys allowed themselves to be seen in the leafless brush along Big Piney Creek only a little way from the fort. Inside the stockade, a big gun roared, sending a shell to pop harmlessly over their heads. As if frightened and demoralized, the decoys headed for the hills to the north, taking care not to go too fast, so that the soldiers would follow.

And that was just what they did. Colonel Fetterman, disregarding orders, instead of going to relieve the wood train, rode northwest along the creek, apparently hoping to cut off the war party which had attacked the train. That was the last they saw of him from the fort.

Meanwhile, the war party left the wagon train and hid, so that the troops, not finding them, would follow the decoys on northward to the ambush.

There two thousand warriors waited with ready weapons, listening with eager ears, not showing so much as a feather above the brush. It was getting on toward the middle of the day when suddenly, through the quiet frosty air, they heard a far-off sound of firing, which abruptly ended. The heavy silence settled around them again as they waited impatiently. Another volley rang out, quickly over. They looked at each other, each seeking confirmation of his own thought in the eyes of his comrades. Was the firing nearer? It had seemed so. Again the heavy silence settled down around them, and held —and held. There was a long wait. Then, not far off, they heard a third burst of gunfire. Like grass in the wind, the huddled warriors stirred slightly at that sound, every man taking a better grip on his bow or war club.

Not long after, away at the top of the long ridge to the south, they saw a tiny movement: little figures of horsemen coming slowly over the skyline and down the trail along that narrow ridge. It was their decoys. Often they halted to ride back and forth across the trail that followed down along the top of the ridge, or to fire from the saddle, as though standing off their pursuers and protecting somebody behind them.

Then all at once the warriors, peering from their chill hiding places, let their breath out in a great sighing cloud, for there they saw the first lines of the bluecoat enemy following the decoys, coming down the trail. Every man pinched the nose of his war pony for fear it might whinny to the horses of the white men and so betray the trap. Every warrior clutched his weapons tensely, waiting for the word to charge.

The bluecoats were in two groups, some distance apart, one following the other down the trail. First came the Pony Soldiers; behind them marched the Walk-a-Heaps. Slowly they came on, stopping from time to time to fire at the decoys. Then the white powder smoke would cover them like a cloud until the rising wind carried it away. So, while the Indians waited, the Pony Soldiers reached the flat at the forks of Peno Creek. This brought all the bluecoats between the jaws of the trap.

And now the Indian decoys rode their tired animals across the little stream at the end of the flat. They divided into two groups, rode off in opposite directions, then turned and rode back, crossing each other. That was the signal for attack.

"*Hookahey!* Let's go!" In a moment all of the warriors on both sides of the ridge were on horseback. They laid on the quirts, dashed out of ambush. The frantic hoofs of their ponies drummed the earth like thunder, and above that thunder sang the high, shrill ululating of their war cries.

The bluecoats halted in their tracks. Because the swarming Minniconjou were nearer, they reached the troopers first. Thunder Hawk, riding in the lead on the dead run, struck the first soldier, counted his *coup*, and swept by unhurt. Oglala and Cheyenne charged up soon after. Arrows began to fly and sting as the Indians circled, closing in from three sides.

The Walk-a-Heaps ran up the ridge, falling back to a small cluster of rocks. There they took cover and fired, the white smoke blooming above the rocks. But the Pony Soldiers did not join the Walk-a-Heaps. They fell back past them and halted about a hundred steps higher up the ridge. From there they fired down at the whirlpool of Indians around the rocks.

The Indians were not much afraid of the single-shot muzzle-loading rifles of the infantry. But two civilians, lying among the rocks, had up-to-date Henry repeating rifles. Their rapid fire soon taught the Indians to beware of them. One Minniconjou, Eats Meat, charged straight through the bluecoats, but fell before he could get clear.

Only a brave man would charge those forty rifles, but the Sioux were full of fight and so outnumbered their enemies that after a few minutes of circling they charged in and cut down the infantry in hand-to-hand fighting. They killed them all in less time than it takes a man to smoke a pipe.

After that the Indians swarmed up the ridge after the Pony Soldiers. It was steep, with snow and ice in places, no place for mounted action. But the bluecoats kept together, fighting bravely, leading their horses back up the ridge back toward the fort, fighting a slow, losing battle. In turn the cavalrymen would kneel and fire, then get up and retreat again. By this time the Indians were so close around them that arrows flew in all directions, hurting and frightening the horses and bringing down the men. In the rear, one bluecoat marched alone with his face to the Indians, moving backward up the ridge, shouting aloud. Perhaps he was a soldier chief. He was armed with a carbine which he swung first to one side, then to the other.

White Bull charged this soldier horseback, with an arrow fixed on his bowstring. The white man waited to shoot. White Bull let fly and pinned him through the heart.

After that, the Indians took courage, swarming up after their enemies. Within a few minutes the Pony Soldiers had won their way back to the top of the long ridge. There they turned loose their horses. The animals all headed back to the fort as hard as they could go.

The Plains Indian fought for loot as well as glory. Every warrior was eager to capture one of those big American horses. While the warriors raced to catch them, the battle waited.

When they came tearing back, they found the bluecoats waiting behind a number of large boulders, nearly shoulder high, which lay in a rough circle on the level top of the ridge. The ridge at the point where the boulders lie is narrow, hardly forty feet across. To the south the ground rose gently to a higher hill, but on every other side the ridge sloped steep as a house roof toward the valley below. The slopes, patched with ice, offered little footing even for a barefoot pony. So the chiefs were heard yelling, telling the warriors to tie their horses in the coulees. There was now no chance that the bluecoats could run away from them.

And now suddenly the weather turned bitter cold; blood congealed as it flowed.

So far, the fight had lasted only fifteen minutes. But wiping out the bluecoats among the boulders took a little more time. The Pony Soldiers had breech-loading carbines which they could fire with some rapidity, and at such point-blank range it seemed they could hardly miss. So the Indians crowded together on either side of the narrow ridge, hanging just below the rim where the soldiers could not see them, but sending arrows up and over, trying to hit a bluecoat. Back and forth the arrows went in hundreds, sometimes killing an Indian on the other side. Sometimes an Indian would show himself. Then the troopers would jump up to fire at him. All the Indians who saw him would shoot back. When all the warriors had swarmed up, crowding the slopes on both sides, they called back and forth to each other across the ridge, "Are you ready? We are ready." Finally Long Fox, on the west side, yelled to his Minniconjou, "*Hopo*, let's go!"

The Indians charged in on both sides, plunged between the boulders, grappled with the soldiers, clubbing and stabbing, while the cavalrymen swung their carbines. The bugler battered his instrument flat on Indian heads. In that slaughter, several Indians fell before the last white man was struck down.

"After all were dead, a dog was seen running away, barking, and someone called out, 'All are dead but the dog; let him carry the news to the fort,' and someone else cried out, 'Do not let even a dog get away,' and a young man shot at it with his arrow and killed it. The last of the cavalry was killed just where the monument now stands." [3]

The Indians did not count the dead white men. Their medicine man had promised them a hundred dead enemies, and they therefore know this fight as The Hundred White Men Killed. Actually only seventy-nine officers and men and two civilians fell on Massacre Hill that day, December 21, 1866. By the time the Sioux had finished stripping and mutilating the bodies, it would not have been easy to make an accurate count.

During the forty-minute fight perhaps twenty thousand arrows had been fired by the two thousand warriors present. The ground was littered with them. Every warrior who thought of it refilled his quiver, or picked up shafts and spitefully shot them into the bare butchered bodies of his enemies.

While the Indians triumphed there among the dead, a relief column from the fort appeared on the hill which overlooked the battlefield. Indians beckoned and called, inviting the new bluecoats to come down and fight. But Captain Ten Eyck heard no firing and could see nothing of Fetterman's command. He stood his ground.

The fact that there was no firing indicates that the Indians had no guns. In fact, only six of the dead soldiers showed gunshot wounds, and two of these, Colonel Fetterman and Captain F. H. Brown, are believed to have shot themselves. Perhaps the other four were hit with bullets from weapons captured on the battleground, or were wounded by their own comrades in the mêlée.

The Sioux carried off their fourteen dead, the Cheyenne their two, moving back toward Tongue River. Their war party had been successful. It was time to go home and dance over the scalps they had taken. In that bitter weather, they would probably have gone home even if they had been unsuccessful.

Meanwhile, in the stricken fort, Carrington and his surviving handful took all precautions to withstand assault, stored the powder magazine with rations for the women and children huddled there, and mined the building so that it could be destroyed with everyone in it, if the hostiles got over the stockade. That night, through the swirling blizzard, Portugee Phillips set out alone to carry news of the disaster 230 miles to Fort Laramie.

Yet Carrington need not have worried. Indian fighting was always hit and run. Sioux warriors never followed up a victory. The truth is, an Indian war party was not organized to make war, but only to give battle. Each war party had a single objective, and when that objective was attained, the warriors went home to complete the ritual with a ceremonial scalp dance.

Indians seldom even tried to defend their own camps. When a camp was attacked, the men commonly fought a delaying action while noncombatants took to the brush. Never having had any notion of ownership of land, it never occurred to the Indian to defend a piece of ground, nor did he care who was left in possession of the battlefield. If he occupied a hill, it was because the hill protected him or gave him an opportunity to deal a harder blow. He might die in defense of a friend or of his family, or for honor, or even (in the heat of battle) for loot— but never for a tipi or a position.

Siege warfare was therefore to him a brand-new thing. When we built forts on his hunting grounds, the redskin was faced with a novel problem. He never got beyond the rudiments of siege warfare, having no weapon with which to destroy fortifications. His one trick, which he worked so successfully and so often on our soldiers, consisted chiefly of two maneuvers: the charge and the retreat; in a word—ambush.

When news of the "massacre" at Fort Phil Kearney was telegraphed to Washington, the buck was passed around military circles with great speed and dexterity. While this was going on, the Commissioner of Indian Affairs took prompt advantage of the confusion by publishing a statement declaring that his poor starving Indians had come to Fort Phil Kearney to plead for ammunition with which to hunt buffalo and save their famished families. He asserted that Carrington had cruelly refused to help them and that the blameless Sioux, thus driven to desperation, had retaliated by attacking Fetterman and his men.

As a matter of fact, the Sioux—who had no guns—had made a very successful fall hunt, killing plenty of buffalo in the same way they killed soldiers—with arrows.

10

HANCOCK AND THE DOG SOLDIERS

GENERAL DODGE was in command of the Department of the Missouri, and even while General Connor was planning the Powder River Expedition in '65 a force was organized on the Arkansas River to strike the tribes on the Southern Plains. The Indian agent, Colonel J. H. Leavenworth, however, had strongly objected to the proposed campaign and had influence enough to stop it.

The Government, anxious to push the Kansas-Pacific Railroad to the west, tried in vain to persuade the Cheyenne Dog Soldiers to leave their unceded hunting grounds on the Smoky Hill and Republican Rivers. There was hardly any trouble during 1866 except for some raids in Texas by the Kiowa and the murder of a Mexican by a drunk Cheyenne in Kansas.

But citizens of the new State of Kansas now had votes. It was commonly said that the Indians had threatened to attack as soon as the grass was high enough to fatten their ponies. Pressure was put on Congress, which appropriated $150,000 for a military expedition into the hunting grounds of the Dog Soldiers.

At the time it marched, the Indians had received their annuities from Major Wynkoop, their agent, and were hunting buffalo. This was in April, 1867.

Meanwhile Major General W. S. Hancock had replaced General Dodge as commander of the Department of the Missouri, and was given command of the Kansas Expedition.

When it came to making hostiles out of friendlies, General Hancock holds the record. He left Fort Riley at the head of the Kansas Expedition—a mixed force of cavalry, infantry, and artillery—of some 1400 men. He also had a pontoon train to help him chase Indians across the Kansas rivers. Ostensibly his force was to protect the Santa Fe Trail and the Smoky Hill Road. Hancock himself declared his mission was to "feel the temper of the Indians" and to separate the sheep from the goats. The celebrated correspondent Henry M. Stanley went along and reported the General's campaign, afterward describing what he saw in his book *My Early Travels and Adventures in America and Asia.*

At Fort Larned, Hancock summoned the chiefs of the Cheyenne and of their warrior society, the Dog Soldiers, to a night council by firelight. His officers turned out in all their gold braid and epaulettes; "the artillery especially made a fine show with their red horsetails." Major (later Colonel) Edward Wynkoop, the Cheyenne agent, acted as interpreter.

"The Indians were dressed in various styles," Stanley reports, "many of them with the orthodox army overcoat, some with gorgeous red blankets, while their faces were painted and their bodies bedizened in all the glory of the Indian toilette. To the hideous slits in their ears were hanging large rings of brass; they wore armlets of silver, wrist rings of copper, necklaces of beads of variegated colours, breast ornaments of silver shields, and Johnson silver medals, and their scalplocks were adorned with a long string of thin silver discs."

The General shook hands with Tall Bull and White Horse, chiefs of the Dog Soldiers, and spoke to them at some length. He had brought them an Indian boy, supposedly a Cheyenne captive, and reported that an Indian girl was to be sent from

Denver and returned to them. He then demanded that they return to him all captives in their hands, called attention to the unparalleled size of his forces, and told them that the Great Father had heard that some Indians were trying to start a war.

He went on to say, "I intend not only to visit you here, but my troops will remain among you to see that the peace of the Plains is preserved. I am going also to visit you in your camps. The innocent and those who are truly our friends we shall treat as brothers. If we find hereafter that any of you have lied to us, we will strike you. . . . When your agent informs me who the guilty are, I will punish them. . . . I have heard that a great many Indians want to fight; very well, we are here, and are come prepared for war."

Hancock pointed out that the Great Father had many more soldiers at his command than there were Indians on the Plains. "You cannot replace warriors lost; we can. . . . My chiefs cannot derive any distinction from fighting with your small numbers. . . . Let the guilty then beware. . . . If a white man behaves badly or does a wrong to you, he shall be punished, if the evidence ascertained at the trial proves him guilty."

This last remark caused a tremendous sensation among the Indians, who could hardly believe their ears.

Hancock went on, "We can redress your wrongs better than you can." At this the Indians groaned.

"I have no more to say. I will await the end of this council to see whether you want war or peace."

During the silence that followed, the calumet was smoked. Then Tall Bull, a leading chief of the Dog Soldiers, shook hands with all the generals, stepped to the middle of the ring, and spoke:

"You sent for us; we came here. We have made a treaty with our agent, Colonel Wynkoop. We never did the white man any harm; we don't intend to. Our agent told us to meet you here. Whenever you want to go on the Smoky Hill you can go. You can go on any road. When we come on the road your young men must not shoot us. We are willing to be friends with the white man.

"This [captive] boy you have here, we have seen him; we don't recognize him; he must belong to some tribe south of the Arkansas. The buffalo are diminishing fast. The antelope that were plenty a few years ago are now few. When they will all die away we shall be hungry. We shall want something to eat, and we shall be compelled to come into the fort. Your young men must not fire on us. Whenever they see us they fire, and so we fire on them. The Kiowa, Comanche, Apache, and Arapaho, you should send and get *them* here, and talk with *them*. You say you are going to our village tomorrow. If you go, I shall have no more to say to you there than here. I have said all I want to say here."

Here the General interrupted: "I am going, however, to your camp tomorrow."

Tall Bull continued, "I don't know whether the Sioux are coming here or not. They did not tell me they were coming. I have spoken."

General Hancock, being a military man, and knowing that Roman Nose was the most celebrated warrior of these Cheyennes, thought him a chief and was angry because he had not come into the fort for the council. Now Roman Nose, though a famous leader of warriors, was not a chief in the tribe and had no authority to make agreements for his people. But Hancock angrily ordered his troops out and, leaving the Santa Fe Trail he had been sent to guard, marched through the deep snow toward the camp, then nearly fifty miles west. Before he had gone far he met Roman Nose and a party of some three hundred chiefs and warriors coming in for the talk to which he had summoned them. Hancock drew up his men smartly in line of battle. This martial display made the redskins suspicious.

Wynkoop rode out alone to the Indian line. A parley was arranged between the two forces. George Bent told me that Roman Nose, holding a strung bow and four arrows, lost his temper and told Chief Bull Bear that he was going to shoot Hancock then and there. The chief begged Roman Nose to think what this would mean to their women and children. When Hancock came up, Roman Nose eyed him sternly. The big buck made a fine appearance, in a blue uniform and gold epaulettes. When Hancock sharply demanded of him whether the Indians wanted peace or war, Roman Nose replied, in bitter sarcasm, "We don't want war; if we did we would not come so close to your big guns." Hancock asked why Roman Nose had not visited him at the fort as requested. The Cheyenne replied, "My horses are poor, and every man that comes to me tells me a different tale about your intentions."

As the Indians drew off, the troops followed, and next day, early in the afternoon, came in sight of the Cheyenne tipis. The camp stood in a "grove of noble elms . . . along the banks of the Pawnee River."

The Indian warriors, outnumbered two to one, were much disturbed to see the troops going into camp so close to their village, fearing another Sand Creek massacre. The white chief, Hancock, had talked very strong. But the anxiety of the warriors was nothing to that of their women and children. Bull Bear had requested Hancock not to come so near. But the General, knowing nothing of Indian custom, could not realize how redskins felt and how contrary to all their ideas camping thus together must be.

Once the wily Crows had invited Jim Bridger's trappers to camp with them, which Bridger rightly interpreted as a trick to put him at their mercy. The Cheyennes felt that day just as Bridger had some years earlier. But Hancock was ignorant of these customs, and apparently regarded any advice offered him as an affront.

Some time after the troops had made camp, four chiefs voluntarily came to report that their women and children had all run away. The General angrily asked *why* they had run away. Roman Nose sarcastically asked him if he had never heard of Sand Creek, three winters back, when soldiers came to a friendly Cheyenne camp and killed all those who did *not* run away.

Hancock was furious at this "treachery" on the part of noncombatants. Manifestly he thought that, if women and children run from you, it must be their fault. Hancock sent several chiefs on army horses to bring back all those people scattered over the snowy prairie, but of course the chiefs found their mission impossible. Considering the General's angry behavior, it is hardly surprising that the chiefs and warriors held council and voted to follow their women. They left all their tents standing, and all their household goods, and took along not even one travois. All they carried with them was lashed on the backs of their lean and weakened pack animals.

Hancock sent Custer to surround the village. That night Custer wrote his wife: "They feared . . . another massacre like Chivington's. . . . I am to pursue them. . . . The Indians are frightened to death." Though a guard was kept over the camp, the "boys in blue" were "continually carrying away mementos of their bloodless victory . . . arrows and knives were picked up by the dozen, also little dolls." An eight-year-old girl, a captive, was found. She had been pitiably abused. General Hancock decided to burn the camp. "The dry poles of the wigwams caught fire like tinder, and so many burning hides made the sky black with smoke." He set the prairie on fire—in more senses than one.

Hancock, now that the time had come to "chastise the

savages," now that he had driven them to hostilities on the Smoky Hill, found that he could not catch them. Pontoon trains and artillery were no match in speed even for a winter-starved pony. Custer and the Seventh rode out and had a parley with Pawnee Killer, but on being ordered to follow the Indians, found that even cavalry could not overtake them. Captain Hamilton's twenty men were surrounded, but bravely repulsed the Indians. There was an attack on a wagon train, and a fight at Fort Wallace. Lieutenant Kidder, with ten men, carrying dispatches for General Sheridan, was found dead and butchered. He was killed by a mixed party of Sioux and Cheyennes.

Hancock blamed the Indian agent, Major Wynkoop, for claiming the Indians were friendly, contrary to fact. Wynkoop declared that Hancock drove the Cheyenne to war, an opinion in which he was backed up by Agent Leavenworth.

Hancock led the largest command seen on the Plains since General Stephen Watts Kearney led the Army of the West to Santa Fe in 1846. Hancock campaigned busily for four full months. During that time, his 1400 men killed four Indians —two of them friendlies.

>>>>>>> **11** <<<<<<<

MEDICINE LODGE TREATY

There was so much trouble with Indians in the West after Sand Creek that when the Joint Committee's *Report on the Condition of the Indian Tribes* was published, assuring the nation that all the trouble on the Plains was caused by white men, there was much public interest, fresh hope for a settlement of the Indian problem, and a widespread demand for a new policy.

To implement this Peace Policy, Congress set up, on July 30, 1867, a Peace Commission to accomplish three main purposes: first, to abolish Indian wars forever by removing their causes; second, to get the Indians to abandon their nomadic life and take up farming; and third, to keep the redskins from interfering with the construction of railroads across the Plains and from attacking frontier settlements.

This was quite a contradictory assignment, since farms and railroads were, along with wagon trails, the principal causes of Indian wars!

The Commissioner of Indian Affairs, N. G. Taylor, presided. Formerly a Methodist preacher, whose "Methodical sanctity still clings to him like a well-fitting coat, most prominent in the florid speeches which he inflicts on the red infidels," he was an earnest man, "full of philanthropic ideas

114

BUFFALO: THE INDIAN'S COMMISSARY

CHIEF SITTING BULL

Leading Sioux Warrior and Statesman

respecting the poor Indian," and was devoting his life to the "improvement of the social status of the American aborigine." An unfriendly Western paper described him as "a simpering White House courtier." He was to match his homiletics against the forensic skill of the chiefs.

Senator John B. Henderson of Missouri was chairman of the Senate Committee on Indian Affairs. He was "the businessman of the Commission, doggedly perseverant in the cause of Western interests." He was at work every moment, and quite impatient at delay in getting the tribes to council and bringing the talks to a close. He was always alert, taking notes and asking pertinent questions.

General J. B. Sanborn, who had served his country "on many a hard field—a good-natured and jovial gentleman, pleasant to converse with, free of access, and pretty thoroughly posted on Indian matters," was selected to superintend the movements of the Commission. Sanborn was regarded as something of a jester, described by a malicious reporter as apt to deliver "oracles in terribly vulgar language" and as having "a loquacious, fanatical spirit created by love of office."

Colonel S. F. Tappan of Colorado loyally supported Commissioner Taylor. He was a small man, rather priggish in appearance, "an agreeable companion but of few words." He took Indian affairs very hard and regarded the United States as an absolute aggressor. Taylor spoke for them both: "Rapidly our race has relieved them of their vast domain, and the remnants of the ancient red nations, encircled by the pressing millions of our people, maintain precarious footholds on their last hunting grounds. These millions will soon crush them out from the face of the earth, unless the humanity and Christian philanthropy of enlightened statesmen shall interfere and rescue them."

To balance the appeasers on the Commission President Johnson appointed also three major generals—William S.

Harney, Alfred H. Terry and C. C. Augur—to represent the War Department. He also asked the commander of the Division of the Missouri, Lieutenant-General William Tecumseh Sherman, to serve.

Harney, the hero of the frontiersmen, erect and vital despite his age, with his venerable white beard and handsome mustaches, towered above his colleagues "like another Saul." That old war horse had seen more of the Plains Indians in war and in council than any man in the group. He believed in straight talk and direct action, and when he learned that Little Raven's Arapahoes had caught up with some Kaws who had stolen their ponies, he made a typical remark: "Hurrah! I hope they kill them all!"

Terry, captor of Fort Fisher, with his sober face and dark imperial, and Augur, with gray sideburns spraying out on either side of his sanguine face and long cigar, had little to say. But Sherman's red beard and high balding forehead was in the front of every argument. He spoke incisively for the Army—until he was called back to Washington.

The Peace Commission proceeded first to North Platte, Nebraska, for a conference with the Northern Cheyenne and Sioux (Oglala and Brûlé): Spotted Tail, Man-Afraid-of-His-Horses, Man-That-Walks-Under-the-Ground, Pawnee Killer, Standing Elk, Swift Bear, Black Bear, Turkey Foot (Turkey Leg), Cut Nose, Whistler, Big Mouth, Cold Face, Crazy Lodge.

The Commission had to wait for weeks while the Indians delayed their coming. During this time they received reports of the Wagon Box Fight, near Fort Phil Kearney, and the Hayfield Fight, near Fort C. F. Smith, in which small detachments were besieged by hundreds of warriors. Though the Sioux and Cheyennes could not wipe out the white forces, they killed as many men as they lost and had a good time skirmishing with the troops.

About the same time news reached headquarters that the Cheyennes had wrecked and burned a railroad train at Plum Creek, Nebraska, south of the Platte. There was one survivor, William Thompson, who was scalped alive and tried to preserve his scalp by keeping it fresh in a bucket of water until he could reach a doctor and have it sewed on!

Captain Frank North and the Pawnee Scouts were promptly sent to Plum Creek. There they encountered some of the raiders, put them to flight, and during a long running fight killed and scalped fifteen Cheyennes and captured two, one the nephew of Chief Turkey Leg. The Pawnees did not lose one man.

When Turkey Leg came to North Platte for the council he brought six white captives, all women and children, and exchanged them for his nephew and the Cheyenne squaw.

With war's alarms all about them, the appeasers on the Commission felt somewhat at a disadvantage in the sessions with their military colleagues. But Taylor and his supporters soon recovered their aplomb and adroitly took advantage of the Indian attacks to bolster the Peace Policy. The Indian Office declared that the government must either send heavy armed forces and fight a hard war with the Sioux, or else make peace with them *on their own terms*. But at length the Indians came in and the council assembled. A group of newspaper correspondents were on hand to report proceedings, chief among them Henry M. Stanley.

Swift Bear opened proceedings. He remarked, "When we make peace we pray to the Great Spirit. We have no witness, but keep our treaties faithfully by praying to the Great Spirit."

Taylor introduced his colleagues, and pleaded for peace, saying they had come to hear the grievances of the Indians.

Those grievances were, first of all, the roads built by the whites through the hunting grounds north of the Platte and along the Smoky Hill River; and secondly, a shortage of guns and ammunition. Pawnee Killer said the railroad could go through if the whites would "stop the Powder River road." The chiefs begged for traders and for ammunition. One of the chiefs declared, "Ever since I have been born I have eaten wild meat. My father and grandfather ate wild meat before me. *We cannot give up quickly the customs of our fathers.*"

On the following day General Sherman replied for the Commission, explaining that if the roads through Indian country damaged the Indians, the government would compensate them. "But the roads will be built, and you must not interfere with them." He reminded the chiefs that some of the Indians were still at war.

"We will give you some presents because you have come up here to see us. But we will not give you much till we come to a satisfactory agreement." Sherman agreed to give the peaceful bands "almost anything they want. . . . But the rest of you must work with your bows and arrows till you satisfy us you will not kill our people."

Instead of presents Sherman gave them advice—that they must learn to support themselves as white men do, that they must learn to cultivate their land, build houses and raise cattle. "A great many agreements have been made by people gone before us . . . but I am afraid they did not make allowances for the rapid growth of the white race. . . . You cannot stop the locomotive any more than you can stop the sun or moon, and you must submit and do the best you can. . . . Our people East hardly think of what you call war here, but if they make up their minds to fight you, they will come out as thick as a herd of buffalo, and if you continue fighting you will all be killed. . . . This Commission is not only a Peace Commission, but it is a War Commission also."

Sherman said he would be back in November to make the treaty. The Indians were much discouraged at not getting their presents and by having the peace treaty deferred. An Oglala declared, "I am poor. You are rich. When you come to our villages we always share with you. Where is the present I am to get? What am I to do? . . . I cannot make powder nor can I make ball. . . . I was raised upon buffalo meat. I want to live upon it. . . . After a battle, when two nations meet and shake hands, they ought to be at peace."

In spite of Sherman's blunt refusal to give arms and ammunition to the Indians, the warriors made such a threatening demonstration (never officially reported) that his colleagues prevailed on him to modify his stand. Arms and ammunition were delivered to the Indians so that Taylor could report the council had ended in a "perfect agreement."

The Commission went next to Fort Laramie, where they arrived about the middle of September, with paper, ink and a pen all ready for Red Cloud to touch. For this chief's name had been so publicized that nobody in the East would consider a treaty satisfactory without his mark upon it. But the Sioux sent word that they were busy hunting and would see the Commission "maybeso next summer."

At Laramie, Taylor put it up to Sherman and the other generals, demanding to know how large a military expedition would be necessary to whip the hostiles on Powder River. Sherman could only reply that, owing to the overhasty demobilization of our armies after the Civil War, no additional troops could be spared from the forces then occupying the South. The hostiles continued to harass our meager forces garrisoning the posts and every train passing over the roads in their hunting grounds. If the Army could not handle the Indians, the appeasers had everything their own way.

The Commission then proceeded to Fort Larned, Kansas, and from that post traveled seventy miles to Medicine Lodge Creek to council with the Southern tribes: Arapaho, Apache, Cheyenne, Comanche and Kiowa. Two ambulances carried

the Commission and the press. These were trailed by thirty
wagons containing supplies, and were escorted by three companies of the Seventh Cavalry and a battery of Gatling guns.
After his plain speaking, General Sherman had been called to
Washington.

The military escort looked good to Major Wynkoop,
agent for the Cheyennes. At first he had gone directly to the
Indian camp. But one day someone came running to warn
him that Roman Nose was gunning for him and was on his
way to the lodge where Wynkoop was staying. Wynkoop
looked out and saw the formidable warrior coming, with ten
braves at his heels and a revolver in his hand. Roman Nose
believed that Wynkoop was the man who had led General
Hancock to the Cheyenne camp.

The agent raised the lodge skins at the back of the tipi,
ducked out, jumped on a fast horse picketed there, spurred
out of the village, and saved his life.

On the way from the fort to the treaty ground, old-timers
amused themselves by filling the tenderfeet with tall tales:
buffalo had been so thick on the prairie that a man could
walk on their backs for ten miles and never touch the ground;
just a while back, they swore, Hancock's outfit had been
compelled to mow a passage through the herds with grape-
shot from their howitzers, and so on. But the party saw
enough buffalo that day to make such yarns seem credible.
On the way some camp-followers of the Commission, then
known by the unflattering name of "bummers," shot the
buffalo for sport, to the vast indignation of the Indians. Satanta burst out, "Have the white men become children, that
they should kill meat and not eat? When the red men kill,
they do so that they may live." The Commission put the culprits under arrest.

Nearly a thousand lodges, sheltering more than five thousand Indians, were pitched along the pleasant little stream.

The tribal camp circles along the wooded banks were surrounded by thousands of ponies grazing on the hills and by the cattle brought along for rations.

The Apache were represented by Wolf Sleeve, Poor Bear, Iron Shirt, and Crow; the Arapaho by Little Raven, Spotted Wolf, Yellow Bear, Powder Face; the Cheyenne by Black Kettle, Big Jake, Bull Bear, chief of the Dog Soldiers, Tall Bull, Heap of Birds, Slim Face, Black White Man; the Comanche by Ten Bear, Young Bear, Painted Lips, Iron Mountain; the Kiowa by Satanta, Kicking Bird, Satank.

The sensation of the meeting was Mrs. Adams, interpretress for the Arapaho. She appeared in a crimson petticoat, black cloth coat, and a small coquettish velvet hat decorated with a white ostrich feather. The Indians regarded her with great respect, for as one of them said, "I have hunted among the Spaniards and the Red Coats, in the mountains to the west and the forests east of the Missouri River. But I have never seen a bird with feathers like *that*. This woman must be the daughter of a great chief."

What followed is recorded in the *Proceedings of the Council*, October 19—20, 1867.

After an issue of uniforms to the Indians, Taylor opened the preliminary meeting. Then several Kiowa chiefs spoke briefly. Satanta, dubbed "the Orator of the Plains," spoke for the Kiowas. He was a tall man and good-looking, with plenty of long shiny blue-black hair, dark piercing eyes, a consuming vanity, and a quick temper. His presence was commanding and he was able to sway the councils of his people. He was respected, too, as a warrior. His weakness was that he loved the sound of his own voice too well, and was perhaps more affected by his oratory than were any of his listeners. He seldom missed a chance to sound off, particularly when he could pose as a great man.

But on that October day Satanta disdainfully declared, "I

don't want to say anything at this talk. I will say what I have
to say at the grand council." Immediately the wrinkled old
Comanche chieftain, Ten Bear, put on his spectacles and in
a shrill voice made the cutting remark: "What I say is law
for the Comanche, but it takes half a dozen to speak for the
Kiowa."

The Comanche were a business-like, practical, and—what
was even rarer among Indians—a skeptical people. They
had no tribal religion, no Sun Dance; each man made medicine to suit himself.

Stung by Ten Bear's challenge, Satanta decided to take the
floor again. First, however, he buried his hands in the loose
earth at his feet, rubbing the sand over them, after which
he went round shaking hands with all present and then stood
within the circle, dignified and ready with his speech. Like
the other chiefs, he had no heart at all for the schools,
churches and farms proposed by the Commission. "His style
of delivery was well calculated to please a savage multitude.
Of formidable and striking appearance and gifted with native eloquence, he compels attention. His name is a thing to
swear by."

"The Commissioners have come from afar to listen to our
grievances," Satanta began. "My heart is glad, and I shall
hide nothing from you. I understood that you were coming
down to see us. I moved away from those disposed to war,
and I also came from afar to see you. The Kiowas and Comanches have not been fighting. We were away down south,
when we heard that you were coming to see us.

"The Cheyennes are those who have been fighting with
you. They did it in broad daylight, so that all could see
them. If I had been fighting, I would have done so also. Two
years ago, I made peace with Generals Harney, Sanborn and
Colonel Leavenworth at the mouth of the Little Arkansas.

"That peace I have never broken. When the grass was

growing this spring, a large body of soldiers came along on the Santa Fe Trail. I had not done anything and therefore was not afraid. All the chiefs of the Kiowas, Comanches and Arapahoes are here today. They have come to listen to the good word. We have been waiting here a long time to see you, and we are getting tired. All the land south of the Arkansas belongs to the Kiowas and Comanches, and I don't want to give away any of it. I love the land and the buffalo, and I will not part with any. I want you to understand, also, that the Kiowas don't want to fight, and have not been fighting since we made the treaty. I hear a good deal of fine talk from these gentlemen, but they never do what they say. I don't want any of these Medicine homes built in the country. I want the papooses brought up just exactly as I am. When I make peace, it is a long and lasting one, there is no end to it. We thank you for your presents.

"All these chiefs and head men feel happy. They will do what you want. They know that you are doing the best you can. I and they will do so also. There is one big chief, lately died—Jim Pockmark, of the Caddoes—he was a good peace-maker, and we are very sorry he is dead. When I look upon you, I know you are all big chiefs. While you are in the country we go to sleep happy and are not afraid. I have heard you intend to settle us on a reservation near the mountains. I don't want to settle there. I love to roam over the wide prairie, and when I do it, I feel free and happy, but when we settle down we grow pale and die.

"Hearken well to what I say. I have laid aside my lance, my bow and my shield, and yet I feel safe in your presence. I have told you the truth. I have no little lies hid about me, but I don't know how it is with the Commissioners; are they as clear as I am? A long time ago this land belonged to our fathers, but when I go up to the river, I see a camp of soldiers, and they are cutting my wood down, or killing my buffalo. I don't like that, and when I see it, my heart feels like bursting with sorrow. I have spoken."

But Satanta, though he had made his speech, still tried to keep his Kiowas talking, and pulled up from his seat the reluctant Black Eagle, "who drew back like a young lady invited to the piano."

Little Raven, chief of the Arapaho, was fat and usually affable, but that day he was plenty wrathy. He announced that he had nothing to say, as all his young men had been sent after some Indians—probably Pawnee—who had stolen their horses. The chief had picked up a little frontier English: "God damn them mean squaws!"

Now that the Kiowas had talked themselves out, Ten Bear observed that their young men had not gone to Washington as he had. There he had learned how to manage things. Now he would speak for them.

"My heart," he said, "is filled with joy, when I see you here, as the brooks fill with water, when the snows melt in the spring, and I feel glad, as the ponies do, when the fresh grass starts in the beginning of the year. I heard of your coming, when I was many sleeps away, and I made but few camps before I met you. I knew that you had come to do good to me and to my people. I looked for the benefits, which would last forever, and so my face shines with joy, as I look upon you. My people have never first drawn a bow or fired a gun against the whites. There has been trouble on the line between us, and my young men have danced the War Dance. But it was not begun by us. It was you, who sent out the first soldier, and it was we, who sent out the second. Two years ago, I came up upon this road, following the buffalo, that my wives and children might have their cheeks plump, and their bodies warm. But the soldiers fired on us, and since that time there has been a noise, like that of a thunderstorm, and we have not known which way to go.

So it was upon the Canadian. Nor have we been made to cry once alone. The blue dressed soldiers and the Utes came from out of the night, when it was dark and still, and for camp fires, they lit our lodges. Instead of hunting game, they killed my braves, and the warriors of the tribe cut short their hair for the dead. So it was in Texas. They made sorrow come into our camps, and we went out like the buffalo bulls, when the cows are attacked. When we found them, we killed them, and their scalps hang in our lodges. The Comanches are not weak and blind, like the pups of a dog when seven sleeps old. They are strong and far-sighted, like grown horses. We took their road, and we went on it. The white women cried, and our women laughed. But there are things which you have said to me which I did not like. They were not sweet like sugar, but bitter like gourds. You said that you wanted to put us upon a reservation, to build us houses and to make us Medicine lodges. I do not want them. I was born upon the prairie, where the wind blew free, and there was nothing to break the light of the sun. I was born where there were no enclosures, and where everything drew a free breath. I want to die there, and not within walls. I know every stream and every wood between the Rio Grande and the Arkansas. I have hunted and lived over that country. I lived like my fathers before me, and like them, I lived happily.

"When I was at Washington, the Great Father told me that all the Comanche land was ours, and that no one should hinder us in living upon it. So why do you ask us to leave the rivers, and the sun, and the wind, and live in houses? Do not ask us to give up the buffalo for the sheep. The young men have heard talk of this, and it has made them sad and angry. Do not speak of it more. I love to carry out the talk I get from the Great Father. When I get goods and presents, I and my people feel glad, since it shows that he holds us in his eye. If the Texans had kept out of my country, there might have been peace. But that which you now say we must live on is too small. The Texans have taken away the places where the grass grew the thickest and the timber was the best. Had we kept that, we might have done the thing you ask. But it is too late. The white man has the country which we loved, and we only wish to wander on the prairie until we die. Any good thing you say to me shall not be forgotten. I shall carry it as near to my heart as my children, and it shall be as often on my tongue as the name of the Great Spirit. I want no blood upon my land to stain the grass. I want it all clear and pure, and I wish it so, that all who go through among my people may find peace when they come in, and leave it when they go out."

"While the talk was being interpreted," Stanley reports, "the Honourable gentlemen were engaged in different things. Harney, with head erect, watched with interest each dusky and painted face of the Indians around the tent. Sanborn picked his teeth and laughed jollily. Tappan read Indian reports about the destruction of the Indian village. Henderson, with eyeglass in his hand, seemed buried in deep study. Terry busied himself in printing alphabetical letters, and Augur whittled away with energy. Agent Leavenworth examined his children, and made by-signals to old Satank, the oldest chief of the Kiowa nation. Under the table sat Commissioner Taylor's [white] papoose, making wry faces at some pretty squaws sitting astride, behind some aspiring youths on ponies, in the background. The correspondents sat *à la Turque* on the ground, their pencils flying over the paper."

The Commissioners briefly explained the terms of the treaty, the principal clause in which provided for reservations for the Kiowa and Comanche between the Red River and the Washita, close to their enemies the Texans; and a reservation for the Cheyenne and Arapaho south of the Arkansas River. In other respects the treaty was identical with that for the Northern tribes. The Cheyenne, then engaged in renewing their Medicine Arrows (their most sacred ceremony), did not arrive until the other tribes had completed their talks.

The Arapaho wanted a reservation separate from the Cheyenne, who—so they said—were always getting them into trouble with the whites. This was unexpected, for the Cheyenne and Arapaho had been close allies, hunting, fighting and camping together since first the white men met them, and probably long before. Though both tribes were of Algonquin stock, their languages differed so much that neither tribe suspected a common ancestry. The Cheyenne tongue is harsh, nasal, choking, sibilant, without liquids. The Arapaho language, on the other hand, is all broad vowels, liquids and soft diphthongs—a tongue as different in sound from Cheyenne as is Italian from German. In fact, the Cheyenne often sang Arapaho songs because the words were more melodious. The Arapaho language was so difficult to learn that very few men not born to it had ever mastered it. Of course, both tribes talked fluently together in sign language.

These tribes were equally brave and warlike, though the Cheyenne patronized the Arapaho because the latter were so few. The Cheyenne warrior was a haughty person, and his women were celebrated for their virtue. On the other hand, the Arapaho was affable and accommodating, an imaginative fellow with a voluminous mythology and an art superior to that of most of his neighbors.

It was amazing that the Arapaho now wished a separate reservation.

The Apache, a small tribe, had come *en masse* and seemed very willing to continue keeping the peace. How little these warriors understood peace, however, is shown by the speech which Poor Bear made when he presented his shield to Mr. Taylor, the great Peace Chief of Washington: "I have slain many an enemy, this shield has saved me many a time from death. When my foe saw this shield he trembled, and I triumphed; go you and do the same."

Still the chiefs of various tribes signed the treaty during the week of October 21-27, 1867, in order to get their presents. But nobody on the frontier could believe that those wild Indians would even try to abandon their wandering habits and become farmers overnight.

In particular the Kiowa appeared determined to behave like juvenile delinquents in peacetime and homicidal maniacs in war. To the anxious frontier people on their lonely homesteads and isolated ranches, the Indian seemed half devil and half child. Yet their own Government continued to treat such gangs of irresponsible armed killers, roving freely over its own territory, as independent nations!

Far back East there were many friends of the Indian—at a safe distance—who advocated disarmament, by which they meant putting our own weapons into the hands of avowed enemies.

12

ROMAN NOSE

THOUGH it was too much to expect that the chiefs who signed the treaty of Medicine Lodge could lead their tribesmen into the White Man's Road immediately, still peace might have followed that agreement, for a time at any rate. But getting Indians to sign a treaty and getting the Senate to ratify it were two separate projects. The Senate dallied. Winter, spring and half the summer dragged by, and the suspicious tribesmen waited in vain for the promised annuities. The chiefs who had signed that document lost face which could only be regained on the warpath. To them and their people it seemed that the Grandfather in Washington had tricked them again.

But of all this the crusaders for peace—at any price to the people on the frontier—were unaware. They were jubilant over their success at Medicine Lodge and made ready to give the Indians everything—except the Union Pacific Railroad. Hawklike the Army watched that line, protecting construction gangs and firing on all Indians who approached the Platte.

The Indian Bureau planned another treaty for the summer of 1868, much heartened by the report, published shortly before, of the Joint Committee to the effect that all Indian trouble on the frontier had been caused by white men. This claim contained a good deal of truth, at any rate up to the time of the Sand Creek Massacre, and was based upon the testimony of such frontiersmen as Kit Carson, William Bent, and John Smith.

But though the trouble before 1864 may have been caused by white men, the trouble existed and had to be coped with. The resentment of the tribesmen all over the Plains over that massacre and the Hancock campaign smoldered in their hearts. They could not forget their relatives whom the white man had butchered, their villages which had been wantonly destroyed, and the loss of their ponies.

No doubt if white men had been kept off the Northern Plains there would have been no trouble there, for the Sioux made no depredations outside Indian country. But the Kiowas and Comanches in the South had raided New Mexico, Old Mexico and Texas for generations. A large proportion of these tribesmen were descended from captives. They were professional kidnappers, horse-thieves and fences, continually riding against the settlements.

Troops were few on the Plains in '68. Even so, the Government might have applied sanctions and have permitted peaceful hunting bands to trade, as they had not been allowed to do for some four years. Instead, while it forbade traders to sell arms and ammunition, the Government allowed Peace Commissions to hand out such presents by the ton; thus the Department of the Interior kept busy arming the hostiles so that they could shoot down officers and men sent out by the War Department!

The crusaders planned to try again that summer of '68, and a Commission proceeded to the Plains. Their slogan was, "Feed them or fight them." Having little luck at Fort Laramie, they proceeded up the Missouri to Fort Rice, carrying lavish presents to the Sioux. These presents, of course, enabled the Indian Bureau to count upon the support of the nefarious

Indian Ring—a gang made up of traders, contractors, and
Indian agents of the baser sort, banded together to exploit
the redskin and the taxpayer alike.

In the past philanthropists and apologists for the Indians
had always protested bitterly against the bribes offered chiefs
to get them to sign treaties. But by 1868 even a visionary could
see that no other method would work. The chiefs had to be
hired to come in, bribed to sign. A flock of missionaries, squaw
men, traders and breeds were sent out to lure the chiefs to
council.

After all their recent fighting, the Indians were much in
need of arms. When the call reached them, some of the hostiles, including the Oglala Bad Faces, went to Fort Laramie,
signed the treaty and carried off the usual presents. Then they
went back to the Powder and continued their war with the
whites.

Sitting Bull and Red Cloud, leaders of the hostile bands,
scorned all the blandishments of the Commission. But Father
Pierre-Jean De Smet was not easily discouraged. He loved
Indians, and the Indians trusted him. With a small band of
friendly Sioux, the Black Robe drove in his buggy far out
to Sitting Bull's camp on the Powder and brought back a
delegation of chiefs to Fort Rice. Here the so-called Treaty
of Laramie was offered to the hostiles.

Gall—also known as Red Walker and The-Man-Who-Goes-
in-the-Middle—was Sitting Bull's delegate. Gall was very
haughty, rehearsed his personal wrongs, and after bragging
that he would take no presents, demanded powder and ball.
Gall touched the pen July 2, 1868.

It is clear that the chiefs who signed the treaty had a very
imperfect idea of the nature of that document. Perhaps the interpreters, anxious for the success of their mission and the
continuance of their wages, avoided trouble by keeping the
chiefs in the dark. Perhaps the eager, philanthropic Commis-

sioners were at fault. It is manifest, at any rate, that the Indians thought the new treaty was just the usual agreement for trade and peace. Still Red Cloud, in spite of all temptations, refused to sign until the Army had actually abandoned all forts on the Powder River Road. The champions of the Peace Policy gloated.

For that treaty contained clauses which, its framers believed, would make it forever impossible for the Army to interfere with Indians off the reservation. And of course, all Indians on reservations would be under the control of the Indian Bureau and the Peace Party who controlled it. That treaty gave the hostile hunting bands everything they wanted, and asked (so they imagined) nothing in return; it was sheer appeasement of the wild Indians of the Northern Plains. True, it contained clauses that the reservation Sioux might find hard to stomach. These provisions required the Sioux to settle down and become farmers, to submit to a census, and to refrain from opposing the building of railroads and wagon roads outside their reservation—a reservation which was to be in that barren region along the Missouri River where there was no longer any wild game whatever. But, since these clauses had not been translated fully to the chiefs whose signatures adorned that document, there was no need to worry—yet. Score a smashing victory for the Peace Party: *this* time they had got the chiefs of the hostiles (some of them) to touch the pen!

All this while the Army was not sitting on its hands. They yet had time to act. For the Treaty of Medicine Lodge, signed in October, 1867, was not proclaimed until late summer, 1868, and the "Laramie Treaty" with the Sioux not until February of the year following.

The Indians loved traders, who brought them the arms and kettles, the blankets and knives which they were powerless to make for themselves. They did not much mind the small forces of blue-coated soldiers who passed through their country and sometimes fought with them. In fact, they liked these fighting men—the only white men whom they at all understood—since they themselves were warriors. But they all hated the settler, the man who fenced and plowed, cut down the timber, burned the grass and destroyed the game. Bitterly they hated and butchered him and all his breed—women and children, even babies. In their opinion, the only good farmer was a dead farmer. For the plow that broke the Plains broke also everything the Indian knew or loved.

But as the number of settlers on the frontier steadily increased, their clamor and influence had more and more effect upon the Government, which dared not punish them to favor redskins. The frontiersmen had to be defended, no matter how often chiefs and Commissioners made treaties. Moreover, it must never be forgotten that certain bands of Comanche and Kiowa had no hand in the treaty-making at Medicine Lodge and did not feel bound by its provisions. Once they became involved in conflict, it was inevitable that their fellow tribesmen should join forces with them whether they had signed the treaty or not.

Thus while the Commissioners were busy pushing their treaty on the Northern Plains, rumors of trouble prompted General Phil Sheridan to move his headquarters from Fort Leavenworth on the Missouri River to Fort Hays on the Kansas plains. He was a man who liked to get his facts first-hand. He had talks with the Cheyenne and Arapaho, as General Sully did with the Kiowa and Comanche. Both at first refused the appeals of the Indians; both afterward yielded. Sully made the great mistake of issuing guns and ammunition to them.

Early in August the Cheyennes perpetrated repeated outrages on the Saline, raping women and murdering without regard to age or sex all luckless whites whom they encountered. The Kiowa and Comanche joined in, using Sully's guns, in Kansas and along the Texas border. Governor Frank Hall of Colorado wired Sheridan: "For God's sake give me authority to take soldiers from Fort Reynolds." That was August 25, 1868. These depredations might have swept the Southern Plains, had not Captain Frederick W. Benteen scattered the warriors with a detachment of cavalry from Fort Harker. The settlers were shouting for protection.

These developments took Sheridan by surprise. He knew there had been no immediate provocation for these raids. General Sherman, too, was besieged in St. Louis by appeals from the frontier for help.

Yet it seemed at first that nothing could be done. There were simply not enough troops available on the border to control the hostiles. The ease with which the Cheyenne had avoided Hancock's futile marchings up and down the Plains had not been lost upon the military mind.

In this crisis, Major George A. Forsyth proposed that a company of civilian frontiersmen be formed of men who knew the country and savvied Injuns, men who could ride and shoot and follow a trail. He thought such a company of scouts might prove useful.

Jim Bridger had proposed this plan two years before, and his views on the subject had been published in the *Kearney Herald* (January 6, 1866) at Fort Kearney, Nebraska. When Forsyth brought it up, General Phil Sheridan approved. On August 29, Major Forsyth marched out of Fort Hays at the head of fifty enlisted scouts, nearly every man a seasoned plainsman, some of them veterans of the Civil War. They carried seven-shot Spencer rifles, Colt's revolvers, and—though somewhat unmilitary and few in number—felt confident that they could outfight twice their weight in Regulars. They headed for the Republican River, where they picked up an Indian trail, and struck the Arikaree Fork on September 16, 1868.

That night they made camp beside the shallow river, opposite a narrow sand bar near the south bank. This island, then covered with willow brush and crowned by one tall cottonwood, was about seventy yards long, forty feet wide. The prairie all around was bare and level. But downstream, opposite the east end of the island, a patch of tall grass covered a few square yards on the mainland just under the low sand bank of the river.

Three big camps, two of Sioux under Pawnee Killer and one of Cheyenne and Arapaho, were only a dozen miles downriver. Forsyth, heading upstream, would have ridden away and left them, had not a few warriors seen his company on the march.

They hurried to carry the news to the nearest camp. Most of the Cheyenne were Dog Soldiers, under their soldier chiefs, Tall Bull and White Horse. There were also numbers of Northern Cheyenne, one of them the famous Roman Nose.

At that time no Cheyenne warrior on the Plains was more renowned for valor and victories. His string of *coups* was endless. Though he was not a chief, all the men of his camp regarded him as their natural leader. He was once offered a chieftaincy, but declined it on the ground that, having spent all his time on the warpath, he lacked the gentle and paternal qualities which a civil chief should have.

Earlier that same year he had attended a council at Fort Laramie, where he was photographed along with Spotted Tail, Old-Man-Afraid-of-His-Horses, and other chiefs. This, almost certainly the only photograph of Roman Nose in existence, shows a big man in early middle life, with an easy, confident bearing, a high forehead, the prominent brows of a fighter, a firm chin, and a large nose; he squints at the photographer, Gardner, with a quizzical, somewhat contemptuous smile. He wears beaded buckskin leggings, a flannel shirt, a buffalo robe —and a single upright eagle feather in his back hair.[1]

The Cheyenne invited the Sioux and the Arapaho to act with them, organized a big party, and set out to look for Forsyth. Roman Nose told them not to wait for him. When his crier made the announcement, many of the people wondered why Roman Nose did not go along with the others. Only a few understood.

The war party, some 500 or 600 Indians, failed to find Forsyth that day, and finally went into camp to wait for morning. When all was dark, eight young men slipped away, contrary to the wishes of their chiefs, hoping to find the white scouts, stampede a few horses, and so be the first to strike the enemy.

"They rode from hill to hill, stopped to listen, and often dismounted and held their ears close to the ground, but could hear nothing. Just before daybreak, however, they saw, far off, the light of fires being kindled. They rode toward them quietly, until they could see the horses and mules scattered about, and then, making all the noise they could and waving robes and blankets, they charged through the herd, to stampede it. A few horses broke loose from their picket-pins, but they secured only seven." [2]

At dawn the main party rode over the hill and saw Forsyth's outfit about two miles away, packing and almost ready to march. *Hookahey!* Immediately the warriors formed a line of battle and charged on the dead run, yelling and whooping. On the open prairie they knew that little band of white men had no chance to live.

But Major Forsyth knew that too. He was an able officer. Quickly he ordered his men to cross the stream to the island. By the time the Indians came within easy range, his scouts had splashed through the shallow channel and were busy making breastworks of their packs. Forsyth sent Jack Stilwell and two others down to guard the lower (east) end of the island. There was little cover, and less time. So Stilwell and his comrades hopped over the narrow channel to the south bank, took cover in the tall grass there, and dug in on the mainland.

By that time the charging warriors swept along the wide, dry, sandy bed of the shrunken stream, intending to ride the scouts down and rub them out. But when they reached the island and faced that determined company of riflemen, the warriors had a sudden change of heart, split, swung to left and right, and swept by on either side. Only one of them—Bad Heart—had the guts to ride through the enemy. The scouts knocked down one Indian and several horses, but not without loss.

Major Forsyth was the first man wounded. Lieutenant Fred Beecher was also hit twice. Until the men had time to dig in, their casualties mounted.

Luckily for them, the soil was all loose sand; within a few minutes they had entrenched themselves and were ready for the second charge. It was not long in coming.

Once more one brave man rode through their lines, and once more the other warriors split and swept by. The smell of mule blood was too much for their excited ponies. Some of them, riding over Stilwell through the tall grass, were shot down.

Finding they could do nothing on horseback, the Indians dismounted and advanced. A few charged zigzag across the stream, flung themselves down on the sand within a few yards of the white men's rifles, dug frantically to throw up breastworks. Only one of these got away. The scouts could not miss at that distance.

The warriors began to wish that their great champion, Roman Nose, would show up, and bring along his war bonnet. In early life he had been named Sauts, the Bat, after that creature so hard to kill or catch. Since he had got his famous bonnet, all believed him to be bulletproof, invincible.[3]

"This war bonnet had been made long ago by White Bull —also known as Ice—a Northern Cheyenne. It had always protected Roman Nose in battle.

"There were certain taboos which were a part of the medicine of this war bonnet and which, if disregarded, took away its protective power. One of these was that the man who wore it might not eat food that had been taken out of a dish with an iron instrument. The food for the owner of this bonnet must be taken from the pot or other dish by means of a sharpened stick. If this law was not complied with the owner of the war bonnet would be hit by bullet or arrow in his next battle. An elaborate ceremony of purification might restore the protective power of the war bonnet, but this ceremony was long and required much time.

"Shortly before Forsyth's command had been discovered, Roman Nose had been invited to a feast by a certain Sioux, and the woman who was preparing the food for the feasters used a fork to take from the frying-pan the bread she was cooking. This was not known when the food was served to the feasters, and Roman Nose ate the bread instead of abstaining, as he would have done if aware of the circumstances. Afterward Eight Horns, one of the Dog Soldiers, noticed that the woman, who was continuing her cooking, was using a fork and pointed out to Roman Nose what she was doing. Then Roman Nose said: 'That breaks my medicine.'

"Tall Bull, who heard of the matter, advised Roman Nose to go through the ceremony of purification at once, but almost immediately afterward and before Roman Nose had done anything Forsyth's scouts were discovered, and there was then no time for the ceremonies. . . .

"Roman Nose had not yet got to the fight. Runners had gone to the camp and told Roman Nose that there was fighting, and a good many Indians were being killed. Then Roman Nose got on his horse and rode up to the battlefield, and

when he got there one of the old chiefs cried out that Roman
Nose had come. The Indians were still all about the island, but
the fighting had stopped and everyone was standing back,
waiting to see what Roman Nose would do.

"Roman Nose stopped on the top of the hill. Tangle Hair
overtook him at this place and they sat down together, and
two or three other men came up and dismounted. Roman
Nose spoke to the others and said: 'At the Sioux camp the
other day something was done that I was told must not be
done. The bread I ate was taken out of the frying-pan with
something made of iron. I have been told not to eat anything
so treated. This is what keeps me from making a charge. If
I go into this fight I shall certainly be killed.'

"While they sat there White Contrary rode up and said:
'Well, here is Roman Nose, the man that we depend on, sitting behind this hill. He is the man that makes it easy for his
men in any fight.' Then, addressing Roman Nose, he went
on: 'You do not see your men falling out there? Two fell
just as I came up.'

"Roman Nose laughed and replied: 'What the old man says
is true.'

"White Contrary went on: 'All those people fighting out
there feel that they belong to you, and they will do all that
you tell them, and here you are behind this hill.'

"Roman Nose said: 'I have done something that I was told
not to do. My food was lifted with an iron tool. I know that
I shall be killed today.' Then he went off to one side and
painted himself and got out his war bonnet, and began to
shake it and to make ready to put it on. . . .

"After he had prepared himself for battle, Roman Nose
mounted his horse, and rode fast up toward where the scouts
were, and behind him followed many Indians. He rode almost
over the scouts hidden in the high grass—the men who had
shot Weasel Bear and White Thunder—and they shot Roman

Nose in the back just above the hips. He fell off his horse at the edge of the grass, but a little later had strength to creep up from the sand to the bank, and before long some young men came down and carried him off. He lived for a little time, and died about sundown." [4]

After Roman Nose fell, other charges were made. Some of the Cheyenne, creeping into the long grass, with a lariat managed to snake out the bodies of the warriors wounded or killed there by Stilwell's party. One of them was knocked over at long range as he was helping to carry the body of one of these warriors. That night Forsyth made plans to send two scouts for succor. He had had twenty-three casualties—among them his surgeon, Doctor Mooers, shot through the head.

The next day was one long fight. One halfhearted charge was promptly repulsed. Most of the time both sides fired at long range. The day following, the fighting was less, and after that day the scouts never saw an Indian.

They spent the time eating dead horses and a stray coyote they killed, or shivering with rheumatism in their wet foxholes under the chill rain, wondering anxiously if relief would ever come.

Stilwell and Trudeau had slipped away through the darkness and hurried to Fort Wallace, over 100 miles away, to get help. Jack Stilwell was just a kid, nineteen years old. The story goes that on the way some Cheyennes halted close to their hiding place, a shallow buffalo wallow, where they had the sparse cover of a few withered weeds which had grown up around their dried-up mudhole. While they cowered motionless, a rattlesnake came weaving in to share their shelter. They dared not move. Still the snake came on. Then Stilwell, who had a cud of tobacco in his mouth, spit in the snake's eyes and drove him away. The men lay quiet until the Cheyennes rode away.

Another pair of scouts, Donovan and Pliley, also went for help.

Forsyth finally got his anxious message through. It read as follows:

"To Colonel Bankhead or
 Commanding Officer
Fort Wallace: I sent you two messengers on the night of the 17th inst., informing you of my critical condition. I tried to send two more last night but they did not succeed in passing the Indian pickets and returned. If the others have arrived there, hasten at once to my assistance. I have eight badly wounded and ten slightly wounded men to take in and every animal I had was killed save seven which the Indians stampeded. Lieutenant Beecher is dead and Acting Assistant Surgeon Moore [Mooers] probably cannot live the night out. He was hit in the head on Thursday and has spoken but one rational word since. I am wounded in two places, in my right thigh and my left leg broken below the knee. The Cheyennes numbered four hundred and fifty or more. Mr. Grover says they never fought so before. There were at least thirty-five of them killed and wounded many more besides killing and wounding a quantity of their stock. They carried off most of their killed during the night. But three of their men fell into our hands. I am on a little island have still plenty of ammunition left. We are living on mule and horse meat and are entirely out of rations; if it was not for so many wounded I would come in and take the chances of whipping them if attacked. They are evidently sick of their bargain.

"I had two of the members of my company killed on the 17th, namely William Wilson and George W. Calver. You had better start with not less than seventy-five men and bring all the wagons and ambulances you can spare. Bring a six-pounder howitzer with you. I can hold out here for six days longer if *absolutely necessary*, but please lose no time.

George A. Forsyth, etc.

P.S.—My Surgeon having been mortally wounded none of my wounded have had their wounds dressed yet—so please bring out a Surgeon with you."

On the 25th of September one of the discouraged men on the island called out that he saw "Injuns" on the skyline. The beleaguered scouts made ready for another attack. Then, to their intense relief, they saw an ambulance with the supposed "Injuns" and knew that they were saved.

By that time the Cheyenne and Arapaho had pulled out and were far away. To them, though they lost nine men, the fight at Beecher Island would have been just another incident in their life of continuous warfare and adventure but for the killing of their great war leader, Roman Nose.

13

SHERMAN AND BLACK KETTLE

Long before General Sherman learned that Forsyth had been attacked by Roman Nose, the General had come to the end of his patience. He declared the Peace Policy a wretched failure and made it plain that he could no longer play ball with the pious visionaries of the Indian Bureau and their corrupt allies in the Indian Ring.

Up to that time the Indian Bureau and its treaty makers had had everything their own way. Sherman's change of front shocked them. Taylor, Commissioner of Indian Affairs, was outraged by the General's remarks. He rallied his supporters, and Tappan wrote of the Army and its officers in scathing terms. He accused Sherman and Sheridan of wishing to "exterminate" the poor Indians and of being in league with the settlers on the frontier. Sherman insisted that he held no brief for the settlers, pointing out that the settlers "instead of helping us, are an absolute charge, for they call for troops to defend them against apprehended danger."

As for the Army's fomenting war, he retorted: "To accuse us of inaugurating or wishing such a war, is to accuse us of a want of common sense, and of that regard for order and peace which has ever characterized our regular army. The injustice and frauds heretofore practiced on the Indians as charged, are not of our making; and I know the present war did not result from any acts of ours."

In particular Sherman pitched into Taylor's right-hand man, Tappan, in an angry letter written the very day after Forsyth was rescued. Sherman described the recent Indian outrages against civilians on the frontier, and declared that even the moderate General Augur had admitted that the hostiles must be "terribly whipped before they can appreciate kindness." Sherman declared, "Either the Indians must give way, or we must abandon all west of the Missouri River and confess, as you say, that forty million whites are cowed by a few thousand savages. Nothing but arrant cowardice or false humanity will account for your utter denial of all testimony on this point." Finally he wrote, "When they laugh at our cordiality, rape our women, murder our men, burn whole trains with their drivers to cinders, and send word that they never intended to keep their treaties, then we must fight them. When we come to fight Indians, I will take my code from soldiers and not from citizens."

Hastily Tappan proposed a bill to create an Indian Department with a secretary who should be a member of the Cabinet—a department with fewer but better-paid agents and inspectors. However, the bill also provided that no state or territory could wage war against Indians. Thus Tappan tacitly admitted that the Indian Ring—and by implication the Bureau —was corrupt and so the main cause of Indian wars. Military men who had served on the frontier agreed fully with General John Pope that the Bureau was in fact an "organized system of fraud and rascality."

Even while Major Forsyth and his scouts were fighting the Cheyenne brave, Roman Nose, the Commissioners sent out by the Indian Bureau were busily negotiating their new "Treaty of Laramie" with the Sioux, a treaty expressly designed to drive the Army from the Indian country. Red Cloud had his way: the forts on the Powder River Road were dismantled and abandoned. The Cheyenne chief, Little Wolf, set Fort Phil Kearney ablaze.

Then many of the hostiles came in to get their presents. Sitting Bull would not come in, would not touch the pen, but Red Cloud signed on November 6, 1868.

Yet, whatever Tappan and Taylor might say, the fat was in the fire. The outrages on the frontier must be stopped. The meager forces of cavalry there were alerted, awaiting the ringing call, "Boots and Saddles."

The Southern tribes were ready enough to fight. Though Black Kettle (now deposed because of the Sand Creek disaster) and other friendly leading men might prevent a few raids and persuade their own relatives to keep the peace, many of the young men went their own way and took to the warpath.

By Cheyenne custom a young man was nobody until he had gone to war, counted a *coup,* stolen a horse, or scalped an enemy. None of the girls would look at him. Besides, war was the Indian's one chance to get something for nothing.

They had excuses: General Hancock had burned their deserted village only a few moons back, Chivington had massacred their relatives on Sand Creek only four winters behind. Apparently there was no strong sentiment in the Cheyenne camp against war.

During the summer and autumn the Cheyenne and their allies had repeatedly raided in Kansas, committing bloody outrages against the whites.

"On the 10th of August, 1868, they struck the settlements on the Saline River. On the 12th they reached the Solomon and wiped out a settlement where the city of Minneapolis, Kansas, is now situated. In this raid fifteen persons were killed, two wounded, and five women carried off. On the same day they attacked Wright's hay camp near Ft. Dodge, raided the

Pawnee, and killed two settlers on the Republican. On the 8th of September they captured a train at the Cimarron crossing of the Arkansas River, securing possession of seventeen men, whom they burned; and the day following they murdered six men between Sheridan and Ft. Wallace. On the first of September, 1868, the Indians killed four men at Spanish Fork, in Texas, and outraged three women. One of these women was outraged by thirteen Indians and afterward killed and scalped. They left her with the hatchet still sticking in her head. Before leaving, they murdered her four little children. Of the children carried off by the Indians from Texas in 1868, fourteen were frozen to death in captivity." [1]

The action of the Peace Commissioners which, according to the official report, "aimed to hold out the olive branch with one hand and the sword in the other," resulted in the establishment of General Hazen at Fort Cobb, with an appropriation of $50,000, in clothing and stores, supplied by the Indian Bureau so that he could gather together and provide subsistence for all friendly Indians there. But, said the same report, this action was "not thereby intended that any hostile Indians should make use of that establishment as a refuge from just punishment for acts already done." The military control over the reservation was as complete as over Kansas, and General Sheridan was informed that "if hostile Indians retreat within that reservation, they are by no means to escape a deserved punishment, but may be followed even to Fort Cobb, captured, and punished." Hazen was not to send out punitive expeditions. He was to act as a peace chief.

Though Spotted Tail and other chiefs had openly declared that the Indians no longer had any justification for war, Colonel Tappan of the Peace Commission stuck "to his long preconceived opinion, that in the present case, as in all the past, our troops and our people were the aggressors, and that the Indians had no alternative but war. . . ."

CHEYENNE CAMP OF BUFFALO SKIN LODGES

(See Chapter 13, Page 143.) (Bureau of American Ethnology)

TREATY COUNCIL OF 1868 AT FORT LARAMIE

(See Chapter 15, Page 164.) (Bureau of American Ethnology)

CHEYENNE HOSTAGES
SEIZED BY GENERAL CUSTER, MARCH 1869

According to General Sherman, "Colonel Tappan stated that the officers of our Army, instead of protecting the Indians against the infuriated whites, had joined the border people in their constant cry of 'extermination.' " [2]

The Army stood ready to chastise the Indians at the drop of the hat. But General Hancock had discovered that, once they were hostile, it was impossible to catch them in summer. They could outmarch the troops.

It was now abundantly clear that mounted Indians could not be overtaken and punished while the grass was green. The Army planned a winter campaign, in which their grain-fed animals would give the troopers the advantage.

Accordingly, on October 15, 1868, General W. T. Sherman sent instructions to General Sheridan, worded as follows:

"As to 'extermination,' it is for the Indians themselves to determine. We don't want to exterminate or even fight them. At best it is an inglorious war, not apt to add much to our fame or personal comfort; and for our soldiers, to whom we owe our first thoughts, it is all danger and extreme labor, without a single compensating advantage. . . . As brave men and as the soldiers of a government which has exhausted its peace efforts, we, in the performance of a most unpleasant duty, accept the war begun by our enemies, and hereby resolve to make its end final. If it results in the utter annihilation of these Indians it is but the result of what they have been warned again and again, and for which they seem fully prepared. I will say nothing and do nothing to restrain our troops from doing what they deem proper on the spot, and will allow no mere vague general charges of cruelty and inhumanity to tie their hands, but will use all the powers confided to me to the end that these Indians, the enemies of our race and of our civilization, shall not again be able to begin and carry on their barbarous warfare on any kind of a pretext that they may choose to allege. I believe that this winter will afford us the opportunity, and that before snow falls these Indians will seek some sort of peace, to be broken next year at their option; but we will not accept their peace, or cease our efforts till all the past acts are both punished and avenged. You may now go ahead in your own way and I will back you with my whole authority, and stand between you and any efforts that may be attempted in your rear to restrain your purpose or check your troops."

When the famous scout and guide, old Jim Bridger, learned that Sheridan intended to attack Indian camps in winter, he roused his infirm body and made the long trip west to dissuade the General. Jim didn't think those "paper-collar soldiers" could weather a blizzard. And after Sheridan—to demonstrate—had plodded through one from Fort Hays to Fort Dodge, he was almost ready to admit that Jim was right. His tents blew away and he lost a lot of mules. Nevertheless, he ordered Custer forward with twelve troops of the Seventh Cavalry from Camp Supply to strike the Cheyenne, then known to be on the Washita River somewhere south near the Antelope Hills and no great distance northwest of Fort Cobb.

Though there was no secret about the location of Black Kettle's camp, Custer had a staff of first-rate scouts: California Joe, Ben Clark, the Mexican called "Romeo," Jimmy Morrison, and a bunch of Osages led by old Hard Rope. He took a big wagon train, with ammunition and provisions for two weeks. On November 21 a norther swept the plains, hiding them in snow, which kept on falling all the next day and night. Early on the morning of the 23rd, when Custer stuck his head out of the tent, the white flakes were still falling on two feet of snow. The little General smiled. "Just what I like! This will keep the Indians from moving around." The command marched off, and was soon lost in the blizzard. In spite of all his famous scouts, Custer had to steer his course by compass.

Meanwhile Black Kettle led a delegation of some twenty Cheyenne and Arapaho chiefs to Fort Cobb to talk with Colonel W. B. Hazen. Now that winter had set in, it seemed about time for another truce, and their enthusiasm for peace, now that the raiding season was over, was vastly stimulated by reports that soldiers were coming from Kansas to fight them on the snow. Black Kettle declared that his people never fought in Texas or south of the Arkansas River, but admitted that north of the Arkansas (in Kansas) they were almost always at war. He blamed white men for the murders in Kansas, professed to be unable to control his young men and keep them all at home. He ended by saying he wished to move his camp nearer Fort Cobb, adding, "My camp is now on the Washita, forty miles east of the Antelope Hills, and I have there about 180 lodges. I speak only for my own people."

After similar remarks by Big Mouth, an Arapaho, Hazen explained that he could not stop soldiers from coming down to attack them. His words are quoted in the Sheridan papers (November 20, 1868):

"I am sent here as a peace chief. All here is to be peace, but north of the Arkansas is General Sheridan, the great war chief, and I do not control him, and he has all the soldiers who are fighting the Cheyennes and Arapahoes. Therefore you must go back to your country, and if the soldiers come to fight, you must remember they are not from me, but from that great war chief, and it is with him that you must make your peace. . . . I cannot stop the war, but will send your talk to the Great Father, and if he gives me orders to treat you like the friendly Indians I will send out to you to come in; but you must not come in unless I send for you, and you must keep well out beyond the friendly Kiowas and Comanches. . . . I hope you understand how and why it is that I cannot make peace with you."

In reporting this council, Hazen adds that the Kiowas and

Comanches told him that, though Black Kettle was no doubt in earnest, he could not speak for most of his young men. Even the Cheyenne braves who accompanied Black Kettle to Fort Cobb were jubilant because he was not able to make peace with Hazen, since now they could capture more mules. They saw no point in a truce of a few moons. Next spring, they said, the Sioux and Northern Cheyennes would come down and help them clean out the entire country. Hazen fed them, and they rode off grumbling because he would not give them everything in the fort.

The very day Black Kettle got back to his camp on the Washita, two Cheyenne war parties, led by Black Shield and Crow Neck, came in from Kansas, where they had been committing depredations, and the whole camp prepared for a big scalp dance. The scalp dance was a social dance, almost the only occasion on which the young men and women could dance together. Dry logs were piled together to make a big fire, and about moonrise, when the drums began to pound, the crier raised his thin voice and summoned the dancers from the scattered lodges up and down the river. Every victorious warrior, smudged with the black paint of victory, wrapped himself and his sweetheart in the same snug robe.

All the dancers formed a circle, facing inward, wedged shoulder to shoulder, moving from right to left. The painted belles of the village, belted with butcher knives, proudly carried the weapons and trophies of their heroes, or flaunted fresh scalps from the top of peeled willow wands. That night the dancers tied themselves together with rawhide lariats so that nobody could quit the shuffling circle until the dance was over. For most of the night their high-pitched triumphant music rose and fell above the steady drumbeat through the dark branches of the moonlit trees.

In the camp were several white prisoners. One of them, Mrs. Clara Blinn, captured on October 6 from a wagon train on the trail between Fort Lyon and Fort Dodge, had lost her husband, but managed to keep her ailing two-year-old son, Willie. Nearly a month before, she had sent a pitiful letter by the hands of a Mexican trader, begging the Americans to buy her from the Cheyennes and to make peace with them.

Moreover, while Black Kettle was away at Fort Cobb, most of the Kiowa and Comanche bands had pulled out and moved over to Rainy Mountain Creek to hunt buffalo.

14

THE BATTLE OF THE WASHITA

IT WAS HARDLY SURPRISING that Chief Black Kettle was uneasy. Perhaps he had heard rumors then current in the camp: of how one of the Cheyenne war parties had heard firing on the Canadian River, but had supposed—until they reached camp—that it was the other war party shooting buffalo; of how Crow Neck, while out looking for a stray horse, saw a dark line of buffalo or soldiers snaking over the snowy hills; of how two Kiowas, coming in from a foray against the Utes, had crossed a plain trail made by many horses wearing shoes.

Certainly Black Kettle took extraordinary precautions. He tied his best horse close to his tipi. He even stationed a sentinel to keep watch. As for his young men, they laughed at rumors. They could not believe that white soldiers would come so far through the snow to fight them. When the dance was over, they all slept soundly.

"Double Wolf went forth to relieve the man who had been on watch since sundown. Everything was still. The bright moon illuminated the surrounding hillsides. A papoose wailed for a moment and was quiet. Soon the insistent, bitter cold penetrated the sentinel's blanket. He stole inside a lodge to warm himself over the dying embers of the fire. In a few moments he too was asleep." [1]

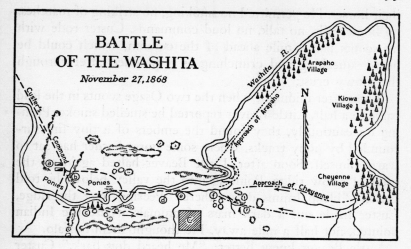

BATTLE OF THE WASHITA

NOVEMBER 27, 1868

Redrawn from a map surveyed and drawn by Frank Rush for *Border Command* by Carl Coke Rister, by permission of the University of Oklahoma Press.

a. Where Custer halted to wait for morning.
b. Ridge from which Custer reconnoitred Black Kettle's Cheyenne camp.
c. Black Kettle's camp. His own tipi stood north of the river.
d. Where Sergeant-Major Kennedy was killed.
e. Where Elliott's men were surrounded and killed.
f. Farthest advance of Elliott's detachment.
The capital C in the box indicates the position of the present town of Cheyenne, Oklahoma.

Meanwhile, Custer's column moved steadily over the moonlit snow toward Black Kettle's camp. Custer had left his supply train on the Canadian River, taking only one ambulance and seven wagon-loads of ammunition to the attack. His troopers were issued 100 rounds each, with coffee and hardtack enough for a single day and a saddlebag full of oats for their horses. He permitted no smoking, no striking of matches, no bugle calls, no talk, no loud commands. Custer rode with his scouts half a mile ahead of the column, which could be heard squeaking and crunching as it plodded after through the snowy crust.

It was after midnight when the two Osage scouts in the lead came to a halt. Little Beaver reported he smelled smoke. Pushing on cautiously, they found the embers of a tiny fire surrounded by pony tracks, where some horse herder had sat to warm himself. Soon after, Little Beaver halted again on the crest of a low ridge. Pointing into the valley below, he told Custer, "Heap Injuns down there." Peering over the ridge, Custer made out a dark mass of animals where the Indian pointed, not half a mile away. He thought them buffalo.

Little Beaver knew better: "Me heard dog bark." Custer heard a dog too, faint and far off, somewhere in the timber to the right. A moment later the intermittent tinkle of a bell came on the frosty air. Custer knew that buffalo were not equipped with bells. And then he heard the crying of a child.

Custer promptly divided his command into four parts, of about 200 men each. He sent Major Joel H. Elliott to attack from the east, Captain William Thompson to the south and west. Colonel Edward Meyers formed his men on Custer's right. Lieutenant W. W. Cook's picked sharpshooters, forty in number, were assigned to the column on the left, along with Custer and the band. The Osage scouts, fearful they might be taken for hostiles and killed in the fight, kept close to the General.

He had no way of knowing how many Indians were down there or what that terrain was like. But there were the enemies he had come to strike. He did not hesitate. He put every man into the attack, leaving no reserves.

Custer had not seen Hazen's report of his council with Black Kettle and that chief's claim to have 180 lodges in his camp. He could not know that nearly all the Southern Cheyenne and Arapaho were on the Washita, together with small bands of Kiowas, whose camps were strung out along the river below for fully fifteen miles. Hard Rope and the Osages kept their fears to themselves. Custer had his men discard their overcoats, sabers and haversacks and waited impatiently until the other columns had had time to take position. Already the east was paling.

As he moved slowly forward, the herd of Indian ponies moved out of his way toward the south. He could see now that the village stood beyond the river, the taper tents, plastered with snow, thrusting up their spiky sheaves of bare poles above the brush along the stream. There was no movement. The village was not so lifeless as it seemed. Suddenly all the dogs in the village began to bark furiously.

Captain Nye's account, previously quoted, continues: "Early in the morning a Cheyenne woman, troubled with rheumatic pains, went out to get firewood. She saw something shining on the hillside, something moving. Soldiers! Hastily she roused her children, sent them scurrying down the creek. Then she followed, afraid to shout lest the soldiers see her and shoot. The savage barking of camp dogs aroused the negligent Double Wolf. He seized his rifle and went to the edge of the frozen river. A woman ran from the timber where she had gone to get her horse.

" 'Soldiers!' she cried.

"Double Wolf listened intently, all faculties alert. Unmistakably there came the noise of many hoofs breaking through the snow, crackling the underbrush. The head of a white man appeared over a fallen tree. Thoughts of the Sand Creek tragedy raced through the Indian's mind; orders about raising the white flag were forgotten. He lifted his gun and fired."

Custer's bugler sounded the charge. He signaled the mounted band to play "Garry Owen," the rollicking war song of the

Seventh Cavalry. The half-frozen musicians set stiff lips to the icy mouthpieces of their instruments, squawked and bleated through a few bars—until the horns froze up. Meanwhile, Cook's sharpshooters were firing into the village. From three sides the cavalry charged in among the tipis.

As it happened, Custer's own men struck the village at the northwest corner, where Black Kettle's big black tipi stood on the edge of the camp. His troopers charged in, cheering. Before the Cheyennes could grab up their weapons and rush from their lodges, the village was already swarming with soldiers. Women and children ran from the tents, jumped over the steep banks of the river into waist-deep icy water, scuttled to hiding in the brush, or ran on through the trees. Because of vermin, Cheyenne men slept practically naked, and many of them ran out into the snow with little more on than their moccasins and breechclouts. But the bitter cold was the least of their troubles. Outnumbered four to one, the bravest of them tried to form a rear guard and defend the women and children streaming from the camp.

Black Kettle had no time to raise his white flag. He did not stop to parley, but slashed the lariat of his pony, jumped on its back, helped his squaw up behind. But already the sharpshooters were throwing lead into his camp. Black Kettle and his wife caught it, slid from the pony's back, and lay in the water. An Osage scout scalped the chief. That same volley laid low the negligent sentinel, Double Wolf.

For once the troops had an adequate number of marksmen along, and Indian casualties ran high. The troopers rode along the slopes on either side of the stream, firing into the Cheyennes hiding under the banks, driving back those who scuttled over the sand dunes or up the bluffs.

So complete was the surprise that the Indians had no chance to catch up their ponies. The victory was so immediate that the fight was soon only a matter of mopping up.

Yet the fight was no pushover for the troopers. The Indians put up a vigorous defense.

Among the bravest were the Indian teen-age boys, reckless and bloodthirsty, heedless of danger, hell-bent on playing a warrior's part. One of these, seeing Major Benteen and his squadron coming through the timber, whipped up his pony and charged alone on the troops. He headed straight for Benteen. The Major, not wishing to kill a boy, raised his upright palm in the peace sign. But the boy scorned surrender. A warrior and the son of a warrior, he shot to kill. He raised his revolver. He fired, barely missing Benteen's head—once, twice, all the time steadily advancing. His third bullet pierced the neck of the Major's horse close to the shoulder. In self-defense, Benteen had to drop him.

Before all the Indians cleared out of the camp they shot Mrs. Blinn through the forehead and cracked the skull of her two-year-old child against a tree trunk. As the troopers advanced, they saw a squaw running off, tugging a little white boy along by the hand. Finding herself surrounded and cut off, she whipped out her butcher knife and disemboweled the child. But that was the last of her.

Seventeen Cheyennes were firing from a depression. The sharpshooters were called forward and, as the Indians raised their heads to fire, drilled every one through the forehead. Thirty-eight more warriors were wiped out in a near-by ravine.

The Indians fleeing down the stream had to leave it at the horseshoe bend a mile or two below the camp. There the water was too deep to wade. They had to come out and cut across the bend and so expose themselves to attack.

Major Elliott, seeing these fugitives, called for volunteers. Sergeant-Major Walter Kennedy responded, as did eighteen others. When they rode off, Elliott called back, "Here goes for a brevet or a coffin!" Two Cheyennes and a Kiowa tried to stand Elliott off and protect the fugitives. Little Rock killed the Sergeant-Major's horse before he himself fell. The other two managed to get away.

As Elliott came on, Buffalo Woman, running through the snow with three children, was too tired to go farther. She sat down in the snow. Elliott's detachment caught up with her, and he detailed Sergeant-Major Kennedy, now dismounted, to take the prisoners back to camp. They started—but Buffalo Woman's heart was strong. She was still in the fight and, keeping a bright lookout, saw a number of warriors heading back toward the captured camp. In order to delay her captor, she halted and tore off strips from her dress and began to wrap these around the bare, half-frozen feet of the children with her. The kindhearted Sergeant-Major let her delay him—until the warriors charged in and shot him down. He fell in the water of a little creek, since known as Sergeant Major Creek. An Arapaho, Little Chief, armed with a hatchet, counted *coup* on him.

Once beyond that creek, Major Elliott found himself confronted by a great many Indians. By that time all the women and children who could get away had escaped, and the warriors could turn their undivided attention to the fight. Most were afoot, but many another came riding from the camps below. They were far too many for Elliott. His retreat was cut off. He backed up to a bend in the little creek and, seeing a depression there full of tall grass, dismounted his men and turned his horses loose.

His position was poorly chosen. Crouching in the tall grass, his men could see nothing and had no proper field of fire. Moreover, the opposite bank of the stream overlooked him and provided abundant cover for his enemies.

I got the story of what followed from the Cheyenne warrior, Roman Nose Thunder, who told me about it many years later in 1913, at the Sun Dance of the Southern Cheyennes not far from Cantonment, Oklahoma.

"At first," he said, "we could see nothing but white smoke where the soldiers were. We could not see the soldiers, but we thought maybeso they could see us. They kept on shooting, fast, but hit nobody. When the Indians saw this they went forward faster.

"I was a young man then and had a fast horse. I rode around, getting closer to the soldiers under the smoke every time. Pretty soon I was near enough to see some of them. They were all shooting—not taking aim—just shooting. So then I charged right in among them. When my horse came alongside the first soldier lying there I wanted to strike him. I had a bow in my hand, and leaned down to strike him. He saw me coming, rolled over, and fired at me. His bullet hit my arm." (Roman Nose Thunder rolled up his sleeve to show a scar on his dark wizened arm.) "But I did not flinch. I struck him in the face, on his cheek. I counted the first *coup* in that fight.

"Then I rode off to look at my arm. It was bleeding, but the bone had not been hit. Afterwards everyone charged in and began to kill the soldiers and count *coup* on them. Warriors of all tribes charged in.

"People were running up from all sides to see the end of the fight. But before they could get close, all the soldiers were dead. The shooting was over.

"The fight did not last longer than it would take a man to smoke a pipe four times. Always remember, *I* struck the enemy *first*."

Meanwhile, Custer had cleared the camp of enemies, rounded up sixty prisoners in one or two large bodies in the middle of the village, and gathered his wounded into an improvised hospital. By that time it was ten o'clock. He tells in his book, *My Life on the Plains*, how he saw "a little bugler boy sitting on a bundle of dressed robes," waiting his turn with the surgeon. His face was covered with blood. He had a wound on his forehead. He told Custer that an arrow had struck him above the eye, had glanced under the skin, and had gone out near his ear. "The arrow, being barbed, could not be withdrawn at once, but by cutting off the steel point the surgeon was able to withdraw the wooden shaft. . . . The little fellow bore his suffering manfully." When Custer asked him if he saw the Indian who had wounded him, the boy shoved his hand deep into his trousers pocket, saying, "If anybody thinks I didn't see him, I want them to take a look at that," and pulled out a scalp.

Custer was surprised to see a party of mounted Indians collected on a knoll about a mile below the village. At first he supposed them to be warriors who had escaped him, caught up their ponies, and got together to watch his movements. But many of the Indian ponies, frightened by the shooting, had sought refuge in the captured camp, and now California Joe requested Custer to give him a detachment to bring in another large herd of ponies he had seen nearby. Custer had no men to spare just then, but told Joe to go ahead on his own hook. Presently Joe returned, driving in 300 horses on the run, aided by a couple of mounted squaws whom he had captured and put to work. Joe was riding his favorite mule, whirling the end of his dragging lariat around his head to urge the herd forward.

It was clear now that the mounted Indians were not from the captured camp. Through his glasses, Custer could see that they were all painted and dressed up for battle, with war bonnets and lances. Their number kept growing. Black Kettle's sister, one of the captives, explained that there were a thousand lodges on the river below.

And now the Indians swarmed in on all sides. The guard left with the overcoats and rations came tearing in, breathless, to report the loss of his charge. But luckily the quartermaster had brought his wagons full of ammunition to the top of the bluffs, and in the nick of time they came skidding down, their locked wheels striking fire from the friction with the snow.

Custer fought off the Indians and had time to check the loot. It consisted of 241 saddles, 573 buffalo robes, 390 buffalo skins for lodges, 160 untanned robes, 210 axes, 140 hatchets, 35 revolvers, 47 rifles, 535 pounds of powder, 1050 pounds of lead, 4000 arrows and arrowheads, 75 spears, 90 bullet molds, 35 bows and quivers, 12 shields, 300 pounds of bullets, 775 lariats, 940 buckskin saddle bags, 470 blankets, 93 coats, 700 pounds of tobacco, the winter supply of dried buffalo meat, meal, flour, uncounted camp kettles, coffeepots, tin cups, water kegs, and assorted clothing.

But the most valuable capture was some 875 ponies, the real wealth of the tribe and its only means of continuing the war or hunting buffalo. Custer knew the Indians would attempt to recover these animals. He sent the Indian women whom he had captured to choose and bridle the animals they wished to ride, and ordered the others shot. The troopers drove the ponies to a point east of the camp and held them on a narrow stretch of land between the river and the hills. They would not allow a white man to touch them. The detachment spent an hour and a half shooting down these horses, some of them beautiful animals—a mighty tough assignment for cavalrymen.

When the camp and the ponies had been destroyed, the Indians seemed to lose heart, and when the troops advanced against them, they slowly retired. By mid-afternoon the stampeding camps had fled from the Washita and were legging it to Red River, west of the Wichita Mountains.

And now Custer found his men without rations, without overcoats, exhausted after two days and a night of marching and fighting, almost without food, in that bitter weather. His wagon train, left behind on the Canadian, might be discovered and destroyed by the savages. Custer gave orders for the return to Camp Supply. With comparatively small loss in men and officers, he had surprised and burned a camp of more than fifty lodges, claimed 103 warriors killed, with sixteen women and a few children, and held sixty captives. It was hardly "extermination," but it was a severe blow, and in the opinion of most men on the frontier in those days, a well-deserved punishment. Texans and Kansans seldom agreed, but on one point they agreed perfectly—neither had any earthly use for Indians. Frontiersmen saw no point in being meek and gentle with these butchers. But in the Eastern States many humane people, who were in no danger of being scalped and slaughtered, were shocked by the success of Custer's raid.

On the other hand, one eyewitness, De B. Randolph Keim, in his *Sheridan's Troopers on the Borders: A Winter Campaign on the Plains*, gives the following list of mutilations of American soldiers at the Battle of the Washita:

"Major Joel H. Elliott, one bullet hole in left cheek, two bullets in head, throat cut, right foot cut off, left foot almost cut off, calves of legs very much cut, groin ripped open and otherwise mutilated.

"Walter Kennedy, sergeant-major, bullet hole in right temple, head partly cut off, seventeen bullet holes in back, and two in legs.

"Harry Mercer, corporal company E, bullet hole in right axilla, one in region of heart, three in back, eight arrow wounds in back, right ear cut off, head scalped, and skull fractured, deep gashes in both legs, and throat cut.

"Thomas Christie, company E, bullet hole in head, right foot cut off, bullet hole in abdomen, and throat cut.

"William Carrick, corporal company H, bullet hole in right parietal bone, both feet cut off, throat cut, left arm broken, and otherwise mutilated.

"Eugene Clover, company H, head cut off, arrow wound in right side, both legs terribly mutilated.

"William Milligan, company H, bullet hole in left side of head, deep gashes in right leg, left arm deeply gashed, head scalped, throat cut, and otherwise mutilated.

"James F. Williams, corporal company I, bullet hole in back, head and arms cut off, many and deep cuts in back, and otherwise mutilated.

"Thomas Downey, company I, arrow hole in region of stomach, throat cut open, head cut off, and right shoulder cut by a tomahawk.

"Thomas Fitzpatrick, farrier, company M, scalped, two arrow and several bullet holes in back, and throat cut.

"Ferdinand Linebach, company M, bullet hole in right parietal bone, head scalped, one arm broken, throat cut, and otherwise mutilated.

"John Myers, company M, several bullet holes in head, scalped, skull extensively fractured, several arrow and bullet holes in back, deep gashes in face, and throat cut.

"Carson D. J. Myers, company M, several bullet holes in head, scalped, nineteen bullet holes in body, throat cut, and otherwise mutilated.

"Cal. Charp, company M, two bullet holes in left side, throat cut, one bullet hole in left side of head, one arrow hole in left side of head, one arrow hole in left side, left arm broken, and otherwise mutilated.

"Unknown, head cut off, body partly devoured by wolves.

"Unknown, head and right hand cut off, three bullet and nine arrow holes in back, and otherwise mutilated.

"Unknown, scalped, skull fractured, six bullet and thirteen arrow holes in back, and three bullet holes in chest."

15

THE DOG SOLDIERS ARE PUNISHED

On January 7, 1869, General Sheridan established a new post some thirty-odd miles south of Fort Cobb, at the east end of the Wichita Mountains. There he found water running in the streams, plenty of timber, and pastures covered with bunch grass. The new post was nearer the center of the Indian country. There was plenty of game in the neighborhood; indeed, when I was stationed there in 1917 an order was still posted in the hospital forbidding patients to shoot buffalo from the windows. He named it Fort Sill.

The Indians were ordered to bring their people to the fort, but except for a few loafers acting as spies on the troops, no Cheyenne or Arapaho showed up. To Sheridan it was obvious that the Indians were simply waiting until the spring grass had strengthened their ponies to take to the warpath. Sheridan sent Custer and his cavalry to find the Cheyenne.

The Arapaho camp, under Little Raven, had come in and camped within forty miles of the post. Custer rode all the way to Red River and never saw a Cheyenne. When he returned, Sheridan sent Weir to round up Little Raven's sixty lodges and bring them to the post. Little Raven was then "rather stout, about fifty years of age, having the appearance of one who lived well and took the world calmly." The officer thought him "remarkably intelligent." At any rate Little Raven was intelligent enough to obey Sheridan's orders.

By the middle of February, '69, Sheridan had let Lone Wolf and Satanta go. Soon after Indians came in to talk, eagerly accepting Sheridan's promise to "let the past be buried," if they would keep the peace. Sheridan made plans to strike all the bands which had not come in. He equipped the Seventh Cavalry for the campaign, and would have accompanied the troops himself had he not been recalled to Washington. With Custer's eleven troops of the Seventh marched a force of ten troops of the Nineteenth Kansas Cavalry.

On Sweetwater Creek, southwest of the Wichita Mountains, Custer found a Cheyenne village. On March 15 he parleyed with the chiefs, led by Rock Forehead or Medicine Arrow. Finding that the camp contained two white women held prisoners, he dared not attack lest the women be murdered, as Mrs. Blinn had been at the Battle of the Washita.

The chiefs agreed to bring the village in and surrender the two prisoners. But, fearing another Sand Creek, many of the Cheyenne fled from their lodges toward another camp of their people. Custer promptly seized several warriors and held them as hostages for the surrender of the two captive white women, in the meantime allowing the scared Indians to return to get their lodges.

After some days of waiting without receiving the white prisoners, Custer threatened to hang the Indians he held. Next day the wretched women were brought in.

Custer marched off to Camp Supply, taking his hostages along. The Cheyenne followed, and pitched their lodges nearby.

For Custer, like Sheridan, plainly told the Indians that the white man no longer regarded the tribes as independent nations. In future, he said, hostiles would be treated as "refractory subjects of a common government," subject to trial in the white man's courts.

The Indians on the Southern Plains no longer had any real choice. Sheridan's new policy of campaigning against them in winter put them at a much greater disadvantage than were the Indians on the Northern Plains. For in the South, though the winters were mild enough for the cavalry to operate on their grain-fed horses, winter grasses and cottonwood bark could not keep up the strength, speed and wind of an Indian pony. In the North it was different, for the bitter weather in Montana made winter campaigning there almost impossible for troops.

Therefore the campaign resulted in a truce with the Southern Cheyenne lasting almost five years, until 1874.

Sheridan was as good as his word, and "buried the past" of those bands which reported at the military posts. But he warned their chiefs that he would hold them personally accountable for any future crimes committed by their people.

There was still one job to do—to bring in the Dog Soldiers.

After the Texas Rangers and the Royal Northwest Mounted Police, the Cheyenne Dog Soldiers rated as the most celebrated band of fighters in the history of the Great Plains—until Major Frank North's Pawnee Scouts put the Indian sign on them.

In the old days, every Plains tribe was made up of bands, each consisting of a number of families, all under one chief. Such a band included men, women and children, who formed a social and economic unit, living and hunting together.

When in summer the whole tribe assembled for the annual Sun Dance, all the bands camped together in a great circle—sometimes a mile across—the lodges standing three or four deep, with the opening or gateway to the circle generally to the east. Each band had its regular place in the circle with relation to this entrance, and could always be found occupying its own proper segment whenever the great camp circle was formed.

The active warriors of these bands organized themselves into 5 or 6 societies of warriors or "soldiers" and these "soldier societies" or warrior societies were the real power and government of the tribe. The duties of the Indian "soldiers" were partly military, partly fraternal; but the members also acted as police in camp and on the trail. The chiefs detailed each society in turn to police the camp and direct the tribal hunting, but in fact the tribal chiefs and band chiefs—unless they were also chiefs of some warrior society—were hardly more than mouthpieces for these organizations.

Each society had its own insignia, rituals, dances, and characteristic equipment.

Most of the year the different bands were scattered over the country, and since members of each warrior society were drawn from all the bands, these societies could not function until the whole tribe met to camp together again. Thus in each band the men would be members of half a dozen different societies.

But the Cheyenne Dog Soldiers changed all this. One day, well over a hundred years ago, all the men of the Masihkota band up and joined the Dog Soldiers in a body. This identified the band with the society, since all the members of the society were always together and so could act as a body in peace or in war. Thus the Dog Soldier society became also a band. Its power and prestige rapidly increased, and as often as not the band was known as the Dog Soldier band, or in their language, *Hotamʹ itanʹiu*, literally "Dog Men."

With such an organization behind them, the chiefs of the Dog Soldiers became very powerful and arbitrary and enforced strict discipline upon their followers, who were always under their thumb. Indeed, Little Wolf, one of their chiefs, became a real strategist and a true commander, planning his battles and compelling his warriors to carry out orders, a thing which no Cheyenne war chief before him had ever been able to do. With such control he was often able to dominate the tribal camp as well. The chiefs could do little without the consent of the Dog Soldiers.

Such a warrior society, led by men like Little Wolf, Tall Bull, Black Sun, White Horse, Roman Nose, and Tangle Hair, inevitably attracted the bravest warriors to join them—not only Cheyennes, but Sioux as well. In fact, this band or society of Dog Soldiers was often called the Cheyenne-Sioux because so many of its members had Sioux blood.

The Dog Soldiers believed their order had been founded by the watchdogs of the camp. From time to time certain members of unusual courage were appointed leaders, and in battle wore a leather sash over one shoulder, with a long trailing tail, known as a "dog rope." As soon as the fighting began, the Dog Soldier who wore a sash drove a picket pin through the tail of his "rope" into the ground, thus staking himself to his post of duty. He was under a vow not to pull it up until he was victorious. He could not retreat without disgrace unless one of his own comrades pulled up the picket pin and quirted him from the battlefield. If his comrades neglected to do this, it was his duty to die where he stood. Naturally only very daring men were chosen for this service.

It was early summer, 1869. Tall Bull's Dog Soldiers, eighty-four lodges of them, with perhaps two warriors to the lodge, were in camp on the headwaters of a small stream flowing into the South Fork of the Republican River not far above the mouth of the Arikaree Fork, near the eastern boundary of Colorado. Among them, as usual, were some Sioux.

One evening their hunters rode in and told the chiefs they had seen white soldiers in a big camp farther down the creek.

Immediately the Dog Soldiers picked up their bridles and blankets, caught up their ponies, and rode downstream. After dark they charged General Carr's command in a sudden thunder of hoofs, wild yelling, and waving blankets, in hope of stampeding the cavalry horses.

To their surprise and disappointment, the animals, though excited, did not break away. General Eugene A. Carr had along 150 Pawnee scouts under Major Frank North and his brother Luther. With 200 troops to back them, these Pawnees took the offensive, ran the Dog Soldiers off, and saved the horses. The fracas lasted only a few minutes, and apparently amounted to very little. One teamster was wounded and one Cheyenne, Yellow Nose, was thrown from his horse in the darkness and had to walk home.

For all that, Tall Bull decided to head north. Though outnumbered, he might have fought off 200 white men. But all those Pawnees made the odds too heavy, especially as he had a camp full of women and children to protect. Tall Bull knew the Dog Soldiers could easily outride the troops, even when taking along their tipis, women, jerked meat, dogs, kettles and all. They could travel fifty miles a day.

Next day the tents came down early; the pack ponies and mounted Indians kept moving all day, and the morning after arrived on White Butte Creek, which flows from Summit Springs. The Dog Soldiers naturally expected to move straight on to the South Platte before night, but Chief Tall Bull decreed a halt. At that season the river was likely to be running bank-full. Here at the Springs they could let their horses rest and wait for the water to go down.

"Tall Bull said, 'We will stop here for two days; then we will rush across the South Platte and go up to the Rock where we starved the Pawnees!'" [1]

In his announcement Tall Bull sneered at the Pawnees with General Carr, forgetting that when the Pawnees had been trapped on top of Court House Rock by the Cheyenne long before, they had managed to slip out of the trap without the loss of a man.

Tall Bull was confident that the white men would not catch him napping. For on the way up to Summit Springs he had made his people scatter and divide into small diverging parties, thus leaving a number of trails to confuse the white men's scouts—if any tried to follow him. So now Tall Bull did not even bother to send scouts to watch his back trail and give him warning of pursuit. Instead he sent his young men north to the Platte to find a ford while the people in his camp loafed through the hot July days.

But hard as Tall Bull had worked to cover his trail, he had made one bad mistake. In his tipi he had two white women taken captive in Kansas. As captives, they had to walk. The print of their shoes, appearing among the pony tracks and moccasin prints, told General Carr and his scouts that they were on the right trail.

With three days' rations on pack mules, the General pushed on, making a forced march until he came to the forks of the trail. There were three trails: the broadest heading east, one heading west, one going on north. The General, unskilled in Indian wiles, would have followed the broadest trail, but Major North and his Pawnees talked him out of that. Carr sent Colonel W. B. Royall, with "Buffalo Bill" Cody as chief scout, on that right-hand trail; the North brothers and part of the Pawnees on the middle, north-bound trail; while he himself and the rest of the scouts and troopers pushed up the left-hand trail diverging toward the west.

As it happened, one of General Carr's Pawnees was first to discover the hostile camp. He carried the word to Major North. But Buffalo Bill and Colonel Royall were too far away to be reached in time. They missed the fight entirely.

The horses of the command were tired and sweating in the

July heat. General Carr halted to let them rest a little and make a battle plan before making the charge.

The Cheyennes were taking it easy that day, smoking, talking, sleeping, not keeping any guard. The women had pulled up the tent pegs and raised the sides of their taper lodges to let the breeze blow through.

Some time before, a number of war parties had gone out from this camp and the Dog Soldiers were expecting them to return any time now. When they saw Indian riders coming over the hill, they were not alarmed. They sat looking out from the shade of their lodges, watching the Pawnees charging along the slope of the hill, listening to the banging of their guns. What they saw was just what they had expected. The Pawnees were behaving just like a successful war party announcing a victory. Even when a few bullets ripped through the lodge skins, the Cheyennes thought it was just an accident.

Then suddenly they saw the blue-clad troopers pouring over the ridge, and knew it was too late to defend their camp.

It was every man for himself. Those who had ponies staked out near their tents quickly cut the lariats, helped their women and children on the ponies' backs, jumped aboard and raced away. Those who had no horses ran for cover, darting out of the camp in all directions. Some ran west—straight into the line of bluecoats coming over the hill from that side. Some ran east—and met the bluecoats there. Some ran north—and found the troopers had surrounded the camp. Only one way lay open—to the south. Already enemies were among their tipis. Running for their lives, they heard at their heels the shrill, triumphant *"Ki-de-de-de"* of Pawnee victors. It was lucky for the Cheyennes that their horses were fresh.

But the Pawnees dashed after them, hard as their jaded ponies could run, caught them helpless among the tents or on the prairie, singly or in small bunches, unable to defend themselves. The Pawnees chopped down men, women and children, scalped them, cut them to pieces. So great was the panic that some Cheyenne warriors ran shamefully away, leaving their women and children to be butchered.

Most of the frantic young folk trusted to their agile legs to get away. But some older Indians, knowing they could not outrun their enemies, took refuge in a small box canyon close by. Once through the narrow mouth of that small gulch, they might defend themselves.

That was a bitter hour for Tall Bull. He saw the day was lost—and through his own fault. He had a fine horse staked beside his tipi. Quickly he helped his wife and six-year-old daughter onto its back, then turned and shot down the two white women, his captives. Leaving them both for dead, Tall Bull jumped up behind his family, kicked his fast war horse into a run, reached the gulch unhit. He made his woman and child hide in the bottom of the gulch.

At the mouth of the little canyon his fine war horse waited, fresh and fast, ready to bear him to safety. Tall Bull pulled out his scalping knife, plunged it between the horse's ribs up to the hilt. Tall Bull, Chief of the Dog Soldiers, had made up his mind to die right there.

The narrow gulch where these few Indians had taken refuge was deep, with high steep banks. It was hard for the chief to clamber to the top where he could shoot at his enemies. But when Tall Bull died, he meant to die fighting, taking an enemy with him. Up he went.

When he looked over the top of the bank, he saw two white men on horses charging toward him. They were Major Frank North and his brother, Luther. Tall Bull raised his rifle, fired, then quickly ducked down to reload.

Listening, Tall Bull heard the two horses come to a halt, then gallop away.

Maybeso he had knocked one of the men out of the saddle. Maybeso he had missed. Maybeso he could get another shot before they were clean out of range. Tall Bull poked his weapon over the rim of the canyon and raised his head to shoot. He found himself looking down a rifle barrel in the hands of a kneeling white man. Before he could stir, a puff of white smoke hid that enemy. The ball crashed into Tall Bull's forehead.

Major North was a crack shot. He had tricked Tall Bull. While Luther galloped away with both horses, Frank had remained, covering the spot from which Tall Bull had fired at him.

Mr. Grinnell continues the account in *The Fighting Cheyennes:* "Shortly after this another head appeared at the same spot—the head of a woman. She reached the top of the bank, pulled her little six-year-old girl after her, and making signs that she wished to talk, walked to Major North, and passed her hands over him, asking him for pity. Major North sent her to the rear, where she would be safe. She proved to be the wife of Tall Bull. She told him that there were still seven Indians alive in the ravine. These were afterward killed, thirteen having already been killed at the head of the ravine."

When Tall Bull's body fell backward into that gulch, the power of the Dog Soldiers crashed down with him. In that hour they had lost their leader, their weapons (fifty-six rifles, twenty-two revolvers, forty bows and arrows, fifty pounds of gunpowder), 300 ponies, 150 mules, 10,000 pounds of dried buffalo meat, their lodges, their clothing, more than fifty of their people killed, and nearly a score made prisoner. Scattered and broken, half-naked and starving, they hurried away to find refuge with other bands. It was a miserable journey for them all. That night it rained hard.

The troops found one of the captive women dead, the other only wounded. The men chipped in and gave this wretched woman most of the money ($1500) which had been found in the camp. They burned all the Indian property, drove off the captured ponies. Somewhat later Colonel W. B. Royall, Fifth Cavalry, set out to overtake what was left of the Dog Soldiers. Every day his command rode twenty to thirty dry, hot miles after the fugitives, until rations gave out and their horses were used up. Yet this time the Cheyennes outran them.

But from that day Kansas and Nebraska suffered little at the hands of Plains Indians. Wagons heading for the Colorado gold fields rolled unmolested up the Smoky Hill.

Now that the middle of the Plains was cleared of hostiles, frontiersmen were eager to have the Army settle the hash of Injuns north and south. In the Northern Plains, they wanted that Powder River country opened, the Bighorns and the Black Hills taken from the hunting bands, and *all* redskins confined to reservations without delay. They hated the guts of the Sioux. But what they thought of the Sioux was mild compared to their opinion of Eastern "humanitarians" who had, they thought, "unsound hearts, white livers, and soft heads."

As for the Kiowa and Comanche on the Southern Plains, "the sooner those butchers were wiped out, the better."

16

RAIDS AND COUNCILS

AFTER THE BATTLE OF THE WASHITA, Sheridan and Custer had returned to inspect the site and to discover what had
become of Elliott and his men. The weather was still cold, and
they found the bodies of the troopers and those of the captives: an unidentified boy, Mrs. Clara Blinn and her child.
Sheridan followed the Indian travois trail. His slogan was
"Punishment must follow crime."

The trail led toward Fort Cobb on the Washita. There General Hazen, the Peace Chief, held sway. Sherman had ordered
Hazen to get word to Sheridan not to pursue "peaceable
Indians." Hazen sent word that all the Indians between Sheridan's position and Fort Cobb were "friendly, and have not
been on the warpath this season."

But the Kiowa held Hazen's messengers as hostages. They
sent Satanta and Lone Wolf to parley with Sheridan's officers.
Custer was eager to attack. But Hazen's letter gave Sheridan
pause. It was the old deadlock between the War Department
and the Indian Bureau. Though morally certain that these
chiefs and their bands were guilty, he was unwilling to subject
the Army to criticism—and so to further interference. He hit
upon another way to stop the raiding—he arrested Satanta
and Lone Wolf.

Lone Wolf, who now wore the moccasins of the late Chief Little Mountain, was a second-rate fellow, vain, touchy, and given to sudden violence. His character did not inspire confidence even among his own people. He never could control them.

Satanta, the strapping boaster, loved to prate, but had more words than brains. He must also have had some inner doubts about his courage, for he allowed the taunting of his comrades to make him forget all his pledges and policies. When they called him "coward," he took to the warpath instantly to save his face. In fact, the Kiowa had no able chiefs after Little Mountain died. Such a small tribe could not produce so great a man in every generation.

No sooner had Sheridan arrested Lone Wolf and Satanta than all the other Kiowa abandoned their chiefs and hit the trail to the southwest, away from the fort and the troops. Sheridan ordered Custer to "tell those Indians that if their villages are not here by sundown tomorrow I will hang them both to the nearest tree."

The chiefs evidently knew that such a threat would only result in making the Kiowa run faster. They sent word to their people that the white chief would give them a feast and extra rations if they came back.

The Kiowa arrived on time. Sheridan scolded them, warned them, and gave them nothing. Satanta and Lone Wolf said they were ready to do all that was required of them. Sheridan released the precious pair. The Indian Bureau had won that round. But for once the Kiowa had met a white man who had no paper to sign, no presents to make. They understood the plain talk of this "no-treaty chief."

The raiding, however, went on just the same, the Indians bringing their captives in to get ransom from our government. If one officer or agent refused to pay, there was always some other white chief to take pity on the wretched captives.

Lawrie Tatum, agent for the Kiowa and Comanche, though a Quaker, began to see that it was high time to temper mercy with justice. Why should not Indians guilty of murder be tried in civil courts and hanged for their crimes like white men?

Among his charges was a sawed-off, skinny old man, Satank or Sitting Bear, part Kiowa, part Sarsi, with high cheekbones, prominent nose and chin, a scraggly mustache and a baleful Mongol glare. His glare was all the more sinister because he had pulled out all his eyelashes and painted the edges of his eyelids with vermilion.

Satank was the meanest, fiercest, and bravest of the Kiowa—who feared him as they feared no one else. They believed he could throw up a knife from his belly whenever he needed it.

When Tatum tried to get Satank to surrender a mule he had stolen in Texas, Satank challenged the agent to a duel to the death—winner take mule. The Quaker declined. The raiding went on.

In 1871 General Sherman came to the Indian country on a tour of inspection. Everywhere he heard accounts of atrocities and depredations.

Meanwhile the Kiowa attacked a train of ten wagons laden with grain for the government. Sherman sent Colonel Ranald S. MacKenzie, Fourth Cavalry, to the scene of the fight. Here is the surgeon's report of what they found:

"Colonel R. S. MacKenzie,
4th Cav
Sir:

I have the honor to report that in compliance with your instructions I examined on May 19, 1871, the bodies of five citizens killed near Salt Creek by Indians on the previous day. All the bodies were riddled with bullets, covered with gashes, and the skulls crushed, evidently with an axe found bloody on the place; some of the bodies exhibited also signs of having been stabbed with arrows. One of the bodies was even more mutilated than the others, it having been found fastened with a chain to the pole of a wagon lying over a fire with the face to the ground, the tongue being cut out. Owing to the charred condition of the soft parts it was impossible to determine whether the man was burned before or after his death. The scalps of all but one were taken.

I have the honor to be, colonel,

your obedient servant,

(signed) J. H. Patzki,

Asst Surgeon, U.S.A."

It was clear to everyone who knew the facts that the Kiowa would do exactly as they pleased—unless forced to act otherwise.

Ever since 1834, when the Dragoons visited their country to restore Kiowa captives taken by the Osage, the Kiowa had been raiding, killing, kidnapping and stealing. But the Kiowa saw no profit in giving up their raiding. They were continually humored, catered to, and rewarded with payment for their crimes. On the other hand, their peaceful neighbors—the Wichita and Caddo—were never given anything or invited to council. Washington treated its enemies better than its friends. The Peace Policy was just what the hostiles wanted.

General Sherman reached Fort Sill May 23, 1871, to hold council with the Kiowa. When the General, accompanied by the commanding officer, visited the office of the Quaker agent, Lawrie "Bald Head" Tatum, he found the agent already at the end of his patience over the misdeeds of his Indian wards. For once an Indian agent and an Army officer were, though unknown to each other, of much the same mind: to have Indian raiders "arrested for murder and turned over to the proper authorities of Texas for trial." Yet Tatum was still unaware of the recent wagon-train massacre committed by his charges. Sherman learned that some of the Indians had been absent during the time of the attack but would soon arrive to get their rations.

They came in to the commissary on Saturday and were told that the agent wished to council with them. When he questioned them about the raid, Satanta boastfully replied: "Yes, I led that raid. I have heard that you have stolen a large portion of our annuity goods and given them to the Texans; I have repeatedly asked you for arms and ammunition, which you have not furnished, and made many other requests which have not been granted. You do not listen to my talk. The white people are preparing to build a railroad through our country, which will not be permitted. Some years ago we were taken by the hair and pulled close to the Texans where we have to fight. But we have cut that loose now and are all going with the Cheyenne to the Antelope Hills. When General Custer was here two or three years ago, he arrested me and kept me in confinement several days. But arresting Indians is played out now and is never to be repeated. On account of these grievances, I took, a short time ago, about 100 of my warriors, with the chiefs Satank, Eagle Heart, Big Tree, Big Bow, and Fast Bear. . . . We went to Texas, where we captured a train not far from Fort Richardson, killed seven of the men and drove off about 41 mules. Three of my men were killed, but we are willing to call it even. We don't expect to do any raiding around here this summer, but we expect to raid in Texas. If any other Indian comes here and claims the honor of leading the party, he will be lying to you, for I did it myself!"

The other Kiowas confirmed Satanta's boast that he had been fighting Texans. All his life he had been selling white captives to the Army—why not again? Tatum informed him that General Sherman was at the fort, that if the General authorized an issue of ammunition and arms to the Kiowa, the agent would give these to them. Tatum immediately reported the matter in writing to the post commander.

Sherman prepared to receive the Kiowa, mounting his cavalry out of sight inside the corral and posting a company of soldiers, their rifles loaded, behind the closed shutters of the rooms opening on the long porch of the commanding officer's quarters.

The Kiowas were warned of danger, but decided to talk with the General.

Sherman, unarmed and in civilian clothes, walked up and down on the porch. He questioned the chiefs. Satanta made no bones about his part in the raid, though he denied that anybody had been tied to the wagon wheel and burned. Again he named the leading Kiowas in the party. Sherman promptly informed the Indians that Satanta, Satank and Big Tree would be arrested, sent to Texas, and tried for murder.

Satanta lost his temper. "I would rather be shot right here," he cried defiantly, pulled off his blanket and reached for the handle of his revolver.

Sherman snapped out a command. The shutters along the front of the house swung open. The Kiowas saw a line of Negro troopers, "buffalo soldiers," looking across the sights of their leveled carbines.

Satanta's braggadocio instantly evaporated. "Don't shoot!" he yelled.

While the Indians hesitated, shifting their feet, uncertain what to do, a trumpet sounded. The cavalry swarmed out of the corral where they had been waiting and quickly barred all exit from the post. The soldiers had caught Big Tree and now brought him to join the council. Chief Lone Wolf, hoping to leave the post, was called back to join the others. He distributed all the weapons he had among his fellow warriors, then, cocking his own carbine, aimed it at Sherman. Colonel

H. B. Grierson grabbed Lone Wolf. They wrestled together and fell on the porch.

Stumbling Bear set an arrow on his bowstring and waited for Sherman, still coolly pacing up and down the porch, to come opposite him. Before he could shoot, one of the Indians seized the chief's arm. His arrow flew wide.

Throughout all this excitement Satank alone remained seated, smoking.

" 'If you men want to crawl out of this affair by telling pitiful stories,' he remarked, 'that is your affair. I am sitting here saying nothing. I am an old man, surrounded by soldiers. But if any soldier lays a hand on me I am going to die, here and now.' " [1]

Sherman saw that the Indians were nerving themselves for a fight to the death. He ordered the troopers in the house to lower the barrels of their guns. It was getting dusk, and Sherman hastened to bring the council to an end.

The General told them that he would arrest Chief Satanta, Satank and Big Tree and that the Kiowa must hand over forty-one good mules.

Perhaps the interpreter was too scared to translate properly. Perhaps he was too wise. Perhaps he made a genuine mistake. At any rate, the Indians went off believing that when they brought in the mules their three chiefs would be released. The guard came marching up, put handcuffs and fetters on the three prisoners, and locked them up.

Sherman was the hero of Fort Sill that night, but he took the praise as calmly as he had the danger. It was left to MacKenzie to take the chiefs to Texas for trial.

Big Tree and Satanta were anything but saucy when led out to take their place in the wagons. But Satank was as full of fight as ever. He was head man in the leading warrior society of the tribe, the Kaitsenko. This order had only ten members, brave men chosen and pledged to lead every desperate charge and to keep their place in the front of battle until they won victory or death. In battle their leader carried a specially made arrow and wore over his left shoulder a black elkskin sash, the end of which trailed on the ground. When his men were about to charge the enemy, it was his duty to thrust the arrow through the tail of his sash, thus pinning himself to the ground. There he was bound to remain, defying the enemy, until the Kiowa had driven them from the field, or, if retiring, until his comrades set him free by pulling the arrow from the ground. If nobody remembered to do this, he was expected to remain and fight to the death. If he pulled up the arrow himself, he would become the laughingstock of the tribe.

So now Chief Satank, the leading warrior of his tribe, felt that his obligations required him to defy the whites. He was so refractory that they had to throw him into a wagon by himself, with two soldiers to guard him. Satank complained bitterly, "I am a chief and a warrior; they treat me like a child." Big Tree and Satanta rode together in another wagon.

As the wagons left the fort with their mounted escort, a Caddo Indian named George Washington rode by. Satank called to him, "Tell my people I am dead. I died the first day out. They will find my bones beside the road." As the wagons rolled along, Satank called out to the other prisoners, "See that tree ahead? I will never go beyond that tree, but die right there." Some Tonkawa Indian government scouts rode with the party. Nye reports: "Satank spoke to a Tonkawa scout who was riding nearby. 'You may have my scalp,' he said. 'The hair is poor. It isn't worth much, but you may have it.' The Tonkawa's squaw whooped to honor the brave old Kiowa."

They had not gone a mile from the post when Satank began to sing the death song of his warrior society:

" '*Iha hyo oya iya iya o iha yaya yoyo.*
Aheya aheya yaheyo ya eye heyo eheyo.

O sun, you remain forever, but we Kaitsenko must die.
O earth, you remain forever, but we Kaitsenko must die.' " [2]

Having fulfilled this ritual, he sat with his back to the guard and managed, not without losing some skin, to slip his skinny hands out of the handcuffs. Then, producing his "magic" knife, he jumped up and went for the guards, gashing one of them in the leg. At this the guards jumped or fell out of the wagon, leaving one of their carbines in the hands of the chief.

Hoping to take one or two soldiers with him, Satank tried to pump a cartridge into the chamber. But the soldiers riding along beside him fired first, incidentally wounding the teamster severely. Still Satank struggled up to continue the fight. Everybody was shooting at him—he was hit several times. Satanta and Big Tree took no part in the fracas, but sat meekly with their hands up.

Satank fell to the ground. There for a time he sat up, bleeding at the mouth and gritting his teeth, until he died. MacKenzie forbade his Tonkawa scouts to scalp the body and ordered the command forward. As the Kiowa never claimed the chief's body, the troops buried him in the post cemetery. The old chief had lived up to his vow, preferring death to dishonor.

The "Orator of the Plains" thereafter blamed all the misdeeds of the Kiowa on his dead comrade Satank. But a Texas jury made short work of convicting him and Big Tree. The pair were sentenced to be hanged.

But Indian-lovers in the East soon brought pressure to bear, and the Governor of Texas commuted the sentences to life imprisonment.

The Army feared—not without cause—that the two war

criminals would never serve out a life sentence. And before long the Kiowa were as saucy and troublesome as ever. One of their chiefs told an officer that he would prefer eating dung on the prairie to living on a reservation.

In the middle of the summer of 1872, a general conference of the Southern tribes was called at Fort Cobb in Oklahoma, though the fort had been abandoned by the Army. Some Cheyennes and Arapahoes turned up, but left before any Comanche or Kiowa arrived. These latter were extremely insolent, strutting and bragging of depredations they had committed on the Brazos River shortly before. They had three white children, they said, and impudently demanded that all the country between the Rio Grande and the Missouri River should be added to their reservation and all white men driven from their lands. They also demanded that their chief, Satanta, be set free and restored to them. Several displayed fresh wounds which they had suffered during the recent raid. They said they would never submit to being cooped up on a reservation.

It was time for the Army to strike again. The last week of September Colonel Ranald S. MacKenzie attacked a camp of some 250 lodges on the North Fork of Red River. He killed two dozen hostiles and captured more than 100 women and children and more than forty head of branded mules, recently stolen from the whites. He was now in an excellent position to bargain with the hostiles, swapped prisoners with them, and compelled them to bring in stolen animals.

By August, '73, though the raiding still went on, Satanta and Big Tree were released and taken back to Sill.

The Governor of Texas had laid down certain conditions for their release—requiring the presence of every warrior at Fort Sill every third day to draw rations and answer roll call.

But the soft-hearted Indian agent ignored these "hard" requirements. The tribes went on with their killing. The Indians refused to give up five warriors who had been raiding. Meanwhile orders came from Washington to stop Comanche rations, and threatening to turn the tribe over to the Army. At once the Comanche, whether in search of food or scornful of the threat, pulled out, heading for Texas.

In October, 1873, in appreciation of the release of Big Tree and Satanta, the Kiowa promised to follow the white man's road and raid no more. Immediately after, a war party of Kiowa and Comanche hit the trail, killing more than a dozen men and taking several prisoners.

But this time a detachment of the Fourth Cavalry intercepted them. In ten minutes the troopers, without losing a single man, had the Indians on the run, leaving nine dead behind them. This disaster made the Kiowa furious. Lone Wolf, whose son had been killed in the fight, no longer had any heart whatever for the white men.

So long as redskins ran free on the Plains, it was clear that there would be no end to the raiding.

17

THAT THIEVES' ROAD

Meanwhile, trouble had been brewing in the North.

Though Red Cloud thought he had gained everything he could hope for from the Treaty of 1868, signing it had placed him in an awkward position. He was no longer a hostile like Sitting Bull, and so took no part in the later battles of his people with the troops. Yet he was no progressive like Spotted Tail, who had seen enough of the white man's civilization at close range to know that the days of the hunter were numbered. Red Cloud tried to remain an unreconstructed Sioux while living on the reservation and eating out of the white man's hand. This committed him to a program of biting the hand that fed him until it finally slapped him down. He became perforce at once an opportunist and an obstructionist. He tried to make the best of both worlds, but had not the wit to see that his attempt was doomed to failure.

The visionaries who promoted the Treaty of 1868 apparently dreamed that Sitting Bull and Crazy Horse, who led the hunting bands, the hostile Sioux, would abandon the Big Horn Mountains and the Powder River country and settle at the agency if they were sufficiently appeased. In this they were badly fooled. Sitting Bull would trade for white men's goods with traders whom he trusted, but he would never accept a present from the government, and even forbade the warriors of his band to take the belongings of white men whom they killed in battle. He knew that no compromise was possible, and held out until there were no buffalo to maintain him.

Another false notion the treaty makers entertained was that the Powder River country was unsuited to white occupation and that no white man wished to settle there.

These two misconceptions left the door open to the frontiersmen, who poured their own pleas into the ear of President Grant. Early in 1870 the papers were headlining a Sioux war scare and printing stories that troops would soon be moving to the West. Caught by surprise, the Peace Party had to act quickly. They sent Chief Red Cloud to Washington on the pretense that he had asked to go. None of the Indians in the party had visited the East before. By the time the delegation reached Washington, they were a scared lot of Indians.

They were somewhat surprised to find Spotted Tail, with another delegation of Sioux, already there. So, true to Sioux form in an emergency, they promptly began to quarrel—over the matter of precedence.

The Sioux were shown the city, the warships in the river, the big guns at the arsenal, one of which was fired for them. Red Cloud measured the gun with his eagle-wing fan. All that armament brought the spirits of the Sioux to a new low, and when Red Cloud began to demand that no more roads be built and that Fort Fetterman be dismantled, President Grant advised him to go back to the Missouri River and start plowing.

Then the Secretary of the Interior took them in hand. Finding the chiefs vague as to their agreements in the Treaty of 1868, he had it translated for them, clause by clause. For the first time they learned that the treaty provided that they must settle down and farm, be counted in a census, must not oppose the building of railroads off the reservation, and that that reservation was to be in the barren, gameless country along the Missouri River. The Sioux were flabbergasted, declared the treaty a swindle, denied that they had ever made such promises, protested that they had been cheated, and demanded a quick trip home. Red Cloud had to be restrained from committing suicide, so the story goes.

That was a facer for the visionaries who had framed the treaty—and the Sioux. They had to act quickly. In the hope of winning sympathy for their cause, they decided to take the indignant Red Cloud to New York and have him make a speech. His sponsors persuaded him to doff his colorful Indian costume; they dressed him up in a boiled shirt, long-tailed coat, and top hat. He spoke at Cooper Institute before a huge crowd.

The chief was a big man, with a very strong face and all the dignity and aplomb of an old-time Sioux chieftain. He was very obviously much in earnest, and, no mean actor, emphasized his remarks with eloquent gestures from the sign language. He was a tall, magnetic man and a practiced orator. He began with a prayer invoking Wakan Tanka, dwelt on the wrongs his people had endured, demanded justice for them, told of his long pilgrimage to Washington to prevent war, and appealed to the crowd: "You have children and so have we. We want to rear our children well, and ask you to help us in doing so." His appeal, "at once simple, strong and heartfelt," greatly impressed the audience. "During the intervals of translation he stood statuesque and impressive, which was quite as striking as the animation of the more earnest passages of his appeal."

Red Dog provided the comic relief. He declared, "When the Grandfather first sent out men to our people, I was poor and thin; now I am big and fat. This is because so many liars have been sent out there, and I have been stuffed full of their lies."

The success of Red Cloud's speech compelled concessions. The government granted the Indians the right to trade as they wished. When the Sioux got home they held a Sun Dance and promptly went to war with the Crows. In the course of the fighting they used the guns given them to shoot at white soldiers stationed at Crow Agency. The agent's earnest appeal for arms for his Crows was ignored by the Indian Bureau. The Crows were friendly—no point in protecting them!

The net result of Red Cloud's visit to the East was an exposé to the Sioux of the true nature of the Treaty of 1868 and a universal conviction that any Indian who trusted the Grandfather was an utter fool.[1] And Red Cloud's hatred for the white men was not diminished by having to explain to his followers how the white men had swindled him.

The failure of the Sioux to go to war in 1870 was a setback to those who wanted a strong military force on the frontier. But it only confirmed the sponsors of the Peace Policy in humoring the Indians. From that time on the Sioux, in particular, so bedeviled their agents that at last one called for troops. But the Indians' friends kept all this hushed up and hastened to make further concessions to the truculent tribesmen.

The Sioux behaved very badly. The tribes were controlled by the warrior societies, the bulk of whose members were young men with more spunk than gumption. In order to maintain any influence a chief had to follow the warriors; he was, in fact, little more than their mouthpiece. Those chiefs who had gone to Washington could not, or would not, try to make the Sioux understand the power of the white man. They did nothing to prevent their people from exhausting the patience of the very people sent out to help them.

When one of the Sioux agents attempted to take the census required under the Treaty of 1868, the warriors made a violent demonstration, forbade him to count their people, and forced him to accept their own estimate of the Indian population. This, as it turned out, was not only ugly but stupid, since the actual count made later showed the Indians' figure to be an underestimate by some thirty per cent. But the warriors at any rate prevented the agent from issuing rations to heads of families. They enforced the old system of turning over all issue goods to the chiefs. To eat at all, every Sioux on the reservation had to obey his chief—who obeyed the warriors.

Meanwhile, the Sioux blithely waged war as usual on neighboring tribes; in '73 they struck the Pawnees in a surprise attack, killing and wounding many, and robbing them of their horses and other property. Those Pawnees, long loyal to Uncle Sam, had served as scouts with the troops year after year and were, in fact, responsible for most of the casualties inflicted on the hostiles in those campaigns. But the government, under the Peace Policy, while continually appeasing the troublesome Cutthroats (as the Sioux described themselves in the sign language), never lifted a finger to help those loyal Pawnees. Under the Peace Policy, peaceful Indians might starve or be killed with impunity. It was only hostiles who were pampered. As one educated Pawnee expressed it, "God help all friends of the United States."

The Sioux, like some other militaristic peoples, could never get it through their skulls that the generosity and patience of Americans meant anything but softness, weakness, cowardice. The more the Sioux were pampered, the meaner and uglier they became.

When the agent at Red Cloud, Dr. J. J. Saville, persisted in saying that he must take the census, he was threatened with death and came near being killed. White men were not allowed to leave his half-finished stockade. And when the agent tried to set up a flagpole, the Indians chopped it to pieces.

Under the Peace Policy, Indian agents were chosen from and by various religious denominations, in the belief that Christian ministers would be lovers of peace and would also be honest in fulfilling their duties. Many of the Sioux were turned over to the Episcopal Church, and Bishop William Hobart

Hare (described by one who knew him well as "a razor sent to do the work of a broadax") went out to visit the agencies and report. His account of hordes of warriors firing their guns and yelling, surrounding and threatening the Commission, opened some eyes. Yet in spite of this experience, he still hoped that the Sioux might be satisfied if they could have their agency in the Black Hills.

On Hare's return, that summer of '74, he found out that General George Armstrong Custer was about to lead a military expedition into the Black Hills to discover trails into that area and find a suitable site for a military post, on the understanding that such a post would "threaten the Indian villages and stock if the latter raided the settlements."

As a matter of fact, Jim Bridger had led Captain W. F. Raynolds through that country years before, and all military men in the West used the Raynolds map. Moreover, Warren, as we have seen, had visited the Hills before.

Bishop Hare protested to President Grant in writing, warning that war must follow, but Grant did nothing to interfere with the War Department's plans.

A severe depression gripped the whole country. The public was tired of spending millions to pacify the Sioux, vainly trying to buy off the warriors. Fat or lean, full or empty, the Sioux were always on the warpath. The public was tired of the false propaganda of the Peace Party. Westerners were making themselves heard, too, as well as railroad builders.

And so General Custer set out to make what one of the Sioux bitterly called "That Thieves' Road."

The march itself was a junket. There was no opposition, no fighting with Indians. Custer rhapsodized about the beauty of the Hills, "grazing whose only fault, if any, was the great luxuriance," streams of "crystal water so cold as to render ice undesirable even at noonday," and went on to make the country's mouth water by declaring, "I know no portion of our country where Nature has done so much to prepare homes for husbandmen and left so little for the latter to do as here. . . . Nowhere in the States have I tasted cultivated berries of better flavor than those found growing wild here. . . . Cattle could winter in these valleys without other food or shelter than that to be obtained from running at large."

Hardly the style for a military report, that. But there was method in it. Custer was only building up to an announcement that was to lead swiftly enough to the end of Indian wars—and of Custer.

Custer appears to have been far less interested in military routes and posts than in the mining and farming resources of the Black Hills. In fact, he took along a party of prospectors and some newspapermen. He himself sent most glowing accounts of the country to the newspapers. An eager public was informed that there was "gold in the grassroots."

That autumn of '74 Red Cloud began to make trouble again, convincing a visiting naturalist, Professor O. C. Marsh of Yale University, that the rations of the Sioux were short and inedible. The fuss over this business resulted in a great investigation, and once more Red Cloud was invited to Washington.

This time he failed to impress the public as he had before. He faltered and hedged and failed to support Professor Marsh when brought to the test. He hastily dropped his charges against the agent, sensing, perhaps, that the President was not much interested in such matters.

And then the blow fell. The Grandfather informed him and the other Indians that the whites were going to take the Black Hills, and that the Sioux had better sell them quick before that happened. The chiefs declared—truly enough—that they could not commit their people to such a deal.

Before he was through, Red Cloud had managed to enrage or insult most of the officials and friends of the Indians with whom he came in contact. And in this emergency, as usual, the Sioux delegation split up and began to upbraid each other.

To make matters worse, a mercenary hotelkeeper took it upon himself to entertain the Sioux. Red Cloud's conducted tour of the city included a visit to a bawdy house—an item duly set down in the bill of his entertainer. During the course of their visit to this establishment, the Indians say, one of the inmates slapped one of the chiefs. To the Sioux such familiarity on the part of a woman was a profound shock.

But that shock was nothing to the one awaiting the chief at the Indian Office. For when Red Cloud, wholly ignorant of the social standards of his pious sponsors, met the Commissioner and other officials for a conference, and openly presented his bill for the entertainment of the Sioux, there was an explosion. The Commissioner, burning with indignation, lectured the chief severely.

Thereafter he was not invited to make any speeches; the church people and humanitarians throughout the country could no longer support him wholeheartedly. Some of the Sioux had been much interested in the strange institution which they had visited, and had cherished a hope that something of the kind might be established on the reservation for their benefit; now they started home in a sadly puzzled frame of mind.

When the Commission went out to bargain for the Black Hills, they found Red Cloud and the Sioux as threatening and stubborn as ever. The government offered to purchase the Hills outright for $6,000,000 or to pay $400,000 a year for the mining rights. But by this time the Indians had such an exaggerated notion of what they should get for *Pa Sapa* that the chiefs would not even consider Uncle Sam's proposition.

The chiefs were not stupid, but they were sadly ignorant of past Indian relations with the United States. Red Cloud, they say, demanded a hundred times the government's offer and also declared that the government must support the Sioux for seven generations to come. The government had brought the Indians from their hunting grounds to the reservation to live like white men: it was only reasonable, he said, that the government should pay all expenses.

It was manifest that the government would have to put heavy pressure on the Sioux to bring them to their senses. The Commission recommended that Congress withhold all rations until the Sioux consented to whatever arrangement Congress deemed fair.

18

ADOBE WALLS AND PALO DURO

Plains Indians lived on the buffalo, which provided them with food, shelter, clothing, in fact, nearly everything they needed or used. So long as men killed buffalo only for their meat and shaggy robes, the great herds dwindled slowly, for the robes had to be taken in winter. But when, in the early '70s, it was discovered that buffalo *hides* were marketable, swarms of hide hunters fanned out over the Southern Plains summer and winter alike. High-powered Sharps buffalo guns and the coming of the railroad swiftly turned buffalo hunting into a mighty slaughter.

The Army and the Government had no interest in preserving the herds. To the military the extermination of the buffalo seemed the surest way to bring the Indians to heel and force them to live on reservations. By 1874 the hide hunters, having slaughtered most of the buffalo in Kansas, moved south of the Arkansas, south of the Cimarron, encroaching more and more on the hunting grounds of the Kiowa and Comanche, the Southern Cheyenne and Arapaho, in what is now Western Oklahoma.

This enraged the Indians, for the Treaty of Medicine Lodge had expressly provided that white men should *not* hunt south of the Kansas line. Troops patrolled the Arkansas River (which

195

served as a "practical" boundary), but made no serious attempt to round up the hunters or drive them from the Indian lands. In fact, large parties set up permanent camps there. Of these the best known was at Adobe Walls, on the Canadian River, in the Panhandle of Texas.

The rapid destruction of their commissary, the buffalo, roused the warriors. Moreover, during the winter of 1873–74 many fights had occurred in Texas, in which some thirty Comanches and Kiowas were rubbed out. Their kinsmen were eager for revenge, and clashes continually took place; for these outrages, however, the wily chiefs always passed the buck to some other tribe.

On top of all this, hostilities were sparked by a Comanche prophet, Isati, Rear-End-of-a-Wolf, who declared that he could belch up cartridges by the wagonload. Isati proposed to hold a Sun Dance, a ceremony which the Comanches had never held before. Mexican peddlers brought whiskey, and there was much war talk.

At first the plan was to attack the Tonkawa cannibals, but when Quanah Parker suggested that they attack the white hunters at Adobe Walls, all the warriors favored his motion. Kiowas and Cheyennes were invited to join. Some Arapahoes went too. A large war party of these four tribes rode off and made their attack on the log camp of the buffalo hunters at Adobe Walls June 27, 1874.

There were twenty-eight white men and one woman in the settlement. By great good luck, the night before the attack the ridgepole of Hanrahan's saloon cracked, and all hands were kept busy until morning bracing it to keep the roof from falling in. The sky was already colored by the sun when they finished, and the men thought it too late to go to bed. Most of them were still up and indoors when the Indians charged.

Isati had prophesied that the white men would not fire a single shot. The Indians lined up on the ridge and waited for the prophet's command. He yelled; all galloped down the slope to the attack.

The beat of those thundering hooves roused the buffalo hunters, who fired through the windows and between the logs of their cabins. At times the Indians came so close that they beat on the barred doors of the buildings, but could not break in. But they killed two freighters asleep in their wagon outside, and another man, named Tyler. It was easy for the whites to stand them off, for some Indian with a bugle blew the charge every time the warriors advanced. Several Indians were shot down in the first attack. Some got behind the stacks of raw buffalo hides near the buildings, or behind the stables and corrals, and sniped at the hunters. But shortly after noon they all pulled out.

The Cheyennes suffered the heaviest loss—six warriors, including Stone Calf's son. Only five Comanches were killed. The Kiowas, Apaches, and Arapahoes lost no men at all. Quanah Parker himself was hit on his shield by a spent ball, and several other Indians or horses were knocked over by the long bullets of those buffalo guns almost a mile away. Altogether they lost some fifteen men.

After the battle a hot-tempered Cheyenne warrior seized Isati's bridle and offered to quirt him, but Isati protested his innocence. "One of you killed a skunk," he whined. "That broke my medicine."

After this defeat the disgruntled tribesmen scattered, and a good many skirmishes followed. Early in July Cheyennes and Arapahoes attacked Pat Hennessy's wagon train; he was burned as he lay tied to a wagon wheel. John D. Miles, the agent, wired frantically for troops, and so at last Lieutenant Frank D. Baldwin came to the rescue, later heading out on the Staked Plains to relieve the hunters at Adobe Walls. By the end of July, over the protests of the Quaker agents, the President put an end to the old unworkable Peace Policy and ordered the army to take over the management of the hostile tribes. Another order required friendly Indians to register before August 3rd. The period allowed was so short that the hostiles could not get in in time to come under the protection of the troops. Those who did not were declared outlaws, and told they must come in as prisoners of war. By the beginning of August, less than 400 tribesmen had come in.

The new plan of the troops was to keep the Indians eternally on the move, giving them no time to hunt, never allowing them to rest or fatten up their ponies for a campaign. It was a war of attrition.

That summer of '74 was hot, and one of the driest Western Oklahoma ever saw. Vast flights of grasshoppers swept over the country, devouring every blade of grass. The creeks dried up to stagnant water holes covered with green scum. It would have been a wonderful time for a campaign if the troops had had as many horses as the Indians and could have carried forage along. As it was, nothing happened until September.

Troops came piling into the Plains until it seemed to the Indians that their whole country was crawling with soldiers. The Kiowa, fearing what might happen if they surrendered at their own agency where they were known, headed for the Cheyenne-Arapaho agency at Darlington, hoping to be better treated. They missed their guess. The commandant put Satanta and Big Tree in irons and marched the whole group back to Fort Sill to be locked up. Before the Quaker agents found out that Satanta was in the hands of the military, the President had approved General Sheridan's suggestion that the murderous chiefs be turned over to the Texans for trial. There was to be no more monkey business by the Indian Bureau.

It was a wet season on the Staked Plains that fall, but the barefoot hostiles plodded toward Palo Duro Canyon—that amazing gorge cut through the flat Staked Plains. Kiowa, Comanche, Cheyenne gathered there, and listened hopefully to the prophecies of their medicine men.

Colonel Ranald S. MacKenzie had several brushes with the hostiles as he led his command north from the Clear Fork of the Brazos. For a time both Indians and troops pursued each other around like a dog chasing his tail. But on September 26 MacKenzie's scouts, plodding across the endless grassy levels of the Staked Plains, suddenly found themselves brought up short by a yawning chasm. Far below they saw the Palo Duro Creek winding through the thronging tipis of the hostiles.

By dawn next day MacKenzie and his troops reached the brink, but could find no way to get down. They rode along, skirting the canyon, and so at last, about sunup, discovered a narrow game trail angling dangerously down across the face of the cliff. Every trooper dismounted and led his snorting, sliding horse along this precarious trail. That line of soldiers clinging dizzily to the canyon wall would have made a wonderful target had the Indians been alert. But MacKenzie got three full companies into the canyon before the heedless hostiles discovered him.

When the shooting began, a few warriors took cover among the rocks and cedars to snipe at the troops. But most of the Kiowas and Comanches lost no time in making tracks. White sharpshooters' had driven off the snipers by the time the whole command reached the canyon floor.

Meanwhile the troopers were charging in waves through the camp in a haze of dust and powder smoke, chasing the scrambling Indians out of the canyon. They did not linger to defend their camp. A tent is no fortress. They even left their ponies to the mercy of the troops. It was a complete rout.

Very few Indians were killed. As for the whites, one bugler was wounded.

There was some long-range shooting while the soldiers

burned the lodges and drove off 1400 captured ponies. But by this time the Army had learned how impossible it was to keep a herd of Indian ponies. MacKenzie ordered them all destroyed.

The day of the fight was cold and clear. But the following night heavy rains fell. The cold deluge chilled the shelterless Indians left afoot, half-naked and hungry in the midst of the vast Staked Plains. All that was dreary enough. But shortly after, Mexicans stole all the horses the Indians had left. From then on life for the hostiles was a dismal progress from one mud puddle to another.

For the Army it was now simply a matter of mopping up. No time was lost. The troops pushed the hostile bands relentlessly across Red River, across the Staked Plains, trapping and defeating one camp after another. On October 9 Lieutenant Colonel Buell struck a big Kiowa camp on the Salt Fork of the Brazos; on the 17th Captain A. R. Chaffee cleaned out another on the Washita River.

Before the campaign ended, fourteen battles had been fought. Band after wild band came hurrying in to the agencies, sick, hungry, ragged and afoot, to surrender.

Early in September the Cheyennes had surprised a family of emigrants named Germaine (sometimes spelled German) on the Kansas plains. They murdered the father and mother, the grown son and eldest daughter, and carried away the four younger girls. Stone Calf held Catherine, 17, and Sophia, 15, while Chief Greybeard took the younger pair, Julia, 10, and Adelaide, 5. Stone Calf hit the trail to the Staked Plains. Greybeard made camp on McClellan Creek, in Wheeler County, Texas.

General Miles was very anxious to save the captives. His camp was on Red River at the edge of the Staked Plains.

His Chief of Scouts was Lieutenant Frank D. Baldwin, Fifth Infantry, holder of the Congressional Medal, brave as he was eager. Miles sent him with one troop, one company, some scouts and a single mountain howitzer to guard a train of twenty-three six-mule teams hauling empty wagons, heading for the supply camp on the Washita River. Baldwin struck out to the northeast. The orders Miles had given him were admirably suited to the man's temper: "Should you find any considerable body of Indians, you will communicate with me, and attack or pursue, *as you deem expedient*." This was on November 4, 1874.

Now Baldwin knew that in case he met Indians the proper military distribution of his forces would be to corral his wagons at the rear under guard and attack with his remaining men. But he knew that his small force, thus divided, would be quite incapable of any strong offensive action. In fact, he had merely an escort for the wagon train, and no men to spare.

But Miles' orders show that he knew Baldwin would never hesitate to attack if he met with hostile Indians.

Baldwin let no grass grow under his feet. He cut straight across country, avoiding trails, and made camp on the night of November 7 in a thick grove of cottonwood trees on McClellan Creek. It was cold weather, but no campfires were kept burning. Long before dawn Baldwin's scouts were out scouring the rough country in their front. The train itself had just moved out when the scouts came racing back to report they had found Greybeard's big camp. Baldwin immediately sent word to Miles that he had found Greybeard and would attack at once.

Baldwin knew that Greybeard's warriors far outnumbered his meager force. He knew too that Miles would hurry to his relief. But before Miles could arrive, it was certain that the Indians would discover Baldwin. Unless he could surprise the camp, all experience indicated that the prisoners would be murdered before he could recover them. He had to strike hard and strike quickly.

He dared not divide his force. He ordered the wagon train into the front line. The infantry yanked off the wagon sheets, climbed into the empty wagons, and lined up with the cavalry, with the howitzer front and center. They moved rapidly forward. Soon Baldwin could see Greybeard's tipis thronging the flat along the creek, hardly a mile away. As soon as his strange chariots reached the top of the rise, he beckoned the trumpeters.

"Charge!"

The troopers yelled, the mules lunged down the slope, the wagons tore through the Cheyenne camp like so many runaway locomotives, while the doughboys aboard cut loose with everything they had. Utterly surprised and disconcerted, the Cheyennes took to their heels, streaking away to the west, heading for the breaks at the edge of the Staked Plains. As soon as the warriors reached rough ground, they took cover and fired at long range at the advancing troops, trying to hold them back until their squaws and papooses could get away. The troops returned this fire with interest and the Cheyennes quickly gave way, falling back to new positions. When Baldwin's force had mounted to the vast levels of the Staked Plains, they saw it dotted with women and children running for their lives, while the warriors stubbornly guarded their rear.

The howitzer went into action. The cavalry charged. That put an end to all resistance, and there was a running fight until the horses of the cavalrymen played out after a chase of ten or twelve miles.

The two Germaine children were found alive, seated on a buffalo robe on a hillside. They had been put in the charge of a young redskin, but as one of the girls was too young to ride and he was in a bit of a hurry, he left them both behind. Why he did not murder them has never been explained. Perhaps he thought the troops might stop, once they had recovered the captives. These sorry waifs, half-starved, ragged, dirty, sunburned, and frightened, inspired the pity of every soldier who saw them.

For this ingenious and successful attack against superior numbers, Lieutenant Baldwin was brevetted Captain and received a second award of the Congressional Medal.

But it was not so easy to find Stone Calf and rescue the elder sisters. Frequent attacks had made the Cheyennes even meaner than usual. Every day Catherine and her sister expected —or wished—to be killed.

But by January Miles had captured some of Stone Calf's Indians. He sent them to that chief, warning him that unless he brought in the girls unhurt, Miles would show him no mercy and hunt him down. Miles offered, however, to give Stone Calf amnesty if he brought in the girls and surrendered. One of Miles' scouts accompanied the messengers. He secretly carried along a photograph of the two girls already rescued, on the back of which General Miles had written:

"To the Misses Germaine:
Your little sisters are well and in the hands of friends. Do not be discouraged. Every effort is being made for your welfare.

Nelson A. Miles
Colonel, Fifth Infantry"

Stone Calf lost no time in accepting this offer. He made the owners of the captives turn them over to him so that no one could do them harm. Before the month was out, he and his band came dragging into Darlington and gave themselves up.

The Germaine sisters were asked to identify warriors who had taken part in the massacre of their family or who had abused them. The Indians pointed out were then put in irons by the blacksmith at the post. They had to put their feet up on the anvil so that he could hammer the rivets properly and bind the fetters upon them. Whether the blacksmith was clumsy or malicious, somehow he managed to pound flesh as well as rivets. One Indian, resenting this, resisted, tried to get away. The troops fired at him as he ran. The shooting frightened other Cheyennes who had just surrendered. They scurried to the sand hills along the river where they had cannily hidden their best guns as they came in to surrender.

There was a sharp engagement. A number of Cheyennes were killed, some soldiers wounded. But after this confusion the Cheyennes gave in again. Several were sent off to prison at St. Augustine, Florida. Those sent included the offenders pointed out by the Germaine sisters, as well as others whom the commandant selected at random.

By this time there was little fight left in the Indians of the Southern Plains. The Army had made good its claim that the Indians could be pacified by destroying their villages and their ponies, thus depriving them of their means of hunting and fighting. Within four months this program was carried out, and, to the intense chagrin of Eastern humanitarians who abhorred military control, hardly any Indians had been killed in the process.

Satanta, who had broken parole, was caught and given a life sentence at the penitentiary in Texas. He stuck it out three years. Then he declared he was heap sick, and was put in the hospital. There were no bars at his window. Satanta sang his death song, then leaped from the high window headlong to his death.

19

COLONEL REYNOLDS ATTACKS

THE PHONY PEACE set up by the Treaty of 1868 had never been more stable than a house of cards. The visionaries and appeasers who had framed it were too ignorant of Indians, too intolerant of facts which did not fit their theories; their paper treaty could not long endure. Their tune had been, "Feed the Sioux and you will not need to fight them."

But those who sang this song soon changed their tune. When the Commission, headed by Senator Allison, drove out from Fort Robinson, Nebraska, to discuss with Spotted Tail and Red Cloud the purchase of the Black Hills in September, 1875, they found themselves in great danger. Their escort, Captain Egan's White Horse Troop of the Second Cavalry, formed in a single line behind the Commissioners seated in council. Immediately afterward one of the Sioux warrior societies rode up and formed a similar line immediately behind Egan's force, so that every trooper was covered by a Sioux warrior in his rear.

When Young-Man-Afraid-of-His-Horses, the hereditary chief of these Oglala, saw what the die-hard faction of his people intended, he attempted to nullify their hostility by forming up his own warriors in a third line behind the second.

It appeared that the discussions of the council would proceed, after all.

But the feeling among the Sioux for their sacred mountains, the most desirable part of their domain, was very strong. None wished to part with the Black Hills, and many were ready to fight rather than yield them.

Suddenly, while the proceedings still hung fire, Little Big Man, stripped for war and brandishing his Winchester, rode into the council between the Commission and the leaders of his people, shouting that he would kill the first chief who dared to talk of selling the Black Hills.

Spotted Tail, the diplomat, then tactfully advised the Commission to return to the fort, a suggestion which they found most welcome at the time. Climbing into the ambulance and surrounded by mounted troopers, they drove off.

But Little Big Man's faction were not content. They surrounded the escort and rode with them in a very threatening manner, jostling the troops, shaking their weapons and yelling in a terrifying manner. The Commission, if they had ever supposed the Sioux a stoical and stolid people, now had their eyes opened to the volatile and emotional character of those Indians. It was a frightening discovery.

General Anson Mills, in his book *My Story* (page 164), describes how one young man "rode furiously into our ranks," intent upon killing one of the Commission. Luckily some of the friendly Sioux rode with the angry mob of hostiles. One of them distracted the young man's fury by pointing out a colt which happened to be grazing on the prairie about a hundred yards away, and advised him to appease his anger by killing that. The frothing warrior galloped out on the prairie, shot down the colt, and permitted the white men to reach Fort Robinson without loss of blood. The Commission made no further effort to negotiate with the Sioux.

They had been so terrorized, threatened and abused that

they were now fully convinced that the fight could never be taken out of the Sioux merely by filling their bellies with beef. On the contrary, during the seven years following the treaty, the Government had spent no less than thirteen million dollars to keep the Sioux quiet—and all to no purpose. For wars and revolutions are not always caused by starvation. Full bellies only encourage warlike men. Most wars, like most revolutions, have been begun by nations or groups who were better fed than their neighbors.

And so with mutinies. It is not the Regulars under strict discipline who mutiny, but the pampered Volunteers.

After Little Big Man's demonstration, the Commission advised that earlier treaties had *not* been abrogated by the Treaty of 1868, which, they claimed, had merely annulled these articles of the earlier treaties which obliged the government to furnish annuities to the Sioux. The Commission now proposed to revive an old treaty of 1865, which had been signed by a few minor chiefs only, and so side-step the government's pledge to keep white men off the Sioux reservation.

The administration was in desperate need of such an excuse. For it was quite impossible for a representative government, with an empty treasury and an unruly population of hard-up, adventurous voters, to hold back the gold rush to the Black Hills. The President might issue his proclamation, the military might threaten and even arrest some miners in the Hills; but the civil authorities immediately set the culprits free, and the Federal Government dared not get tough with its own citizens on behalf of hated, troublesome redskins.

Accordingly, the Commissioner of Indian Affairs reported: "However unwilling we may be to confess it, the experiences of the past summer prove either the inefficiency of the large military force under the command of such officers as Generals Sheridan, Terry, and Crook, or the utter impracticability of keeping Americans out of a country where gold is known to exist, by any force of orders, or of U. S. cavalry, or by any consideration of the rights of others."

The moment the country realized that the stubborn Sioux would not sell the Black Hills, all popular reluctance to invade the Hills vanished. Many large parties moved in, organized communities, and immediately called for troops to protect them from the very Indians whose lands they had illegally occupied. The Indians had no vote, no press, no lobby. The administration found it simpler to "interpret" the treaties than to force its own citizens to vacate the Hills.

It therefore occurred to certain officials that if military force were used to drive the wild bands into the agencies, it would be easy to bulldoze the tame Indians at those agencies into signing away the Hills. At that time no one doubted that the veterans of the Civil War could whip the Sioux in short order, particularly under a President who had led the Union armies to victory. This is not to say that Grant and his advisers deliberately planned to start a war to cover up a "steal" of the sacred mountains of the Sioux. The speed with which the Army had cleaned up the Southern Plains and brought the Indians there to heel in '74 and '75 made the Army overconfident. It was eager to deal with the Northern tribes in the same manner.

Moreover, the Commissioner of Indian Affairs repeated a statement made in '74 that "a general Indian war is never to occur in the United States," and declared that none of the hostile bands of Sioux could "bring 300 men into the field." He believed that "conflict with separate tribes will hereafter be a rare occurrence, and only in the nature of skirmishing."

The fact was, hardly anyone in the East thought the Indians could put up a real fight. Westerners knew better, but were tickled at the prospect of a showdown.

Action was precipitated by one E. C. Watkins, a United States Indian Inspector, who, having toured the agencies, reported to the Commissioner of Indian Affairs (November 9, 1875) on the "attitude and condition" of "Sitting Bull's band, and other bands of the Sioux nation under chiefs of less note but no less untamable and hostile." Watkins complained that the Sioux attacked more friendly tribes, and he very much resented their "lofty and independent language to government officials."

Watkins expressed his opinion that the hostile Sioux numbered only "a few hundred warriors, and these never all together." He believed that a thousand soldiers, if sent to attack the Indian camps in winter, would be ample to punish and capture them.

Watkins based his plea for war against the Sioux on the administration's sacred obligation to fulfill the stipulations of the treaties! He also made room in his report for a tribute, paid in glowing terms, to settlers on the frontier, to civilization, and to humanity.

When this report was received, a conference was called. Those attending were the President of the United States; the Honorable Z. Chandler, Secretary of the Interior; his Assistant Secretary; the Honorable E. P. Smith, then Commissioner of Indian Affairs; the Honorable William W. Belknap, Secretary of War, then on the eve of being impeached for corruption, and an Army contractor who was later to spend several years in the penitentiary. These gentlemen decided, in violation of the treaties, that the Sioux must settle upon their reservations or be punished by the military. Therefore on December 3, 1875, the Secretary of the Interior wrote officially to the Commissioner of Indian Affairs: "Referring to our communication of the 27th ultimo, relative to the status of certain Sioux Indians residing without the bounds of their reservation and their continued hostile attitude toward the whites, I have to request that you direct the Indian agents at all Sioux agencies in Dakota and at Fort Peck, Montana, to notify said Indians that unless they shall remove within the bounds of their reservation (and remain there), before the 31st of January next, they shall be deemed hostile and treated accordingly by the military force."

The winter of 1875-76 was extremely bitter, even for that severe Northern climate. Sitting Bull's camp, nearer than most other Sioux camps in the buffalo country, was still some 240 miles from Standing Rock Agency. Not all the runners sent out to these camps were able to make it through the snow. Few of them even reached their destinations before the end of January, when the time allowed for coming to the agencies expired. Not one got back within the time allowed for the wild bands to come in.

The haste demanded of the Indians was probably inspired by the anxiety of the Army to launch a winter campaign. For, once the grass was up and the fleet ponies had shed their winter coats, it would be very hard to catch the Sioux on cavalry horses loaded with ammunition, rations, and equipment. The Army had a heavy score to settle with the Sioux—the "massacre" at Fort Phil Kearney, the abandonment of the Powder River forts, the many insults and accusations flung at it by the Indians and their voluble white friends throughout ten long years of the Peace Policy.

But you cannot hurry an Indian. The hunting bands of Sioux had not learned to jump at the crack of the whip.

True, old Two Moon and his band of Cheyennes talked of going in when the weather had moderated; and He-Dog, the Sioux, having a like purpose, parted with his lifelong friend, Chief Crazy Horse, and led eight lodges of his immediate followers to join Two Moon's camp on Powder River. It is possible that, had more time been allowed, other groups might have drifted into the agencies after the spring hunt.

But Crazy Horse and Sitting Bull were in no mood to drag their families and possessions through snowdrifts and howling

(Bureau of American Ethnology)

ISSUE DAY, CAMP SUPPLY (ARAPAHO)

(See Page 236.)

CUSTER BATTLEFIELD

Scene of the Battle of the Little Big Horn taken from the spot where Custer fell, looking toward the river and the site of the Indian Camp.

blizzards for hundreds of miles across the barren plains and badlands. They knew there was no food for them at the agencies. In nearly every tipi could be found some agency Indian who, to keep from starving, had left home to camp with the hunting bands. They sat still and covered their ears.

"No sooner had war been declared upon Sitting Bull for not bringing his women and children through the snow from Powder River to the Missouri than it was discovered that the winter was too severe to permit a military expedition to march from the Missouri to Powder River! 'It was thought advisable to postpone the expedition' from that side, 'the snow being so deep and the number of men badly frozen so great.' Therefore General George Crook, or 'Three Stars' (as the Sioux called him from his insignia of rank), was ordered to attack the hunting bands from the south. He made elaborate preparations for a winter campaign." [1]

Crook left Fort Fetterman, Wyoming, on March 1, 1876. He had a strong outfit, admirably equipped. Part of his baggage the General hauled in wagons, but put his main trust in his tough Army mules and pack saddles. Crook led his men to Tongue River and on down that stream, looking for Indian signs. Finding none, he crossed the divide. Heading for Powder River, he found some pony tracks. Fearing his outfit had been discovered, he made camp to deceive the enemy. The shoes of his mules were too smooth to carry them safely through the broken country into which the Sioux trail led.

On the night of the 16th, Crook sent Colonel J. J. Reynolds to follow the Indian trail and find the village, which he supposed to be that of the Oglala chief, Crazy Horse, estimated to contain more than 100 lodges.

The Indian Bureau had prevented employment of Indian scouts for the campaign. Accordingly, Crook's scouts were few in number, their chief being Frank Grouard, known to the Sioux as Sitting-with-Upraised-Hands, a name sometimes abbreviated to Grabber.

Grouard had been captured by Sitting Bull some years before and adopted into his family. Frank was a smart young man, soon learned to speak Sioux, and before long had become one of the best scouts and hunters in Sitting Bull's camp. General Crook and other officers have amply testified to his skill and efficiency, as have my old friends, Chief White Bull and Chief One Bull, nephews of Sitting Bull.

Other scouts with Crook were jealous of Grouard and secretly spread among the officers a story that Grouard was still in sympathy with the Sioux and was leading the troops into a trap. This yarn appears to have disturbed Colonel Reynolds and his officers, making them overcautious and distrustful of their chief of scouts. According to Captain Anson Mills, there was some ill feeling and jealousy among the officers.

It was sixty degrees below zero. All night long through the snow Grouard followed the Indian trail on foot, until he reached the bluffs above the village. A heavy fog hid everything. But he heard the tinkling bells of Indian ponies. Creeping part way down the hill, he got below the rising fog and saw the village, hardly a mile away. An old crier was out haranguing the camp in his high-pitched, far-carrying voice. From his remarks, Grouard learned that Indians had seen the troops and reported them, that scouts had been sent back by the lower trail to find out who they were, but that the scouts had found nobody.

That was good news.

The camp stood in a low, flat bottom, close to Powder River—105 tipis scattered through the cottonwood timber and willow brush. Grouard recognized some of the Oglala horses, which he had often seen in the camp of Crazy Horse during his captivity. Says he, "I knew this village by the horses." [2]

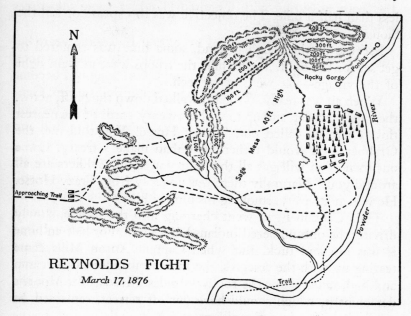

REYNOLDS FIGHT

MARCH 17, 1876

Redrawn from the map made by Captain Anson Mills, by courtesy of the War Department, showing the attack of Colonel J. J. Reynolds, Third Cavalry, upon the Cheyenne camp of Chief Two Moon in the belief that it was the Sioux village of Chief Crazy Horse. The Indians escaped in the rock hills to the north of their camp.

Grouard thereupon reported that he had found the camp of Crazy Horse.

Reynolds asked Frank what should be done. Grouard proposed that the troops be divided, one detachment to charge the camp, another to follow in reserve, a third to round up the ponies, and a fourth to cut off the retreat of the Indians by occupying the slope between the tipis and the rocky, broken hills, impassable to horsemen, which rose a thousand feet within less than half a mile. The objective was to capture or kill the Sioux.

Because of the rough ground, some time was required to get set for the fight. Meanwhile, the troops were in plain sight of the village—yet were never seen.

When all was ready, Grouard walked down the bluff, across the sagebrush flat, and up to within twenty yards of the nearest tipi. There he called out, "Crazy Horse! You told me, the Grabber, you would rather fight than make a treaty. Come out then. You will get all the fight you want. Soldiers are all around you!" Naturally there was no reply from Crazy Horse. He was miles away, smoking his pipe in his tipi.

Then Captain Egan went charging into the village, slowly driving the outnumbered Indians before him. For half an hour it was nip and tuck. But when Captain Anson Mills came tearing up with the reserves, the Indians abandoned the camp and high-tailed it for the rocky hillsides. Meanwhile, Moore's detachment, which should have cut off retreat, remained on a hillside, firing into the village.

There was nobody to hold the Indians. They found refuge among the rocks, where the few of them who had guns kept up a hot fire on the camp. In spite of the complete surprise, only one Indian buck had been killed, one old woman wounded, and one blind squaw taken prisoner. Four troopers were killed, six wounded.

Reynolds found the camp "a perfect magazine of ammunition," but apparently never thought of using it to shoot the ponies. He told Grouard to have his scouts drive the ponies. Now, eighty head of horses is about all one man can hope to wrangle, even when all are accustomed to running in one bunch. It was absurd to expect half a dozen scouts to wrangle 700 frightened animals. So Captain Egan volunteered to take over the ponies.

Reynolds also found the tipis full of agency-issue goods.

This, the Army held, showed that the Indian owners of these goods were in cahoots with the Sioux at the agencies, "that the proceeds of raids on the settlements had been taken into those agencies and supplies had been brought out in return." Of course, if there had been any raids on settlements, the tipis would have contained goods captured on those raids. All the Indians in Two Moon's camp were legally entitled to rations and agency-issue goods until the first of February. Many of them were agency Indians, and all who were not intended becoming agency Indians as soon as the weather moderated.

Reynolds might have called Crook to his relief. Reynolds might have shot the ponies. Reynolds might have put his wounded and weary, sleepless men into the snug tipis to rest by the fire and eat as much as they liked of "tons" of dried buffalo meat. But the Colonel decided to burn the camp and skedaddle.

Even then, he might have saddled 200 ponies with captured Indian saddles, loaded them with buffalo beef and shaggy robes, to feed and protect his exhausted command. Instead, he burned everything—leaving one lodge standing for the old blind squaw—and then, with only one day's rations, led his hungry men out on those bitter cold plains to plod back through the snow to Crook's camp.

On the way back, Cheyennes and Sioux recaptured the unguarded ponies. The warriors also got away with Crook's beef herd, leaving the troops short of supplies.

"We had no beef," John Bourke writes (in his book *On the Border with Crook*), "as our herd had been run off on account of the failure to guard it; we were out of supplies, although we had destroyed enough to last a regiment for a couple of months; we were encumbered with sick, wounded, and cripples with frozen limbs, because we had not had sense enough to save the furs and robes in the village."

Reynolds, as Crook reports, "left so precipitously that our

wounded men were left to fall into the hands of the Indians."
The Sioux believe some Cheyennes ate the flesh of one trooper.[3]

Crook immediately put Colonel Reynolds under arrest and
filed charges against him. His disheartened, red-eyed, frost-
bitten troops plodded back to their posts through a howling
blizzard.

Meanwhile, the half-naked Cheyennes and Sioux, with the
ponies they had recaptured, their wounded, and their frozen
families, trailed after He-Dog and Two Moon, until they
reached the camp of Crazy Horse. With them trailed the ribby
snow-starved cattle taken from Crook's command.

Neither Cheyenne nor Sioux any longer had anything to
say about going to the agency. The haughty Cheyenne, who
had not been on the warpath at all, were burning with indignation. It was the Sioux who had been ordered to the agency,
not the Cheyenne; yet the soldiers had charged on and destroyed their village. As for the Oglala, they were furious,
especially at Sitting-with-Upraised-Hands, who had lived so
long among them and now was leading soldiers to attack their
families. There was no more talk of peace. When they had
rested and eaten, they all set out again to the camp of Sitting
Bull.

Of this fight, General Sherman reported: "The result was
only the destruction of the tents or tipis of the Indians, with
their contents."

General Sherman was mistaken. The result was Sitting
Bull's War.

20

THE BATTLE OF THE ROSEBUD

M EANWHILE, the freezing Oglala and Cheyennes set out to find succor in that bitter weather. And at last, cold and hungry, in the Blue Mountains on Beaver Creek, some sixty miles down the Powder, they found the camp of Sitting Bull.

Sitting Bull heard their story, took them in, fed them, gave them horses and saddles, robes, and powder and ball, and told his people to double up and let the refugees have some of their tents. He made them welcome. Right away he sent runners to summon the chiefs of the hunting bands to a big council on Tongue River, and soon after moved his camp to that stream.

When Sitting Bull first heard of that attack, he made up his mind. Ever since the Black Robe came to smoke with him eight years before, he had put up with everything and kept the peace. He was a patient, gentle, long-suffering man, as many great fighters have been. Probably he would not have resented an affront to himself; it was the business of a chief to bear and forbear. But now his people had been wantonly attacked. He had come to the end of his patience. He was angry, and when he was angry he was a different man. At the council on Tongue River, he said: "We are an island of Indians in a lake of whites. We must stand together, or they will rub us out separately. These soldiers have come shooting; they want war. All right, we'll give it to them!"

Many a white man lost his horses and his scalp that season. Sitting Bull had accepted the challenge. There is a limit to what a man can bear.

Runners sped away in all directions, to every camp of the hunting bands, to every Sioux, Cheyenne, and Arapaho agency west of the Missouri—all the agencies. They rode hard, and when they arrived, slipped from their fagged ponies, dived into the tipi of the chief, and spoke the words of Sitting Bull: "It is war. Come to my camp at the Big Bend of the Rosebud. Let's all get together and have one big fight with the soldiers!"

That word swept the camps, the agencies, like a prairie fire. All the restless young men, patriotic and adventurous, weary of lazy starvation at the agency, opened their ears. They began to trade for guns, for powder and ball, for horses, and as soon as the grass was high enough to feed their ponies, their women struck the tipis and they hit the trail to the Rosebud. Red Cloud, who had been in Washington, seen countless white men, and measured their big guns with his fan, despaired of victory; he advised his people to cover their ears and sit still. But his own son, Jack Red Cloud, rode away with the rest; he would not listen to the old man. For this was the day of young men, and Sitting Bull's medicine was good; it was what the young men wanted.[1]

As summer approached, the War Department prepared to launch its long-delayed "winter campaign." The plan adopted in Washington was, in its essentials, the same which had failed so miserably in 1865—to send several columns into the heart of the Sioux country and strike the hostiles all at once from several directions. This plan was known as the Yellowstone Expedition.

Two columns under General Alfred H. Terry, commander

of the Department of Dakota, were to march, one from Dakota and one from Montana. General Custer and the Seventh Cavalry were a part of Terry's command. The third column was to head north from Wyoming under General George Crook, commander of the Department of the Platte. Terry had 1450 men, Crook only about 1050. He marched from Fort Fetterman toward the end of May, heading for the Big Bend of the Rosebud, where it was believed that Sitting Bull, Crazy Horse, and their warriors were encamped in force. The basic idea was to destroy the camps and horses of the hostiles and so bring them to surrender. The plan might have worked in a "winter campaign"; hardly in summer.

On Tongue River, Crook had a brush or two with Indians. There he was joined by 260 Indian scouts—Shoshones and Crows. This brought his force up to more than 1300 men. Washakie was the principal chief along. Frank Grouard was chief of scouts.

Crook, who had already shown his mettle as an Indian fighter, knew well enough that he could never catch mounted Indians with an ambulance and a wagon train. He was a great believer in mules, and his mobile pack train was the admiration of the Army. So now Crook parked his wagons under guard and—to the utter indignation of his infantry commander—mounted his doughboys on the braying draft mules.

On June 16 the command reached the headwaters of the Rosebud, planning to follow it down and surprise the hostile village.

Crook, like many another commander of that day, entertained a mistaken notion that, if they saw him coming, the Indians would run away. In the earliest times, when Indians had no horses and no long-range weapons, their wars necessarily consisted of hand-to-hand fighting, and they naturally rated that man bravest who actually touched or struck the enemy with a weapon held in his hand. Later, when armed only with bow and arrows, the Indian still counted it no honor to kill with them, and felt that he had also to strike the body of the man he had shot in order to claim the glory of the *coup*. So, when Europeans brought horses into his country and the Indian learned to ride, his custom of counting *coup* turned warfare into a dangerous game of tag, a hit-and-run affair. He could dash up, strike an enemy, and immediately get away on his fleet pony. And when the white men turned up with their deadly long-range weapons, that sort of tactics was much encouraged, and so the white men came to think of the warrior as a hit-and-run fighter who never attacked unless he had the advantage of surprise or overwhelming numbers.

But when Crook marched down the Rosebud, times had changed. So many redskins had got revolvers and rifles of their own that they could no longer be kept at a distance by the troops, and so were emboldened to revert more and more to the old-time tactics of hand-to-hand conflict—the only kind of warfare in which they could achieve the honor of the *coup*. This change was also much encouraged by the fact that Indians never had enough ammunition to keep up a long-range battle for any length of time.

Crook appears not yet to have been fully aware of these trends in tactics among the hostiles, and certainly no general then realized how full of fight the wild bands were.

Crook was also unaware that some Cheyenne hunters had seen his command that day and were hightailing it through the Wolf Mountains to Reno Creek, a tributary of the Little Big Horn, where the hostiles were encamped circle on circle, twenty miles away. He thought the hostile camp was much nearer.

The hunters rode into the Cheyenne camp, howling like wolves, to signal their discovery that the valley of the Rosebud was "black with soldiers." Immediately an intertribal council was held; the chiefs laid plans to surprise the troops.

Some would have it that they planned to ambush the troops in the canyon of the Rosebud. But this was obviously impossible, since they had no means of knowing where Crook's command would be when they reached it, or in what direction he would march from the point where the hunters had seen him. I have talked to many, both Sioux and Cheyenne, who were in this war party. None of them had ever heard of any plans for ambush in the canyon of the Rosebud.

A great war party—almost 1000 men—was organized. Of these about 100 were Cheyennes, the rest Sioux. Crazy Horse led the Oglala; Sitting Bull, the Hunkpapa. There were also Sans Arc, Brûlé, Minniconjou, and small parties of other Teton Sioux tribes. Half these Indians had guns. It took some time for all these men to paint, arm, and mount themselves. After they had paraded around camp in their regalia, they headed off in the darkness through the Wolf Mountains toward the Rosebud.

It was almost mid-morning next day when the hostiles, coming up the Rosebud, halted to send out scouts. Members of the warrior societies formed a line in front of the mass of warriors to keep any from slipping away to make a premature attack and so spoil their plan to surprise the troops.

The chiefs sent four scouts to the top of the highest hill on the west side of the river to see if they could spy Crook's outfit.

At that time, about 9:30 in the morning, the command had halted on the other side of the same big hill, had unbridled their horses, and were allowing them to graze on both sides of the shallow, boggy river. General Crook, with his beard in two braids, lazed in his canvas suit by the spring, casually playing cards with his officers. From his position under the bluffs of the north bank, the open country rising to the top of the big hill was not visible.

Four of his watchful Indian scouts were riding up that hill

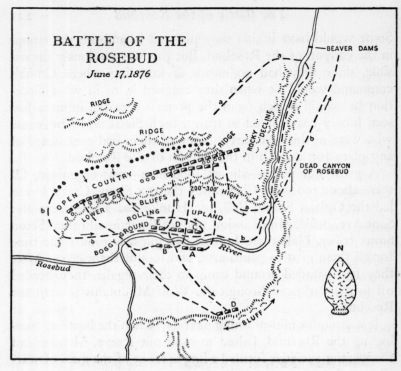

BATTLE OF THE
ROSEBUD
June 17, 1876

BEAVER DAMS

RIDGE

RIDGE

RIDGE

ROCKY DECLINE

DEAD CANYON
OF ROSEBUD

OPEN
COUNTRY

LOWER
BLUFFS

ROLLING
GROUND

BOGGY GROUND

200-300 HIGH

UPLAND

River

Rosebud

N

BATTLE OF THE ROSEBUD

JUNE 17, 1876

The defeat of General George Crook by the hostile Sioux and Cheyennes. Redrawn from the map made by Cyrus Townsend Brady for his *Indian Fights and Fighters* from a sketch by Captain Anson Mills; by permission of Mrs. Katharine M. Brady.

Black dots indicate hostile Indians.

Small circles indicate Government Indian scouts.

A = Mills' Battalion.	River and back again.
B = Noyes' Battalion.	
C = Henry's Battalion.	bbb = The route of the
D = Van Vliet's Battalion.	hostiles circling
E = Chambers' Mounted In-	Crook's command as
fantry and Pack Train.	they rode back to
aaa = Mills' line of march	their camps on Reno
down the Rosebud	Creek.

on his side at the same time the Cheyenne and Sioux scouts were coming up the opposite side. The Crows got to the top first, saw the Sioux, and fired on them. The Sioux fired back, wounding one of the Crows.

The sound of these shots told the hostiles waiting below that it was now too late for surprise. *Hookahey!* As one man they quirted their ponies, broke through the line of Indian guards, raced up the hill and over it in a great wave to the attack. Already their own scouts were far ahead, chasing the Crows back to Crook's command.

It was about two miles from Crook's position in the valley under the bluff to the top of the hill to his north. He did not hear the shots. But Captain Mills' Negro servant heard the yelling. Mills, according to his own account published in his autobiography, *My Story* (pp. 401 ff.), mounted a high piece of ground and saw on the northern skyline "great numbers of moving objects, looking somewhat like distant crows, silhouetted on the clear sky above the horizon." He soon came to the conclusion that they were "Indians in great number."

Crook had not expected the hostiles to carry the war to him, but made his dispositions quickly, sending his troops to occupy the bluffs north of the stream where they might have a field of fire in the direction from which the hostiles were charging down. Mills was on the right of the line and led his troops at the foot of the ridge, driving the leading warriors back a little by the impetus of his advance.

Even at such a moment Captain Mills, a cavalryman to his fingertips, could not but admire the skill and horsemanship of his enemies.

"These Indians" he continues, "were most hideous, every one being painted in most hideous colors and designs, stark naked, except their moccasins, breech clouts and head gear, the latter consisting of feathers and horns; some of the horses also being painted, and the Indians proved then and there that they were the best cavalry soldiers on earth. In charging up towards us they exposed little of their person, hanging on with one arm around the neck and one leg over the horse, firing and lancing from underneath the horses' necks, so that there was no part of the Indian at which we could aim.

"Their shouting and personal appearance was so hideous that it terrified the horses more than our men and rendered them almost uncontrollable before we dismounted and placed them behind the rocks.

"The Indians came not in a line but in flocks or herds like the buffalo, and they piled in upon us until I think there must have been one thousand or fifteen hundred in our immediate front, but they refused to fight when they found us secured behind the rocks, and bore off to our left. I then charged the second ridge, and took it in the same manner and fortified myself with the horses protected behind the larger boulders and the men behind the smaller ones. . . . On our right we were absolutely protected by the jagged and rough places down to the Rosebud Canyon. so we were most fortunate in securing this position."

In this second charge, the trumpeter's headstrong horse ran away, carrying the musician straight through the Indians in the open. A bullet broke both his forearms so that he could not handle the reins at all; but with admirable presence of mind, the trumpeter managed to guide the horse with his legs and so circled back to his comrades, where he flung himself from his saddle and thereby saved his life.

There were many brave charges and rescues on both sides. After their first attack, the Indians fell back. A Cheyenne chief, Comes-in-Sight, whom I used to know in Oklahoma, was one of their best fighters. Valor ran in his family, for when he rode to battle his young sister tagged right along. Comes-in-Sight was showing his courage by riding up and down at a gallop along the soldier line, letting them fire at him, when all at once his horse was hit, turned a complete somersault, and left him lying on the bare prairie between the lines.

Unhorsed as he was, he knew he might easily be overrun and killed by the Crows, or picked off by some sharpshooter in a blue coat. Bullets kicked up the dust all around him. The Crows let out a whoop and headed for him on the dead run. He was too far from the Cheyenne line to outrun them, and bravely turned to face his enemies.

Then he heard hoofs thundering up behind him. Someone rode by, turned the horse round, called to him, and reached out a hand. It was his sister. Comes-in-Sight swung himself up behind the girl and they galloped back to the Cheyenne line in safety.

For this reason the Cheyenne call the Battle of the Rosebud by a name which means "Where the Young Girl Saved Her Brother's Life."

By this time the soldiers on the left of Crook's line had their hands full. The fighting on the west flank was hottest. But even Mills, sheltered among the rocks, had to call for reinforcements; though Crook's command outnumbered his enemies, it was for a long time nip and tuck whether he could save his command at all. The hostiles made one fierce charge after another. The troops and the Indian scouts with them charged in turn. Every man Crook had, including his packers, joined the desperate fight.

Things got so lively that each unit was too busy to watch what the others were doing, and Crook's line was soon very irregular. The hostiles, whooping, thundered down on the left flank, swept through the troops, riding down soldiers, "knocking them from their horses with lances and knives, dismounting and killing them, cutting the arms of several off at the elbows and carrying them away."

As Captain John G. Bourke suggests, this fondness for cutting off the hands and arms of enemies for trophies was characteristic of the Cheyenne, and may account for the sign used to designate this tribe in the sign language of the Plains Indians—usually interpreted as Cut Arm or Striped (Turkey) Arrow Feathers. By the same token, the Sioux, designated as Cutthroats by a sweeping gesture across the throat, may once have been headhunters.

Down the hill they went, helter-skelter, all mixed together in the dust and powder smoke. Only one troop could hold its ground. Vroom's command was the very center of this maelstrom, but managed to form a ring and stand its ground.

"Captain Henry led the counter-charge which reached the lost troop. It cut its way through a desperately fighting mass of red men. Never had the soldiers found the Indians so willing to give blow for blow, so ready to stand up and fight, so apparently reckless of death. When Vroom was rescued, a retreat began to a less advanced position.

"Hard upon the heels of the retiring troopers pressed the Sioux. War cry, rifle shot and lance thrust; scowling, painted, savage faces; tossing war bonnets; rearing, kicking ponies; mounting clouds of dust and smoke—the soldiers knew fear for the first time. But Henry, riding at the very rear, called out encouragement and his coolness steadied them. He winced once, but his face was turned toward the enemy. The troopers were too busy fighting to notice what had happened. They beat the charge off. Then the captain turned to them a countenance so ghastly it chilled them through. A bullet had struck him full in the face, practically tearing the whole visage out under both eyes. His mangled features were covered by a great surge of blood. He was swaying with the shock. For a time he sat his horse, but the vertigo of wound sickness overcame him soon. He fell.

"The Sioux instantly sensed that a leader was down. With the same valor they had displayed all afternoon, they charged.

Back, back they drove the troops. The ponies of their warriors plunged over the very spot where Henry lay. His end seemed certain.

"But from a quarter utterly unexpected came help. The Shoshones and Crows had fought hard but futilely for the whites. The Sioux drove them back and they had been rather out of the fight for the last few minutes. Now they saw the fall of Henry as soon as their foes did.

"Every old plainsman knows how the Indian warrior shows his greatest daring in rescuing dead or wounded comrades from the enemy. The scouts knew the Sioux would be on the ground about Henry in a minute, scalping him, counting *coup*. Here was something they understood. With their war cries echoing from the farthest bluffs, they plunged headlong into the thick of the hostile array. Old Washakie of the Shoshones was there. So was Luishaw. Of the Crows, Alligator-Stands-Up and Plenty Coups were foremost.

"Rearing, snorting horses, kicking up a dust cloud so dense the riders could hardly see—knife thrust and tomahawk blow —the Sioux ranks opened. Washakie, Alligator-Stands-Up and their warriors stood over Henry's limp body.

"The hostiles fought desperately with the scouts. It created a diversion which stopped the Indian advance at its height. Royall and Vroom had time to catch their breath. Now they came back up the hill, driving Crazy Horse's warriors, reoccupying the ground held so heroically by a handful of savage scouts, and getting possession of the captain's unconscious body.

"But there was no possibility of holding the position. Fighting as they went, the soldiers and their Indian allies retreated, taking the wounded officer with them. Henry subsequently recovered and eventually rose to the rank of brigadier general. The fight around his body was the fiercest mêlée of the battle." [2]

Meanwhile Crook clung stubbornly to his original plan—the assault on the village—which he supposed was at the other end of the canyon below, barely six miles away. He ordered Captain Mills, with eight troops of cavalry, to ride down the valley and attack the village, perhaps also hoping in this way to draw off the warriors who were making it so hot for him. Mills set out, and—as there was no village to defend where he was going—the warriors let him go unopposed. His departure only made it all the hotter for the troops who were left on the field.

Mills proceeded down the level valley until he had almost reached the point where he expected to find the village, when suddenly he was overtaken by orders to return. Much disappointed, Mills rode up out of the canyon and cut across the open on his left, coming in behind the Indians, who were still fighting Crook's forces along the bluffs. The appearance of his force from a new direction may have puzzled the Indians. At any rate, they swung in a great insulting circle around behind Crook's lines, passed over the very ground where he had been playing cards when the fight began, captured a few animals, and killed a young friendly who was back there painting his face and making ready for battle.

Then they rode home to celebrate their victory, leaving four scouts behind to keep an eye on General "Three Stars" Crook.

When Mills got back to the command, Crook said to him: "The doctors refused to remain with the wounded unless I left the infantry and one of the squadrons." [3] Under these circumstances, not being able to support Mills in his attack on the village, Crook felt that he must call him back.

A number of officers and John F. Finerty, a newspaper correspondent, have published statements indicating that Mills had to be recalled because Crazy Horse planned a deadly ambush in the canyon, which has been variously described as "a narrow gulch," "a natural trap," and "a gorge." This theory or legend does not square with the facts of topography, as anyone can see who will visit the battlefield. It is true that the valley does narrow where the river bends to the left, but there is no "dangerous defile," no "canyon" worthy of that name. At its narrowest, the valley is about half a mile wide, and in places nearer two miles. On either side are high bluffs with patches of timber. Probably in those days there were fallen trees here and there and some of the flimsy stick corrals that the Indians sometimes made to hold their horses. But the notion that Plains Indians would fell trees to build a barricade, or lay an ambush in such a broad, level valley, is fantastic, and certainly if Crazy Horse wanted to lure the troops down the valley, he made no visible effort to do it. Mills had no difficulty leading his men at a trot down the stream, and certainly saw no decoys in his front.

Very few of those warriors knew how to handle an ax; cutting wood was women's work. Some of these braves afterward lived in Oklahoma near my home. John Homer Seger, their superintendent, used to laugh when telling how, after they had agreed to work, they would try to cut a log in two or fell a tree by striking it with the blade at right angles to the bole. He had to teach them how to hew. So far as is known, there was only one woman with this party, the young sister of Chief Comes-in-Sight.

The hostiles could not possibly have known that Crook expected to find their village at the end of the canyon. And why on earth should they lay a trap in a canyon for troops whom they were mauling so severely in the open?

Perhaps the authors of this story are not to be blamed for their misconception, considering the beating they had undergone. After that day, they could believe the Indians capable of anything.

One other point about this battle needs clarification. Captain Mills pays tribute to the hostiles in these words: "These

Indians lived with their horses, were unsurfeited with food, shelter, raiment or equipment, then the best cavalry in the world; their like will never be seen again. Our friendlies were worthless against them; we would have been better off without them." [4]

This criticism of the Crow and Shoshone scouts with the troops that day seems harsh and unfair, and is not shared at all by the dozens of old Cheyenne and Sioux warriors who were in the fight and with whom I have talked, such as the Sioux: White Bull, One Bull, Old Bull, Elk Nation, Gray Eagle, Bob-Tail-Bull, and the Cheyenne: Young Two Moon, Bob-Tail-Horse, Hump, Comes-in-Sight. They all rate the Crows as equal to, and the Shoshones as superior to, the white soldiers. In fact, though most of the Sioux call the Battle of the Rosebud "The Fight with Three Stars," I have heard a Sioux chief describe it as "The Fight with Our Indian Enemies."

Yet Indian scouts were seldom expected to do battle for the troops. It was, as a rule, their duty to find the enemy, not to fight him, and though we do not know what Crook's instructions to his scouts may have been, we do know that Custer did not require his scouts in that campaign to fight the Sioux, and that one of General Terry's officers actually put a scout under arrest for attacking the enemy. [5] The Crows and Shoshones with Crook on the Rosebud fought with desperate valor—a courage inspired by the fear that the troops "could not protect them."

True enough, it is difficult for a tortoise and a hare to fight in close co-operation, and that made it hard for the troops, when working with the Shoshones and Crows. On their nimble ponies, these masters of hit-and-run tactics charged and countercharged, far outrunning the slower troops both in attack and retreat. And it may well have seemed to officers unaccustomed to Indian fighting that the Crows and Shoshones were merely riding hither and yon and never fighting shoulder to shoulder with the troopers and doughboys in the line. For when the troops charged, they charged to a new position, whereas their Indian scouts simply took after the enemy and followed him until he turned and chased them back. In like manner, when retreat was the order of the day, the scouts' ponies readily outdistanced the heavier cavalry horses.

But a cool consideration of what actually took place on that hard-fought field will show that the Sioux and Cheyennes are right in their estimate of the valor and skill of the Indians opposed to them. In fact, apart from holding the line—not their job—the Shoshones and Crows did more than their share of the fighting, and might even be considered a deciding factor in preventing a general massacre of Crook's outfit.

To begin with, they discovered the enemy, thus preventing surprise at a time when the troops were dismounted and their horses and mules unbridled and grazing. Had the Sioux got down into that valley before the cavalry was mounted, the day might have ended very differently.

Moreover, the scouts, posting themselves in the open on the unprotected left flank, certainly prevented the Sioux from out-flanking Crook on that side, a movement which at several times during the battle might well have been fatal to the white forces.

The fiercest fighting of the whole day occurred when Captain Vroom's men were surrounded and almost overwhelmed, and the whole line was shaken and falling back. Here again it was the Crows and Shoshones who saved the day, driving back the Sioux and Cheyennes in hard-fought hand-to-hand conflict.

Again, it was they—not the white soldiers—who saved Captain Henry from death and mutilation. And any old Sioux or Cheyenne who was in that fight can tell you of many individual exploits and feats of courage performed by Crows and Shoshones, many rescues besides that of Captain Henry.[6]

Had there been as many Crows and Shoshones as there were troopers and infantrymen, and all as well armed, there might have been more mourning than dancing in the hostile camp on Reno Creek.

For the Indian warrior had many advantages over the white soldier in fighting on the Plains. He knew the country, was accustomed to the climate, and the tools by which he made his living were also the weapons with which he made his war. In order to find game, he had to learn to scout and trail and creep up to surprise the animals he shot, until these things became second nature. A young Indian was not allowed to hang around camp, but was always out on the prairie with his pony. He lived in the open, and was forever on horseback, whether traveling, herding, hunting, racing, trailing, scouting, raiding, or merely sitting around. To live he shot running animals from the naked back of a galloping horse. He was (as General Crook himself remarked in his report to the Secretary of War) "a cavalry soldier from the time he has intelligence enough to ride a horse or fire a gun."

The Secretary, on his part, paid this tribute to the Plains Indians employed as government scouts: "They are unequalled as riders, know the country thoroughly, are hardly ever sick, *never desert,* and are careful of their horses. Moreover, I have never seen one of them under the influence of liquor, though they have had every opportunity of getting it."

Crook made a report that year about these friendlies which should settle the question of the relative merits of the friendlies and the enlisted men. It occurs in the report of the Secretary of War, 1876-77: "I have seen our friendly Indians, riding at full speed, shoot and kill a wolf, also on the run, while it is a rare thing that our troops can hit an Indian on horseback, though the soldier may be on his feet at the time."

Some of the other officers admitted that, to use Mills' words, they had been "humiliatingly defeated," that they were "lucky not to have been entirely vanquished."

Considering the length of the engagement and the number of men engaged, the actual losses on both sides were light. Crook reported a loss of nine dead and twenty-one wounded, evidently omitting the casualties among his Indian scouts. There are no exact figures for the hostiles' losses, but from all I can learn I believe them to have been between one and two per cent—which is about as high as Indian casualties usually went.

Crook reported that his troops "drove" the hostiles from the field. Yet they came trooping back next day and accompanied him for some distance on the march back to his base on Goose Creek. There he remained until the end of June, hunting and fishing, making no effort to find Indians.

Reynolds, against whom Crook had filed charges, did at any rate burn the village he was sent to attack; Crook did not even come within sight of the village he was heading for. The hostiles put him out of the campaign.

On receiving Crook's report on the Battle of the Rosebud, General Sheridan sent orders back: "Hit 'em again and hit 'em hard." Crook, licking his wounds on Goose Creek after his defeat, grumbled, "I wonder if Sheridan could surround three Sioux with one soldier." The power of the allied tribes was beyond anything the Army then dreamed of.

Crook knew he could not move without reinforcements, but his inactivity laid him open to some criticism—particularly after the news came that Custer had been destroyed. The troops sang a satirical comment on his Fabian tactics:

> I'd like to be a packer,
>   And pack with George F. Crook,
> And dressed up in my canvas suit,
>   To be for him mistook.

I'd braid my beard in two long tails,
    And idle all the day,
In whittling sticks and wondering
    What the New York papers say.

21

CUSTER'S LAST STAND

WHILE CROOK retreated southward, the Sioux and Cheyennes, exulting in their victory, struck their camp on the headwaters of Reno Creek and headed west to the valley of the Little Big Horn River. They called the stream the Greasy Grass because the rich forage there made their ponies so fat. Crossing the winding, shallow stream, the long cavalcade rolled up the flat on the west bank through clouds of dust. Chiefs Sitting Bull, Crazy Horse, and Two Moon led. The warrior societies guarded the straggling column on both flanks and in the rear. Each tribe followed in its turn, and the cavalcade was so long that the Cheyennes, who had been honored by the Sioux with the first place, had their tipis up and supper cooked before the Hunkpapa at the tail end could halt to form their camp.

The Cheyenne camp circle was farthest north downriver, the Sans Arc Sioux next, with the Minniconjou just above, then the Oglala a little farther from the stream. Farthest south, near the slough where the river bed had been long before, the Hunkpapa went into camp along with Blackfoot Sioux, Two Kettles, and Santees. The camp stretched fully three miles along the stream, all of 2000 tipis, each with one or two or three warriors, more than half of them seasoned fighters.

Before sundown the parched, dusty valley had become a city as orderly as though the Indians had been encamped there for moons. Within each tribal circle each band had its traditional position, each family tent its established place within the band.

The young men watered the ponies at the heavily wooded stream under the ash-gray bluffs towering upward toward the eastern divide. Then they herded the animals out to the grassy benches west of camp, beyond which the far-off Big Horn Mountains loomed against the sunset. Some drove their ponies along the flat north or south of camp.

The buffalo scouts found no game on the Little Big Horn. Such large camps always scared the game away. Buffalo did not mind singing, but would never stay within earshot of an Indian drum. So the great camp rested, letting their horses graze, looking after their wounded, mourning for the dead. At night there were social dances.

It was not yet ten days since Sitting Bull had had his vision at the Sun Dance, in which he saw soldiers and enemy Indians falling from the sky like grasshoppers, head down, right into the Sioux camp, and heard a voice from above crying, "I give you these because they have no ears."

Since that Sun Dance the Indians had bested "Three Stars" on the Rosebud. But they knew the vision had nothing to do with Crook, for he had not come within twenty miles of their camp. Confidently they waited for the fulfillment of Sitting Bull's vision. Meanwhile they cleaned their guns, sharpened their knives, and renewed their war charms. The hearts of the Sioux and Cheyennes were big. Their medicine was strong. One thing only smelled good to them—gunpowder.

Yet they sent out no war parties, danced no war dances. They were not yet the aggressors. Let the soldiers come. Let the white men fire the first shot.

The Indians knew that soldiers were somewhere on their

trail leading up the Rosebud River, and the camp was full of rumors.

As a matter of fact, General George Armstrong Custer, commanding the Seventh Cavalry, with twenty-eight officers and nearly 700 men, had left his camp on June 22 to follow Sitting Bull's broad trail. He was under orders from General Alfred H. Terry, commander of the Department of Dakota, to proceed from the mouth of the Rosebud and scout for the hostile camp, then supposed to be on or near the Little Big Horn.

General Custer had had a rather awkward hand in exposing the corruption of President Grant's administration, and was then in disgrace. But Terry regarded his services as indispensable for the campaign against Sitting Bull, and wires had been pulled to give him back his command. His success on the Washita in 1868 had greatly impressed Sheridan, to say nothing of Custer himself. Now he was eager to conquer the Sioux and so regain the popular prestige which he had long enjoyed as "the boy general," "the flower of cavalrymen," a victor who during the whole Civil War had never lost a gun or a flag. In those days military men might aspire to the highest office in the gift of the American voters, and Custer had hopes and ambitions which he had never dared voice.

But that night before the battle, his Ree and Crow scouts, having located the hostile camp, assured him that he would find more Sioux there than he could handle. To reassure them, Long Hair revealed his secret ambition, told them he was staking his whole career upon this battle—told them that if he won it, if he conquered Sitting Bull, he would become the Grandfather—President of the United States. He promised them that if they ran off the Sioux ponies before the fight, he would befriend their people when he sat in the White House.

Custer could not believe that the hostiles would stand before him. Like most commanders of that day, he was obsessed with

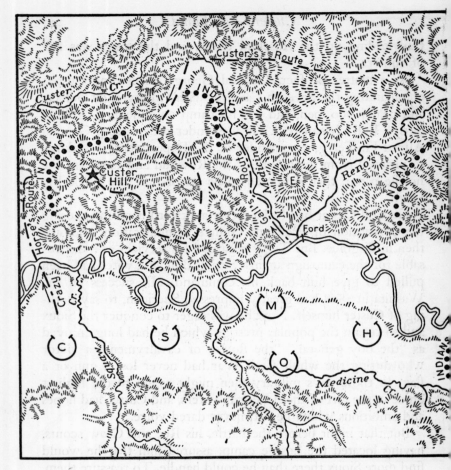

BATTLE OF THE LITTLE BIG HORN

JUNE 25, 1876

General George Armstrong Custer's last stand against hostile Sioux and Cheyennes on the Little Big Horn River, redrawn to include data supplied by Indian participants in the fight, from the map originally prepared by Lieutenant James E. Wilson and revised by Edward S. Godfrey for publication in the *Century Magazine*, January, 1892.

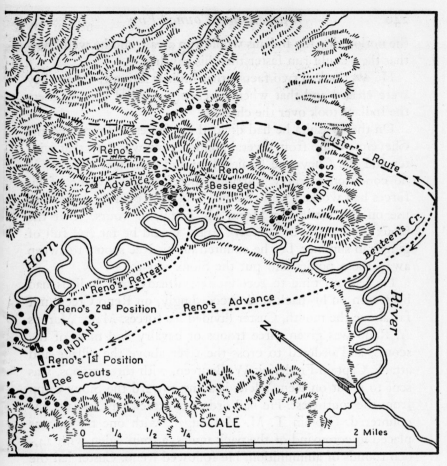

Large broken circles with capital letters inset indicate location of tribal camp circles, as follows:

C—Cheyenne, including some Arapaho lodges
S—Sans Arc Sioux
O—Oglala Sioux
M—Minniconjou Sioux
H—Hunkpapa Sioux, including some Two Kettle and Blackfoot Sioux lodges. Altogether, these camps contained around 2000 lodges.

Small dots indicate positions of hostile Indians.

the notion that the Indians would run away, and he well knew that they could run faster than his cavalry.

He overlooked two facts—that Indians ran only when they were chased and that when an enemy stopped chasing them the Indians took over the chasing.

On the Washita he had divided his forces and attacked the Cheyenne camp from several points. Snow was deep that winter and the Cheyenne ponies, lean and half-starved, were in no condition to carry warriors; therefore the division of his forces had worked well enough. The same plan he decided to use on the Little Big Horn. He knew, of course, that the Sioux ponies, full of "greasy" grass, would be fat and full of ginger in summer, but he counted on his Ree scouts to sweep away those ponies and put the Sioux afoot.

He had no time to reconnoiter; already two Indians had been seen on his back trail. Accordingly, on Reno Creek, not far above the mouth, Custer divided his forces. Major Marcus A. Reno was given three troops of cavalry and most of the scouts, and ordered to cross the river above the village and attack. Captain Frederick W. Benteen, with three troops, was sent to scout on Reno's left, heading toward the Sioux camp from the southwest. He had orders to attack any Indians encountered. Captain T. M. McDougall, with one troop, was placed in command of the pack mules, a train laden with 24,-000 rounds of ammunition. He followed Reno. Custer led the remaining five troops of the Seventh downriver on the high east bank, seeking a crossing below to attack the camp from that side. Such a plan against overwhelming forces required, for its success, a simultaneous attack on three sides. But as Custer and Benteen both had three or four miles farther to ride than Reno, Reno arrived before them.

He crossed the river and saw, barely two miles ahead, the thronging tipis of the Sioux. As yet there were no Indians in his immediate front. Sitting Bull, in fact, had not yet learned that troops were approaching.

But early that morning two Hunkpapa young men, away from the camp looking for strayed horses, had found the trail of the soldiers. Following it along, they came upon a pack which had fallen from the back of one of the mules. Breaking it open, they found it full of hardtack. They sat down and began to eat.

Suddenly some bluecoats came riding back along the trail and fired at them. One of their bullets killed Deeds. The other boy made his escape. Brown Back carried his news to camp: that soldiers were coming. Fat Bear brought the warning to Sitting Bull.

It was not yet time for the midday watering, and most of the ponies were out grazing on the prairie. Before Sitting Bull could rally his warriors, a shrill war whoop vibrated through the camp. Everyone rushed out, pointed, stared upriver to the south. Yonder, under a towering cloud of dust, they caught the glint of gun barrels, saw the flutter of a guidon, the blue shirts of the troopers. The dark column broadened suddenly into line. White smoke bloomed along it, and the Sioux heard the crackle of the carbines. Lead whistled overhead, smacking the tipi poles. The soldiers were coming on the gallop straight for the Hunkpapa camp. In that camp all was confusion.

"Old men were yelling advice, young men dashing away to catch their horses, women and children rushing off afoot and on horseback to the north end of that three-mile camp, fleeing from the soldiers. They left their tents standing, grabbed their babies, called their older children, and hurried away, frightened girls shrinking under their shawls, matrons puffing for breath, hobbling old women, wrinkled and peering, with their sticks, making off as best they could, crying children, lost children, dogs getting in everybody's way and being kicked for their pains, nervous horses resisting the tug of the reins, and over all the sound of the shooting. . . . The Hunkpapa stood their ground bravely, covering the retreat of their women and children down the flat. Veterans of that fight say, 'It was sure hard luck for Major Reno that he struck the Hunkpapa camp first.' . . . As fast as the Sioux were mounted, they rode out to meet the soldiers on the flat. Those who had guns fired occasionally, falling back slowly, trying to cover the retreat of the women streaming to the north. Every moment reinforcements came up, and the firing grew constantly heavier. . . . While this was going on, the Sioux on the right flank swept down on the Ree scouts, recaptured the pony-herd they had taken, and sent the Rees flying." [1]

Reno's gallant charge, had it been continued, might have swept through the Indians in his front, though they outnumbered him ten to one. But Reno was new to Indian fighting. He could not realize, in the face of all those enemies, that they would give way before him if he pushed the charge home. Moreover, Custer had promised to support his attack with "the whole outfit." But now Custer had disappeared beyond the bluffs across the river. Left to his own devices, Reno relied upon the tactics of the Civil War in which he had earned his rank, threw up his right hand, halted the command, ordered his men to dismount and fight on foot.

Once the Sioux saw the soldiers dismount, they knew their wives and children were safe. Now the warriors could give all their energies to fighting. They swarmed around, flanking the blue line on the west, firing from the rear, forcing the soldiers back to the timber. There the troops, facing south and west, lined up behind a cutbank where once the river flowed. The Sioux moved forward over the ground the troops had abandoned.

Where was Custer?

Men began to drop around the Major. Bloody Knife, Indian scout, stood at Reno's side. Suddenly a bullet splashed the

(See Page 256.)

CHEYENNE LEADERS OF THE DULL KNIFE RAID, 1878

Standing, Little Wolf; seated, Dull Knife.

(See Page 291.) (Bureau of American Ethr

THE GHOST DANCE

The solemn religious ritual of the Plains Indians which brought about the Battle of Wounded Knee and the final surrender of the Sioux.

scout's brains over the Major's face. At that moment Reno made his decision. If he remained in the timber, the Sioux could creep up under cover, attack his flanks and rear. He had not enough men to occupy all that timber. A position on the high bare bluffs across the river seemed to offer safety, if only he could reach it through the horde of savages.

Suddenly he gave an order. Few of his troopers heard it. But those who did not, as soon as they saw their comrades riding off, mounted in haste to follow. Their retreat became a rout. Every man rode hell-for-leather, devil take the hindmost.

A thousand Sioux rushed after Reno's fleeing troopers, transfixing them with arrows, knocking them from their horses with war clubs or rifle barrels, riding over them. The Indians say it was just like a buffalo hunt. "It was easy to kill them. We shot them in the back. They put up no fight at all." The troopers forced their frantic horses to leap into the river from the top of the five-foot bank. Those who got across scrambled up the steep bluffs and flung themselves down, panting, on the ridge. They had left some comrades— whether alive or dead they knew not—in the timber. Nearly half the command were reported killed or missing.

Meanwhile Custer's trumpeter, John Martin, had come tearing back to Captain Benteen, bearing a message hastily scribbled by the General's adjutant:

"Benteen. Come on. Big village. Be quick. Bring packs. P.S. Bring pacs."

Now, almost an hour later, Benteen came in sight of the village, saw the flight of Reno's men, pursued by what he estimated to be not less than 900 Sioux. Benteen and McDougall joined Reno on the beleaguered bluffs. They had no idea what had become of Custer. But the Sioux up there gave them plenty to do. For a time they were heavily engaged. Their position, overlooked by higher ground, was a hot corner.

But all at once the hordes around them melted away. In the quiet that followed they heard volley fire far off down-river. Custer was attacking.

Custer had promised to support them. Now it seemed he surely needed their support. Angry officers demanded that Reno order an advance. Lieutenant W. B. Weir indignantly led his own troop off without waiting for orders, and at length Reno and his command followed downriver along the top of the bluffs. Unwilling to leave his wounded, carrying them in blankets, he could travel only at a snail's pace.

For some days before the battle, Custer's officers had noted that the General lacked his usual buoyancy. But the prospect of a fight was always a shot in the arm to Custer, and it is clear that he went into battle that 25th of June full of zest and confidence. As his five troops jogged along the bluffs before Reno's attack, he had jauntily reined up his horse and waved his hat to Reno. Later, seeing the women streaming north after Reno attacked, he sent back word that the Indians were "running," and his later written message to Benteen showed no lack of confidence, rather eagerness to attack.

So Custer's troopers trotted along the ridge, kicking up a great cloud of dust, making steadily for the ford which crossed the river near the mouth of Reno Creek. Five Sioux warriors, accidentally caught in his path, circled away, frantically flailing their ponies to safety. As Custer moved toward the ford he saw nobody to oppose him. There below, just across the stream, lay the "big village" he had hoped for. He had reached it before Gibbon and Terry; the glory of conquering the Sioux would be all his. Already he could see a mass of frightened Indians—women and children, boys and old men—stampeding westward from the camp, streaming out upon the grassy benches beyond. Where was Reno? Where was Benteen? No matter: victory was in his hands.

But not all the Indians were running. Bob-Tail-Horse had

not been able to catch his war pony in time to join the attack on Reno. He was still in the camp. Bob-Tail-Horse was a small, wiry man, very dark in complexion, a quiet man with a cold courage rare even among his daring, warlike people.[2] Heading toward the ford, he encountered three other Cheyennes, Roan Bear, Calf, and another whose name no one remembers. There were only the four of them; but four was the Cheyenne medicine or lucky number, and the little group gained some assurance from that fact. They promptly forded the river and, all abreast, rode forward bravely at a walk— four against more than two hundred.

Mad Wolf, an older man of many war honors and a noted councilor, rode after the four young men with White Shield, his friend, advising them against their rash advance. "No one must charge on the soldiers now: they are far too many." Mad Wolf and White Shield turned aside along the river. But Bob-Tail-Horse and his three comrades paid no attention. They rode steadily forward, a tiny group to withstand the blue columns pouring down the slope. Yet these four brave men seemed to daunt the troops. The soldiers halted.

Bob-Tail-Horse and his three friends still moved forward until they came up behind a little ridge. There, since the troops did not come on, they decided to do a little shooting. At that moment the five Sioux who had fled from before the troops came along and joined forces with the four Cheyennes. They all fired, and saw one of the soldiers fall.

Then the troops opened fire, holding their position. A dense cloud of powder smoke covered the hill, drifting slowly down toward the river. It was hard for the Indians to see anyone to shoot at. But they could not miss such a big target. For a while there were only these nine Indians defending the ford.

Why Custer halted when he did must always remain a mystery. His eagerness to attack shown in his messages earlier, after he saw the village, can hardly have been lessened when he saw the Indians skedaddling from their camp. Was he waiting for Reno, for Benteen, for the ammunition train? Or did the sublime courage of Bob-Tail-Horse and his friends really daunt Custer, making him fear an ambush along the river? It must have seemed very strange, not to say incredible, to the troops that four warriors would ride out to attack them without any backing whatever. It certainly looked like a trap.

I have gone over that battlefield with old warriors who were in the fight and have talked with many others who took part. All of them without exception, both Sioux and Cheyenne, agree that a dashing charge down the hill, across the river, and through the camp would have overwhelmed all resistance, destroyed Bob-Tail-Horse and his friends, killed many Indians, and cut the camp in two. It was a perfect setup for a swift, spirited attack in Custer's usual style. It would have ended the fight—or at any rate given Custer a position on the flat where no one could approach him under cover.

Whatever Custer and his officers thought when they saw Bob-Tail-Horse riding boldly forward and powder smoke blooming from behind the little ridge near the river, their halt was a fatal mistake. For the firing soon brought mounted warriors on the run swarming downriver by the hundred. They were fresh from chasing Reno, full of fight, sure of victory. They forded or swam the stream, heading north up the dry gulch, taking cover wherever that dry, eroded hillside afforded it, driving the troops before them.

Now Custer's men remounted to move forward. But the moment for a successful charge had passed. The ground in front was alive with warriors, white with smoke.

The gray horse troop took position on the hill where the monument stands now. Other troops to a distance of half a mile were along the ridge to the west and down the slopes toward the river. The Indians swarming up the gulch which cut into the ridge drove in the troopers there first of all. Some retreated on horseback. Others who had lost their horses were slowly fighting their way on foot to join the men of the gray horse troop.

Some of the bolder Indians charged through the retreating lines, and as these troopers were shot down or ridden down, the Sioux and Cheyennes snatched up their guns and ammunition, and the firing upon the troops became constantly heavier.

Even then, after the Rosebud battle in which they captured some weapons, not half the warriors had firearms. Many of the cavalry horses by this time were down, dead or kicking; others broke away and were taken by the Indians. Many of the troopers, slowly retreating up the hill and along the ridge, fought only with revolvers or hand to hand. Perhaps some of the carbines jammed. Few reached the crest. There were too many warriors under cover in that broken ground sniping at them through the dust and smoke.

Yet to the end those troopers held their line as they retreated back up the hill to Custer's position with the gray horse troop. Though nearly half those men were rookies who had never fought Indians, they did not flinch or run. They fought hard, maintaining their lines to the end under that withering fire, outnumbered as they were ten to one. Every Indian eyewitness is in agreement as to the unflinching valor of Custer's men.

Only one man is remembered by the warriors as showing more valor than the rest. That was Sergeant Butler. He ran out to a little knoll up the slope from the ford and for a long time stood off all the warriors singlehanded. "That soldier with the three chevrons on his sleeve," they say, "he was the bravest of them all."

The hill where Custer stood, where the monument stands now, might have made a strong position and offered a fine field of fire if he could have occupied the top. But before he reached it, mounted Indians swept up the reverse slope and attacked over the top. Even had Custer gained it, there were so many ravines and washes on that rugged field he must have been destroyed in the long run by snipers.

By that time there had been a good deal of hand-to-hand fighting, of counting *coups,* of clubbing and stabbing and shooting at close range, and not a few individual charges across the broken lines of the dwindling command. Riderless cavalry horses—bays, sorrels, and grays—were running and charging all over the field. This prolonged the fight. For, once victory was certain, the warriors could wait for that while they chased after the animals, every man eager for the honor and profit of a captured horse and for the ammunition in its saddlebags.

Thus, for a time, all the surviving troopers stood together near the hilltop, wholly surrounded, fighting and falling, bravely dying one by one under a hail of arrows and bullets. They knelt or lay on the barren slope, firing over their dead horses or the body of a fallen friend, until only a handful remained alive. When a bold Cheyenne named Bearded Man charged into their ranks, they shot him down.

One soldier ran away hard as his horse could go, heading back toward Reno's position. Some Indians, including Did-Not-Go-Home, were hot on his trail. All at once he put his revolver to his temple, fired, and tumbled down dead. The warriors were amazed at this suicide.

Now that the horses had all been captured, the Sioux and Cheyennes raced to the attack. The troopers no longer had any hope of holding their position near the hilltop.

All at once the last ten of them jumped up, advanced down the slope toward the river, firing steadily at the Indians in their front. Two of these led, one wounded, bleeding from the mouth. White Bull, Sitting Bull's nephew, shot one. A Cheyenne got the other. Still the eight remaining troopers steadily advanced, forcing White Bull and his comrades to give way and take cover. Indians farther down accounted for the eight troopers, the last of Custer's men.

Sitting Bull's vision had been fulfilled. These soldiers, these white men who had no ears, who would not listen, had come to his camp and met the doom that he had prophesied.

It was a great victory, one that warms the hearts of Sioux and Cheyenne to this day—a victory all the more satisfactory because it was such a hard fight. For a while the warriors were busy, stripping and scalping the dead, finishing off the wounded, gathering the spoils.

But the soldiers with Reno still lived. From the hilltop to which he had progressed toward the sound of the firing, Reno and his officers could see no troops, only huge hordes of Indians riding, a great cloud of smoke and dust. Then the firing ceased.

And now the Indians came swarming back to make things hot for Reno on the parching bluffs. He managed to hold his position. Before the sun went down he had lost eighteen killed and forty-three wounded. The Sioux, now armed with new breech loaders and copper cartridges, occupied the high ground and sprayed his troops with bullets.

Next morning the hostiles charged close up to Reno's lines and almost drove the troops from their entrenchments. But before sunset Sitting Bull called off his warriors.

"The soldiers were in a tight place. Everybody, both whites and Indians, agree that, if the Indians had charged all at once from all sides, a retreat must have followed, and a second retreat under Reno must have become a rout. There was no place to run to: every soldier would have been rubbed out. Many have wondered why the Sioux let these soldiers go. The books say that they stopped fighting because they feared the troops coming with 'Red Nose' Gibbon and 'Star' Terry. But that is nonsense: the Indians could easily have killed all of Reno's men before the infantry arrived, and then have run away on their fleet ponies. Long before noon the women were already striking the tents.

"The truth has never been told about this: it was Sitting Bull who saved Reno.

"About noon he came to the Sioux line again. He told the young men to stop shooting. 'That's enough,' he yelled, 'let them go! Let them live, they are trying to live. They came against us, and we have killed a few. If we kill them all, they will send a bigger army against us.' " [3]

In *The Army and Navy Journal* President Grant wrote: "I regard Custer's massacre as a sacrifice of troops, brought on by himself, that was wholly unnecessary. He was not to have made the attack but effect the juncture with Terry and Gibbon. He was notified to meet them on the 26th, but instead of marching slowly as his orders required in order to effect the junction on the 26th, he entered on a forced march of eighty-three miles in twenty-four hours, and thus had to meet the Indians alone on the 25th."

Perhaps Benteen summed it all up best: "Too many Indians; good shots, good riders, and the best fighters the sun ever shone on."

22

SLIM BUTTES

M ANY OF THE INDIANS with Sitting Bull when Custer attacked his camp had joined him not to fight white men, but to hunt buffalo, since everybody knew that there would not be enough rations at the agency to feed them all. These Indians naturally took part in the defense of their camp, and when the battle and their hunting were over soon headed back onto the reservation, moving toward their agencies. Forty lodges of Sioux, led by American Horse or Black Shield, had reached Slim Buttes when General George "Three Stars" Crook, with 2000 men, came plodding through the sticky gumbo of Moreau River. Crook's purpose was "to jump them before they could get to the agency."

Under the treaties these Indians had a perfect right to hunt off the reservation. The military, according to the treaties, had no lawful authority over Indians on the reservation. But that did not stop the Army.

Captain Anson Mills, at the time escorting a train of wagons toward the Black Hills to get supplies for Crook, happened upon this Sioux village, surprised it, and chased the Indians into the rocks beyond their camp. Those who were not killed scattered, finding such concealment as they could. Some of them ran to Sitting Bull's camp at Twin Buttes on Grand River.

American Horse, with only four warriors and some fifteen women and children, holed up in a cave at the dead end of a small gulch. While Sitting Bull was organizing a war party to relieve the Sioux at Slim Buttes, American Horse and his four comrades stood off the soldiers most of the day. Twice they charged on him, only to be repulsed. A white scout, nicknamed Buffalo Chip, and one soldier were killed, an officer and eight men wounded. By that time Crook had come up and sent Frank Grouard forward to urge the Indians to surrender. American Horse yelled back, "Come and get me!"

While Crook kept his soldiers firing into the mouth of the cave, the Sioux rifles flashed back. Finally Crook induced the women and children to come out. The Oglala warriors stayed in their hole, shouting that Crazy Horse would avenge them.

But the relief was long in coming from such a distance through the mud, and accomplished nothing when it came. At last American Horse was led out, clutching his bowels which protruded through his ripped belly. Mortally wounded, he nevertheless stood proudly upright as he gave up his gun to "Three Stars." The chief wrapped a blanket tightly around his wound and sat before the fire until he suddenly fell over dead. . . .

The news of Custer's disaster shocked the people of the United States, coming as it did at the very time when the whole country was celebrating the centennial of our independence. At last the country waked up to the fact that the Sioux were dangerous enemies. As soon as the War Department could act, adequate armed forces, admirably equipped, were rushed into Sioux country. At the same time, many young men at the agencies forked their ponies and set out to join Sitting Bull.

In July a force under General Wesley Merritt managed to stop a band of Cheyennes heading from Fort Robinson to Sitting Bull's camp. Buffalo Bill, scout for Merritt, on this occasion killed the Cheyenne, Yellow Hand.

The Sioux were full of fight after their victory. But it was impossible for Sitting Bull to hold such a big camp together. Game inevitably deserted a country overrun by such hordes of Indians. In order to eat, the Sioux had to scatter. Each band and camp went hunting on its own, making it easier for the soldiers to deal with these separately. As time passed, more and more of Sitting Bull's followers dropped away or were lured into the agencies.

Colonel* Nelson A. Miles, who had tamed the Southern Plains tribes so swiftly in '74, now commanded substantial forces in the Yellowstone country. Colonel E. S. Otis, in command of an escort with a wagon train, had a brush with the Indians under Sitting Bull. To him the chief sent the famous note, written at his dictation by the fugitive half-breed Johnny "Big Leggins" Brughière:

"I want to know what you are doing on this road. You scare all the buffalo away. I want to hunt in this place. I want you to turn back from here. If you don't, I will fight you again. I want you to leave what you have got here and turn back from here.

I am your friend
Sitting Bull

"I mean all the rations you have got and some powder. Wish you would write as soon as you can."

Otis pacified the Sioux by leaving some bacon and hardtack behind as his wagons rolled away over the prairie. Nobody was killed on either side.

On October 20 and again on the following day Sitting Bull and Miles met between the lines and held parley. Brughière was interpreter. Sitting Bull denied that he was looking for trouble with white men, and accused Miles of being the aggressor. Miles proposed to relieve the chief of his old and help-

*Later, General Miles.

less people. Sitting Bull indignantly refused and announced that he would winter in the Black Hills. The second parley ended in suspicion and disagreement, and immediately after the Colonel reached his lines the troops fired on the Sioux. One Indian was wounded. The others rode off and left the infantry.

Miles had induced Johnny Brughière to desert Sitting Bull and serve him as scout and interpreter. With his help, Miles induced a number of leading Sioux and their dependents to go downriver to the agencies. The chiefs went on the steamboat, their families overland. Using these hostages as a lever, the white men forced a good many Indians to come in and surrender. They did so very reluctantly, knowing that they must give up their horses and their guns, their only means of making a living. The only way an Indian could keep the peace was to stop trying to keep anything else.

Though Miles was bustling about the Yellowstone, trying to keep Crook from "stealing my hostiles," getting them to surrender as fast as he could, Bear Coat was frank and, in his way, friendly to the Indians he was sent to fight—and fought so successfully. Said he, "The art of war among the white people is called strategy or tactics; when practiced by the Indians it is called treachery."

He tried, as often as any other officer in the Army, to apply the maxim stated by Buffalo Bill: "The whole secret of treating with Indians is to be honest with them and do as you agree." But Sitting Bull and some other redskins failed to see Bear Coat in this light. To them, he was simply another trouble-maker, starting another fight.

While Sitting Bull and General Nelson A. "Bear Coat" Miles wrangled and fought along the Yellowstone River, Congress enacted a law (on August 15, 1876) providing that until the Sioux relinquished all claim to the Powder River country and the Black Hills, no subsistence would be furnished them.

When the Commission turned up at Red Cloud Agency, the chief knew that he and his people had no choice but to sign the paper laid before them. Red Cloud declared, "You have come to save us from death." At all other agencies it was the same. The nature of this agreement was put clearly at Standing Rock by Bull Ghost, who, as soon as he had signed, demanded, "We have now agreed; when do we eat?"

The Commission reports, "Our cheeks crimsoned with shame."

But now the public, angered by the behavior of the Sioux and by Custer's disaster, no longer cared a hoot for the blushes of the pacifists. Army officers had replaced civilian agents on Sioux reservations. General Crook talked very plainly to Red Cloud, ordered Spotted Tail to Indian Territory (now Oklahoma) to inspect lands there to which the Sioux might migrate, and proceeded to enlist agency Indian scouts to serve against the hostiles with Sitting Bull and Crazy Horse. Unconditional surrender was the tune now. Before Crook was through, he had deposed the stupid obstructionist Red Cloud and had put Spotted Tail at the head of both agencies.

Sitting Bull's war was over, and though it had cost the Government millions of dollars, the new "agreement" in fact provided ample reparations for the money spent. In the words of George E. Hyde in his book (p. 293) *Red Cloud's Folk*: " 'Here are beef, flour, and blankets (said the United States) for your lands in Laramie Plains and between the forks of the Platte, which we took from you before 1865; and here (said the United States) are the same beef, flour, and blankets for your lands in Nebraska which we took before 1870; and (said the United States, with an air of vast generosity) here are the same beef, flour, and blankets for the Black Hills, the Powder River, and the Bighorn lands which we are now taking from you.' In all fairness, that is very near the true meaning of the 'agreement' of 1876."

MACKENZIE AND DULL KNIFE

AFTER CUSTER FELL, the Sioux at the agencies were restless, and Red Cloud, who had signed the swindling treaty and was eating Uncle Sam's rations near Camp Robinson, Nebraska, was sympathetic enough to the hostiles still fighting the troops. His Oglala were thought to be ready to join Sitting Bull or to ride out and fight on their own hook. No one knew when they might start.

The attitude of Red Cloud and his fellow chief, Red Leaf, was not reassuring. He refused to take orders, moved his camp to Chadron Creek, and, it was reported, was talking war. Other chiefs attempted to talk General Ranald S. MacKenzie into marching his men away.

General Sheridan, placed on the defensive by Custer's fall, protested that the hostiles could never have defeated Custer without the aid of agency Sioux. Still he maintained that there were too many warriors at the agencies for his troops to control. Red Cloud's behavior was nothing new, but now it could be no longer tolerated. Fearing an outbreak, Crook ordered MacKenzie and his Fourth Cavalry to join with the Pawnee Scouts and disarm the Sioux.

When Red Cloud woke up on October 24, 1876, he found that his hated enemies, the Pawnees, had stolen all the ponies from his camp, which was entirely surrounded by United States troops. His warriors had to give up their guns. The women took down the lodges, and the whole outfit, under guard, was marched to the agency. Crook put Spotted Tail in charge of Red Cloud's Indians and informed the tribesmen that Red Cloud was now deposed. Crook said that the Great Father was feeding them and that they must pay for this not in words, but in deeds. They must give him their young men to serve as scouts against the hostiles. He advised the sullen chiefs that it would be dangerous to oppose his proposition.

These plain words had their effect. The day when Red Cloud's Sioux could bully an agent and terrorize a Commission had passed forever.

For once, General "Three Stars" Crook had enough men and equipment for a smashing attack on the hostiles. His command was organized at Fort Fetterman, ready to push through the snow and attack the Sioux village of Crazy Horse. General MacKenzie commanded the cavalry. Crook's plan was to send his 800 cavalrymen to attack and destroy the camp; the infantry, with long-range rifles, would follow to do the mopping up.

Before the command could move beyond Cantonment Reno, some of his Indian scouts brought in a prisoner, a young Cheyenne named Beaver Dam. Questioned by MacKenzie, Beaver Dam reported Crazy Horse camped on the Rosebud, and many Cheyennes under Dull Knife and Wild Hog on the headwaters of Powder River. And before MacKenzie's troopers could find Crazy Horse, his Indian scouts found the Cheyenne village, of about 200 lodges, near at hand, tucked snugly away in the Big Horn Mountains. Two of the scouts, Red Shirt and Jackass, remained perched among the icy rocks all night to watch the village below them, while the troops, a long dark column, snaked over the moonlit snow on their trail. It was bitter cold—thirty degrees below zero.

In those 200 lodges of the Cheyenne camp there must be, according to frontier rule of thumb, 400 warriors able to bear arms, many of them fierce and skillful fighters, renowned for their impetuous valor and looked up to by every tribe on the Plains. The wrangling Sioux could be talked or tricked into surrender; but the Cheyennes would have to be whipped. It was not in their blood to play safe.

MacKenzie had almost as many Indian scouts—allies would be a better name—with him as there were warriors in the Cheyenne camp: 155 Arapahoes, Sioux, and Cheyennes, ninety-one Shoshones, fifteen Bannocks, one Ute, one Nez Percé, and 100 of the invincible Pawnee Scouts, led by Major Frank North and his brother, Captain Luther North. For, after Custer fell, the Indian Bureau could no longer prevent the Army from calling out agency Indians to fight hostiles.

The valley where the Cheyennes were encamped is like a crater on the moon, almost circular and walled in—except for three or four narrow passes—by high, unscalable mountains. The shallow stream, heading north, cut straight as an arrow across this crater, its course clearly marked against the surrounding snow by its narrow hedge of dark cottonwood timber and willow brush.

Three-fourths of this craterlike valley lay open and almost unobstructed. But the southwest segment of the crater, the left bank upstream, was uneven, broken, gashed by a network of deep gullies, cutbanks, ridges, knobs, swales, and cliffs. The camp stood spang in the middle of this valley, most of the tipis in the open on the right bank of the stream. However, ten tipis at the upper end of the camp stood across the stream, close to the cutbanks and gulches where the Cheyennes, if attacked from downriver, might quickly find cover.

The Cheyennes were not unaware that troops were in their country, and sent out four scouts—among whom was my friend, young Two Moon—to locate the enemy camp. They

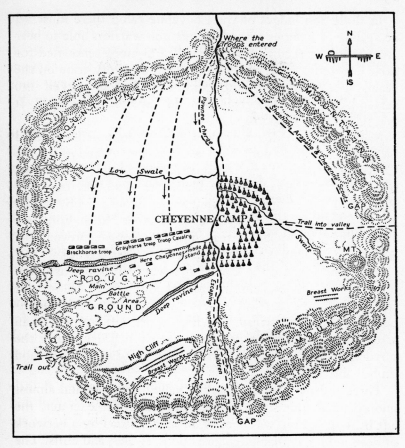

Where the Troops entered

HIGH MOUNTAINS

Pawnee charge

Shoshoni-Arapaho-Cheyenne Scouts

GAP

Low Swale

CHEYENNE CAMP

Trail into valley

Blackhorse troop   Grayhorse troop   Troop Cavalry

Swale

MT

Deep ravine   Here Cheyennes made stand

ROUGH

Main   Battle

Escaping women and children

Breast Works

Area   Deep ravine

GROUND

HIGH MOUNTAINS

Trail out

High Cliff

Breast Works

GAP

CAPTURE OF DULL KNIFE'S VILLAGE

NOVEMBER 26, 1876

Redrawn from the map in George Bird Grinnell's *The Fighting Cheyennes* by permission of Charles Scribner's Sons. Here General Ranald MacKenzie destroyed the Cheyenne Camp on the headwaters of Powder River—the Red Fork.

found it, and soon learned that there were Indians of various tribes with the troops. Two Moon predicted "a big fight."

Black Hairy Dog was Keeper of the Sacred Medicine Arrows and therefore the most important man in the Cheyenne tribe. He immediately proposed that they move out and camp with the Sioux. The chiefs also urged a move. But Last Bull would not have it so.

"Crow Split Nose, chief of the Crooked Lances, spoke to the people, and had an old man come to his side and call it out, saying: 'I think it would be a good idea for the women and children to tear down the lodges, and take them up to that cutbank where there is a good place to throw up breastworks. They should do this at once.' The old man repeated this, and in a short time those of the people whose horses were nearby packed them and were ready to move. Meantime, however, Last Bull, chief of the Fox Soldiers, had called to his old crier and ordered him to call in the Fox Soldiers. When the Fox Soldiers had come together, he ordered them to permit no one to leave the camp. Many people had already started for the place advised by Crow Split Nose, but were turned back by the Fox Soldiers, and told to return to the camp and unpack. Last Bull said: 'No one shall leave the camp to-night.' He said also: 'We will stay up all night and dance.' A little later Crow Split Nose and Last Bull met, and Last Bull said to the other: 'You will not be the only man killed if we are attacked by the white soldiers; what are you afraid of?'

"Crow Split Nose replied: 'I do not care for myself; I am thinking of the women and children. I want to get them up there where they will be safe, so that only we men will be left in the camp ready to fight.'

"'You will know in the morning what is to happen; wait till the morning.'"[1]

The Cheyennes had recently made a successful attack on the Shoshones or Snakes. And to keep anyone from slipping

away in the darkness, Last Bull had ordered a dance to celebrate that victory. Let other tribes run and hide from the
troops; the Cheyennes, he declared defiantly, would stand
and fight.

So the people built a "skunk"—a huge pyramid of firewood
—and by moonrise had formed a great circle, men and women
shoulder to shoulder facing inward about the blazing logs.
And all night long the defiant warriors and their women
stamped and sidled sunwise around the fire, all swaying and
singing together as one creature, carrying the grisly trophies
of their victories. One brandished the withered hand and arm
of a Shoshone squaw; High Wolf proudly displayed his necklace of dried human fingers; while another warrior clutched
triumphantly a buckskin bag containing the right hands of
twelve Shoshone babies. Fluttering overhead, tied to spears
or willow wands, fresh scalps danced a mad jig in the firelight.[2]

One prancing warrior wore a buckskin jacket stripped from
the body of Tom Custer on the Little Big Horn; another
painted victor pranced under the hat of a cavalry sergeant,
while a third wore, instead of a blanket, a blue mackintosh
cape picked up after Custer's last stand. That night the Cheyennes danced their last triumphant victory dance to the pounding of the war drum and the rise and fall of high-pitched
voices on the frosty air. All night long the passionate drum-
ming, singing, and whooping went on.

Last Bull had about 400 warriors, and he meant to keep
them there. He was so willing to fight, so contemptuous of
caution, that he posted no guards in the narrow defiles through
which enemies entering the valley bowl must come.

It was almost morning, dark and foggy, when the drums
ceased to beat and the tired dancers returned to their lodges
and their beds. Black Hairy Dog had not insisted on moving
the camp. Perhaps he remembered how, forty years before,
a warrior society had severely flogged the Keeper of the Medi-

cine Arrows for opposing their wishes. But the anxiety had
not died in his heart. He had staked out his horses close around
his lodge before the dance began, and he did not go to bed
when it ended. Instead, he led his horses far up the hill among
the rocks. There, vigilant in the misty darkness, he heard the
sound of the enemy rushing through the canyon to the north,
where the stream cut through the rim of mountains, heard the
songs and war whoops of the Pawnees and the Snakes, the
shrill monotonous piping of eagle-bone whistles, hoofbeats
and the clatter of arms. Throwing his voice over the weary
camp in a high-pitched crier's tone, he called his people to
battle. Even as the people ran from their lodges, they heard
guns downstream, saw the flash of firing in the darkness before
the dawn. Bullets crashed through the lodge poles overhead.

Cheyennes at the lower end of the village had little time to
clothe or arm themselves, and no chance at all to catch up
their ponies. Many of the animals, hearing the confusion in the
village, ran—strangely enough—toward the troops and so
were captured. Warriors snatched up a rifle in one hand and
a belt of cartridges in the other, fighting a rear-guard action to
protect their families, but with no hope of holding the village.
Sleeping naked as they always did, many went into the fight
almost unprotected from that bitter weather.

A few tried to hold the enemy in a dry creek bed choked
with brush, which entered the main stream just below the
camp. One of these was Dull Knife's son, who jumped out
and fired his rifle at Captain Luther North, then leading the
charging Pawnee scouts. The young warrior was somewhat
to North's right, but the Captain managed to twist round and
defend himself. Their guns cracked together. The Cheyenne
went down, and the Pawnees, riding over him, counted their
coups on his body.

At the upper end of the village many of the Cheyennes had
ponies at hand. The Pawnees' horses stuck in the mud crossing

the creek. This small delay allowed the Cheyennes above to saddle up, snatch their shields and war bonnets. It also gave time for women and children to scuttle away up the deep gulches and ravines stretching southwest toward the mountains from the left bank above the camp.

Once within the valley, the Shoshone, Arapaho, and Cheyenne scouts with the troops swung to the left, cutting off all escape to the hills on the east side. The Pawnees drove straight through the camp, while the cavalry, wheeling into line, swept down the left bank of the stream opposite the camp, until they were suddenly brought up short by a deep gulch manned by Cheyenne riflemen.

MacKenzie made out these Cheyennes through the lightening mist and ordered Lieutenant John A. McKinney, with Company M of the Fourth Cavalry, to dislodge the warriors.

The gulch, too deep to cross, stopped McKinney, and as his small force wheeled by fours to get round the gulch, all the Cheyennes lining its walls almost under the bellies of the cavalry horses fired together. They knocked McKinney dead from his saddle with six wounds, hit a number of other men and horses, and stopped the advance. McKinney's men headed back, breaking up the formation behind them, leaving their trumpeter pinned under his fallen horse.

The Indians rushed out to count *coup* and get the weapons of the men who were down. But Captain Hamilton rallied his men, charged in, and cut down two warriors with his own saber. Such an action was a rare feat, for when charged by cavalry the Indians always scattered and sabers were of no account. Experienced Indian fighters like Custer never took sabers into an Indian fight.

This counterattack won the day. Twenty Cheyennes— nearly every one there—were killed. The completeness of the victory is shown by the fact that no less than thirty dead warriors were abandoned to the troops before it was all over.

Little Wolf, that famous war chief with the heart of a bear, in order to divert the fire of the soldiers from Indians who were trapped in a gulch, exposed himself, standing in the open. Many bullets kicked up the snow around him, but he was never hit. From that time on, with the Pawnees in the village, the Snakes and Arapahoes on the slopes, and the troops in the valley, the Cheyennes spent the rest of the morning saving each other and their few remaining horses. There were many brave rescues and feats of arms performed by men on both sides. One charge was made by twenty Cheyennes, all wearing war bonnets.

The high cliffs echoed and re-echoed the rifle volleys, the strongheart songs of the women, the yells of the infuriated redskins, the hoofbeats of the charges. But the Cheyennes fell steadily back up the slopes to find refuge among the rocks. Neither the Indian scouts with the troops nor the soldiers cared to follow them there. That was a job for the infantry.

Meanwhile William Rowland, who had married a Cheyenne woman, took a few Cheyenne Army scouts and crept up to a position where he could shout across to the hostiles. Dull Knife and Rowland shouted back and forth across no-man's-land. Dull Knife declared he had lost three sons in the fight and was ready to make peace. But Little Wolf and others were more warlike; they called out, "Go home, you have no business here. We can whip these white soldiers alone, but cannot fight you Indians too." [3]

They would not believe that any full-blood Cheyennes were with the troops, and threatened to call on the Sioux for aid, come back, and clean out the whites. "You have killed and hurt a heap of our people," they shouted. "You may as well stay now and kill the rest of us."

The troops did not take up that challenge. It was evident that the Cheyenne were still as fierce and full of fight as ever, in spite of their heavy loss (nearly ten per cent). They kept firing into the troops all afternoon. The command had lost one officer, six men killed, and twenty-six wounded. The Pawnees and Snakes took sixteen scalps. General Crook had made it clear that he would punish severely any Indian scout who killed a child or a woman, and the scouts had remembered his words.

More than 700 Cheyenne ponies were captured; 100 of these the Pawnees packed with plunder.

A little after midday the Pawnee scouts and two troops of cavalry set to work to destroy the Cheyenne camp. Good weapons they saved; everything else was first damaged or destroyed and then burned. By nightfall all was ready for the flames.

"First, all the fat and marrow preserved by the squaws in great bladders and paunches were laid upon the lodge-fires, upon which were then piled the cords and cords of fuel gathered as the winter supply. The crackling flames roared and bellowed in their skyward rush through the covering of hide and canvas, but before the lodge-poles could fairly ignite, the explosion of kegs and cans of powder sent all the belongings of Cheyenne domestic life rocket-like to the zenith.

"Never were orders more thoroughly executed. Experience had taught the troops in bitter lessons the preceding winter that villages only half destroyed were scarcely to be considered injured at all, and on this occasion the determination was to let not one square inch of canvas, of hide, of robe, or even of gunny sack be available for future use by the discomfited enemy.

"Lodge-poles, not more than half burned, were broken into smaller fragments and thrown upon what is no rhetorical flourish to call the funeral pyres of Cheyenne glory. Axes, spades, picks, shovels, hammers, scissors and knives were burned to deprive them of their temper: holes were knocked in the bottom of canteens, kettles, pans and all other utensils, before subjecting them to heat; saddles were smashed, bridle-reins cut, bits broken, and then thrown to the conflagration." [4]

Tons of buffalo meat were consumed, along with 1000 blazing saddles, curling hides, and sizzling tallow, adding its brisk crackle to the popping of exploding ammunition.

Captain John G. Bourke, in his book *On the Border with Crook*, wrote:

"The roar of the flames exasperated the fugitive Cheyennes to frenzy; they saw their homes disappearing in fire and smoke; they heard the dull thump, thump of their own medicine drum, which had fallen into the hands of the Shoshones; and they listened to the plaintive drone of the sacred flageolets upon which the . . . Pawnees were playing. . . ."

During the night brave young Two Moon sneaked back to the ruined camp and recovered a few buffalo robes to keep his friends from freezing.

MacKenzie did not need to call up the infantry to clean the Cheyenne out of the valley, for by next morning (November 26) all had slipped away six miles through the frozen hills to huddle and try to sleep about great fires, on the embers of which they roasted the flesh of the few horses they had left. Bitterly the ill-clad refugees suffered in that frightful cold. Eleven children froze to death, and half-naked old folks saved themselves only by putting feet and hands into the warm entrails of the butchered horses. For some time after, it was rough on small parties of white men in that neighborhood. Anybody with a coat or blanket was doomed to slaughter, if the Cheyenne caught him.

They followed along the Big Horn Mountains to Lake De Smet and Tongue River and so to the camp of Crazy Horse on Beaver Creek. The Sioux were very hospitable, but Crazy Horse would not join the fierce Cheyenne in desperate reprisals. Already he was considering the advisability of surrender to the whites.

His refusal to join the resentful Cheyenne in their war only made them stiffen their necks and harden their hearts against him. And when they learned beyond a doubt that their own people were fighting with the troops, they made up their minds. Dull Knife and Little Wolf surrendered. But on one condition—that they might enlist with the Great Father's young men to attack Crazy Horse.

Spotted Tail was eager to bring Crazy Horse in and so improve his position with the white men. He knew their strength and foresaw the inevitable end. General Crook, always preferring to gain his ends peacefully, favored Spotted Tail in this venture, and by January, 1877, Crazy Horse was in a mood to come in to Camp Robinson. Little Wolf and Dull Knife never had a chance to get back at him.

But Crazy Horse was soon to meet a bloody end.

With only 200 lodges, the chief felt lonesome in the Big Horn country after Sitting Bull had struck out for Canada and his allies, the Cheyenne, had gone to join the whites. And all the time the white men kept sending word that he had better come in and surrender. General Crook sent Spotted Tail, the uncle of Crazy Horse, to persuade him to come in and surrender at Red Cloud Agency. Spotted Tail prevailed. Crazy Horse agreed. There was no use fighting any longer.

Though Spotted Tail had induced Crazy Horse to come in, Red Cloud rode out to meet him and so appear as the one who brought him in to the Oglala agency.

The leading passion of the Sioux, as of all Plains Indians, was a love of prestige. This love of honor made them brave in battle and generous in camp. It was the motive at the bottom of the most of their many virtues. But with every virtue there goes an appropriate vice, and the Sioux—perhaps because they were so numerous—were cursed with jealousy even more than other Plains tribes. And among a race of warriors, where every man carried arms, jealousy was only a thought away from homicide.

Ever since the great treaty of 1851 on Horse Creek, when the Commissioner appointed Stirring Bear head chief of all the Sioux, almost every leading chief who had any influence with the whites cherished a secret longing to have that empty honor conferred on him.

For to the Sioux empty honor was enough. He craved no power, no wealth, but he lusted for public acclaim. Like an actor, he did his works to be seen of men, and had his reward in this world.

So now when Crazy Horse, that renowned fighter, reached Red Cloud Agency, there were many there who resented his coming, and some—among them mixed-bloods and inter-preters, hangers-on at the agency—who hoped to fill the hearts of the whites with suspicion and so bring the great chief down.

Crazy Horse had discussed surrender with Sitting Bull. But Sitting Bull replied that he did not wish to die just yet. Crazy Horse said no more.

He surrendered in May, 1877, about the time Sitting Bull crossed the line into Canada. At the agency he found Red Cloud's Oglala. Probably what followed was not the work of any one man, but a kind of tacit conspiracy among many who hated, feared, or were jealous of so great a warrior.

That summer of '77, rumors were abroad that Crazy Horse was planning to murder his old enemy, General George "Three Stars" Crook. When Crook attempted to enlist some Sioux scouts to fight the Nez Percé, then fighting their way 1600 miles from their Oregon reservation toward Sitting Bull's camp in Canada, there was a misunderstanding which made the white officers suspect Crazy Horse planned another war. Crazy Horse proposed to take his lodges along and do a little hunting on the campaign—as Crook himself was in the habit of doing—and it may be that the officers feared to arm Crazy

Horse and his warriors and send them back to the hunting grounds, women and children and all.

At the agency Crazy Horse married a mixed-blood girl. She fell ill with tuberculosis, and the restless chief asked permission to take her to the Brûlé agency of his uncle, Spotted Tail, there to put her in the care of Dr. V. T. McGillycuddy, whom he trusted.

Permission was refused. But Crazy Horse could not let his young wife die in a tangle of red tape. Fresh from the independence of his roving life, he set out on September 4, riding slowly along beside the travois of the invalid, heading for the doctor. A body of Indian government scouts was sent to bring him back. They rode up to stop him. The chief raised his hand; they halted.

"I am Crazy Horse!" he shouted. "Do not touch me; I am not running away."

Somehow the scouts found his medicine too strong for them. None had war honors enough to entitle him to lay hands on a man with the record of Crazy Horse. None of them had the courage to face that small but valiant warrior. They fell in behind and escorted the chief to Spotted Tail's camp.

It was not only the Indian scouts who feared Crazy Horse. It is clear that Army officers stationed at those agencies were also afraid of him. The garrison at Spotted Tail did not number a hundred men—an island in an ocean of restless Sioux. Those officers knew—none better—that Crazy Horse and his warriors had repeatedly whipped far larger forces, including those of Crook himself on the Rosebud. Apparently some of those officers had a bad case of nerves, and the Indian agents were even more rattled than the officers.

At Spotted Tail Agency they told Crazy Horse he must go back. He agreed reluctantly, at the same time expressing misgivings that "something might happen" to him at Red Cloud. The agent, Lee, did his best to reassure Crazy Horse, persuading him that no evil was intended him and that no one would harm him if he returned. The agent arranged to have a number of the chief's friends go back with them and allowed Crazy Horse to ride a pony. Somebody slipped him a knife.

Meanwhile, at Red Cloud Lieutenant W. P. "White Hat" Clark expended much misdirected zeal in reporting all the malicious rumors current about Crazy Horse and his "evil" intentions. The chief's trip to Spotted Tail without permission created a sensation, and even Washington took alarm. Apparently it was believed that he had intended to murder General Crook, that he planned to skip the reservation and start another war; just where his guns and horses were to come from was not considered. By the time the chief and the agent reached Fort Robinson, orders had come down from Washington to put Crazy Horse under arrest. He was to be imprisoned without trial in the Dry Tortugas, Florida, for life.

The agent had promised the chief that General Bradley, commanding officer of the post, would talk with Crazy Horse and hear his defense against the accusations in the air. But when they arrived at the post, Bradley informed Lee that Crazy Horse must immediately be turned over to the officer of the day.

In vain Lee protested that he had assured Crazy Horse he would be heard and would not be harmed if he returned to Red Cloud.

The fear in which Crazy Horse was held is shown by the fact that no one had the nerve to tell him he was under arrest. They merely asked him to go with the officer of the day, apparently encouraging him to believe that he would be able to talk with General Bradley in the morning.

By that time a good many warriors were on hand, some of them comrades of Crazy Horse, others government scouts from the bands of Red Cloud and American Horse. Each group lined up facing the other, watching the chief.

"Quietly, his blanket folded over his arm as though he were going to his lodge between two friends, Crazy Horse let himself be taken past a soldier walking up and down with a bayoneted gun on his shoulder and in through a door. Only then did he see the barred windows, the men with chains on their legs, and realize it was the iron house. Like a grizzly feeling the deadfall on his neck, the Indian jumped back, drawing the hidden gift knife to strike out around him, but Little Big Man grabbed his arms from behind. Trying to wrench free, Crazy Horse struggled into the open, dragging the stocky Indian through the door. The scouts raised their guns, Red Cloud and American Horse ordering: 'Shoot in the middle; shoot to kill!' the officer of the day knocking the scout guns down with his sword as fast as they came up.

"And between them the chief, like a trapped animal, was heaving, plunging to get free, growling: 'Let me go! Let me go!' as the angry bear growls, the knife flashing in the late sun. Then with a mighty jerk he threw himself sideways and Little Big Man had to drop one hand, blood running from a slash across his arm. But Swift Bear and other old Brûlé friendlies already had Crazy Horse, held him while the officer of the day tried to use his sword against him, yelling: 'Stab him! Kill the son of a bitch!'

"The guard came running up, lunged with his bayonet and, hitting the door, jerked the weapon free and lunged twice more. At the redness of the steel a noise of alarm, of warning rose from the watching Indians. Crazy Horse pulled at his old captors once more. 'Let me go, my friends,' he panted. 'You have got me hurt enough.'

"And at these soft words all the Indians suddenly dropped their hands from him as though very much afraid. Released, Crazy Horse staggered backward, turned half around, and sank to the ground, his shirt and leggings already wet and blood-darkened." [5]

A good many different stories are current as to the details of this killing. I have preferred the Indian story; the friends of Crazy Horse, at any rate, had nothing to hide.

That night Crazy Horse, mortally wounded but still a prisoner, lay dying under a red blanket in the adjutant's office. The bayonet had passed through both kidneys. His parents and a friend or two were admitted. Before he died, he whispered to his father, "My father, I am bad hurt. Tell the people it is no use to depend on me any more now."

24

THE DULL KNIFE RAID

WHEN Crazy Horse surrendered, Dull Knife, his Cheyenne ally, then encamped with him, made his decision also.

All that winter after the MacKenzie fight, Dull Knife and his band of Northern Cheyenne had remained in camp on Powder River with Crazy Horse and his Oglala Sioux. But times were changing. Two Moon's Cheyenne gave up their guns to the white men and enlisted as scouts to help round up the Sioux. Chief Lame Deer was defeated, killed. Dull Knife, more the counselor than the warrior, thought it time to join the general movement. In the spring of 1877 he and his band surrendered.

They were promptly ordered to the Cheyenne-Arapaho agency at Darlington, near Fort Reno, in what is now Oklahoma. On the fifth of August a detachment of the Fourth Cavalry brought 937 of them to Fort Reno. The commandant promptly turned them over to the Indian agent, John D. Miles.

Miles found Dull Knife's band a handful. By that time there were no longer any buffalo in the Southern country. Many of the Southern Cheyenne had taken no part in hostilities since the battle of the Washita, and most of them had set out in good faith to follow the white man's road.

And now here came Dull Knife's warriors from a country

where game still abounded. They were no agency Indians; until only a few moons before they had been on the warpath. At every gathering, in every lodge, they bragged of their warlike exploits and taunted the Southern Cheyenne. Dull Knife's people did not like this "hot country"—a land choked with tall grass, weeds, and trees—a country with too much rain and dew and too little snow. Before the summer was out, many were stricken with malaria.

Dull Knife's people did not like agency rations—bacon and flour and baking powder, and beeves that were all horns and skin and bone. The warrior society which policed their camp flatly refused to allow the agent to issue rations to heads of families. They took the law into their own hands, declared they had never agreed to come south, and kept stirring up the Southern Cheyenne.

The sudden influx of all these people made heavy inroads on the rations, and there was no game to fill their empty bellies. Agent Miles testified later before a committee of the Senate that he had never received enough rations to feed his Indians more than nine months out of the year. He declared, "They have lived, and that is about all."

For almost a year Dull Knife and his people stuck it out. Then they requested to be sent back to their own home. As Little Chief put it, they were "homesick, and heartsick, and sick in every way." With Dull Knife was Little Wolf, that great fighter, one war chief who was a disciplinarian and a strategist —a man with a heart like a bear. Little Wolf, or Old Little Wolf, as he is sometimes called, was a tall, dark Indian, with long braids reaching to his waist, who liked to wear a large, shiny metal cross hanging on his breast. His cheekbones, nose, jaw, and brows were so prominent that his knobby head resembled a medieval carving, or the end of a walking stick. But, though no beauty, he was all man, and spoke plainly to the agent: " 'These people were raised far up in the north among the pines and the mountains. In that country we were always healthy. There was no sickness and very few of us died. Now, since we have been in this country, we are dying every day. This is not a good country for us, and we wish to return to our home in the mountains. If you have not the power to give us permission to go back there, let some of us go on to Washington, and tell them there how it is, or do you write to Washington and get permission for us to go back north.' The agent's answer was: 'I cannot do this now. Stay here for one more year and then we will see what we can do for you.'

" 'No,' replied Little Wolf, 'we cannot stay another year; we want to go now. Before another year has passed we may all be dead and there will be none of us left to travel north.'

"The agent said to him: 'I am told that some of your people have gone off already.'

" 'I do not know that any have gone,' replied Little Wolf.

"They talked a little longer without result and the Cheyennes went back to their camp and continued to discuss the matter, trying to decide whether they should wait another year or go now. Soon after this some of the Indian policemen came to the camp, saying that they had been sent by the agent, who declared that three of their young men had run away and that he believed they were all going. He had sent the policemen to stop them.

"Little Wolf said to the policemen: 'You go back and tell the agent that we intend to move a little way up the river to camp there, and that then we will come and see him again.'

"They moved camp as he said they would, but before they had had time to go in to see the agent some troops came up to the camp, bringing with them a howitzer and told the Indians that they must go back to the agency. The troops camped close by the Indians and they stayed there for four days longer, when a messenger came from the agency asking

Little Wolf to go in and talk with the agent. He went, taking with him two men, Wild Hog and Crow.

"When Little Wolf entered the agent's office he asked: 'What do you want with me; why did you send for me?'

"The agent said: 'Three of your young men have run off, and now I want you to give me ten of your young men, to hold here as prisoners until I get back the three that have gone off. The soldiers will go after these three, and when they have brought them back I will give the ten men their liberty.'

"Little Wolf stood up and after he had shaken hands with the agent, and with some army officers who were there, he said: 'I will not do what you ask. If you follow those three men, you cannot find them. Three men who are travelling over the country can hide, so that they cannot be found. You never could get back these three and you never would set my men free. You would keep them always.'

"The agent said to him: 'If you do not give me these ten men, I will give you no rations. I will give you nothing to eat until I get them. You shall starve until they are given to me. So you must give me those men, and I want them at once.'

"Little Wolf answered again: 'I cannot give you the ten men you wish, to be held for the three who have gone. I will not give them. I am a friend to the white people, and have been so for a long time. I went to see my Great Father in Washington, and he told me that he did not wish any more blood spilled; that we ought to be friends and fight no more.' The agent's reply was that he must have these hostages and must have them quickly.

"Then Little Wolf said to him: 'You and I have always been friends, but to-day I cannot do for you what you ask. I do not want any trouble, nor do I wish to have blood shed at this agency, but I cannot do what you ask.' For some little time they talked in this way, the agent insisting that he must have the men—that he would have them.

"At last Little Wolf stood up and again shook hands with all present and said: 'My friends, I am now going to my camp. I do not wish the ground about this agency to be made bloody, but now listen to what I say to you. I am going to leave here; I am going north to my own country. I do not want to see blood spilt about this agency. If you are going to send your soldiers after me, I wish that you would first let me get a little distance away from this agency. Then if you want to fight, I will fight you and we can make the ground bloody at that place.' " [1]

Little Wolf and Dull Knife conferred. Ed Geary (Edmond Guerrier) offered to act as mediator, but found the Indians in such an ugly mood that he hurried back to the agency. Early next morning some 300 Northern Cheyennes, including eighty-seven warriors, hit the northern trail to rejoin the Sioux. It was September 9, 1878.

Two days they marched unmolested, making camp on Little Medicine Lodge River for the night. About sunset a scout on the ridge signaled frantically that soldiers were coming. "Little Wolf ran out of his lodge" according to Grinnell, "and called out to the young men: 'Do not any of you shoot until the troops have fired. Let them shoot first. But do you all get your arms and horses and I will go out and meet the troops, and try to talk with them. If they kill any of us, I will be the first man killed. Then you can fight.' "

The commander of the troops sent a scout forward asking Little Wolf to surrender and return. "Little Wolf replied: 'Tell them that we do not want to fight; that we will not go back. We are leaving this country. I have had no quarrel with anyone. I hold up my right hand that I do not wish to fight with the whites; but we are going to our old home to stay there.' " [2] Still hoping for peace, he rode out for further parley. The soldiers fired at him. The Cheyennes charged, and the battle began. It lasted from mid-afternoon till dark, but the troops could not get near the Cheyenne camp.

Both parties remained on the field, and fought again from dawn until mid-afternoon. After that the troops pulled out, leaving three dead men. Five Cheyennes had been hit, but none killed. Content with their victory and needing rest, the Indians remained there that night, heading north in the morning.

On the fourth day, near the Cimarron River, a gray horse troop charged them, but were so outnumbered that they soon withdrew. The Indians made camp.

"Soon after a third force met them, coming from Fort Dodge and Dodge City. This time the Cheyennes were outnumbered. With the troops was a large number of citizens. But the fight was brief. For some reason, the whites made only one charge. Then, not being able to break the Indian lines, they sounded retreat on the bugles, and pulled out.

"Now the Cheyennes were angry. Up until then, they had refrained from depredations upon citizens, only taking some needed horses and cattle as they rode along. But now that the citizens had come out to fight them, they felt justified in attacking all white men whatever.

"Late that afternoon, the white men returned, with a number of wagons. Using these as a fort, or base of operations, they fought and fought hard all day.

"By this time the Indians saw that they would have to outmarch the troops. That night they left and skipped to the Arkansas River. Before they crossed, they came upon some hide-hunters skinning buffalo. The hide-hunters were scared out of their skins, but the Indians were so glad to see the fresh buffalo-meat—eighteen freshly killed cows—that they let the white men go, only taking their Sharps rifles and long cartridges. Then they hurried across the stream above Fort Dodge.

"North of the river, troops again attacked them, but the Cheyennes dug in on a hilltop and stood them off. They had to leave many horses, broken down by the long, hard trip, at this point.

"But that night, tired of continual fighting, anxious only to get home, the Cheyennes made tracks. For three days they went on as hard as they could go, and almost without stopping. The women jogged along, heavy for want of sleep; the babies rode, silent, heads lolling, in their cradles; old men crouched in the drags, tight-lipped and patient, or singing brave heart songs to cheer their relatives; on the flanks and in the rear rode the young men, quirting their jaded ponies; while out in front rode Little Wolf, tireless and fearless as a bear.

"They reached Frenchman's Fork of the Republican River, in Nebraska. There again the Cheyennes saw troops, but managed to avoid them. They forded the South Platte, somewhere near Ogallala, and finally made camp for a rest near the mouth of White Clay Creek on the North Platte. The long running fight was over.

"Little Wolf wished to push on. But Dull Knife was a gentler soul; he was home now, and that was enough for him. So Little Wolf went on without him. Dull Knife, childlike in his trust, went towards Fort Robinson and surrendered." [3]

The men were allowed to keep their bows and knives, but were ordered to turn in their guns. All their horses were taken from them.

For three months Dull Knife's people lived happily at Fort Robinson, filling up on army rations. They had to report for roll call when the evening meal was served, but at all other times were free to come and go about the post or even to hunt in the hills. Captain Wessels warned them that if anyone slipped away, all would be imprisoned.

One day Bull Hump was missed. Though he was brought back, all the Cheyennes were shut up in a barracks guarded by sentries. The officers informed Dull Knife that orders had come from Washington to send his people south again. Dull

Knife replied firmly. "You may kill me here, but you can never make me go back."

The Plains Indians have always had the fundamental trait of free men—the basic virtue of democracy—the inability to tolerate injustice and abuse.

Captain Wessels stopped the Indians' rations. There were five or six inches of snow on the ground, and the thermometer stood at zero. They had no fuel. For five days the Cheyennes starved in their cold barracks. They ate the snow on the window sills the first two days. When that was gone, they had no water. Wild Hog, a leading warrior, went out to parley with the officers, got into a scuffle with a soldier, stabbed the man, and was put in irons. Then all agreed that the time had come to fight.

There were about 150 of them, the majority old people and children. But they said: "We must all die, but we will not die shut up in this house like dogs; we will die in the open, and die fighting." So they opened their bags and put on their best clothes and gay beaded moccasins, painted their faces, brushed their hair, and made ready for the last battle.

At the time of their surrender, all the men had been searched. But they were not entirely helpless. They had saved five good rifles and eleven pistols. These weapons, taken apart, had been concealed under the dresses of the women. The triggers, gun screws, and springs had been worn as ornaments by the children. But now the desperate warriors assembled the guns, distributed their scanty ammunition, and prepared to break from that bleak prison. Each one tied a blanket around his neck and another around his waist, to leave his hands free. They all— young men and maidens, withered old squaws, gray-haired old men, wide-eyed children—hugged and kissed each other good-bye.

Then the warriors stationed at the windows shot down the sentries, smashed out the window frames, helped their people through. The moon was full and bright, and the soldiers tumbled from their barracks before the Indians streaming from the fort could reach the creek to satisfy their thirst. Many broke through the ice in crossing, and plunged on through the snow, cold and wet, with freezing clothing, the troops hot on their heels. Those warriors who remained behind to guard the rear were soon shot down. Others, who were young and had no babies to carry, soon outdistanced the old people and children and others weakened by starvation or breathless from their long run toward the hills three miles away. Dull Knife and a few others turned off and hid among some rocks and were never discovered by the troops.

Some fifty Indians were shot down before the rest could reach the bluffs beyond the frozen river. But once in the bluffs, the Cheyennes stopped the cavalry in its tracks. The troops went back to barracks, but the Cheyennes never halted. That night they pushed on seventeen miles through the snow, and in the morning stopped another pursuing troop in its tracks, and that night slipped away in the darkness. In one brush a troop horse was shot down. He provided the first food the Indians had tasted in seven days.

Captain Wessels pounded the rifle pits of the Cheyennes all one day with artillery, but could not blast them out. The pursuit kept on for six whole days. Time after time the cornered Cheyennes slipped through the soldiers' lines by night and fled through the darkness and the snow.

They made their last stand forty-four miles from Fort Reno, among the Hat Creek bluffs. There, in a washout, huddled the last thirty-one survivors of that desperate running fight. Many were wounded—most were half-frozen—all were exhausted.

The commander sent a demand for surrender. Three Cheyenne rifles gave him his answer—a ragged volley of the Indians' last cartridges. Three hundred troops advanced on the double, ringed the washout, and fired down upon the huddled, helpless refugees.

Then, out of that pile of death, three ragged, bloody warriors staggered up, shouted the war whoop, and charged. Two of them carried knives; one had an empty pistol. Ringed by 300 rifles, the three were shot to pieces.

The Dull Knife Raid was over. Of the chief's 150 people, sixty-four had been killed, seventy-eight—among them fifty wounded—were taken prisoner, ten were missing. Of the survivors, only twenty were sent back to the "hot country."

Meanwhile Little Wolf had taken his people into the Sand Hills and lived very well all winter on antelope and cattle. It was not until next spring that Lieutenant W. P. Clark (who had served as chief of scouts and therefore knew Indians well) found his old friend Little Wolf and persuaded him to go into Fort Keogh. There General Miles persuaded Little Wolf and his warriors to enlist as scouts for the Sioux campaign. They performed valuable service, and were allowed to remain in their beloved North country.

25

TO THE VICTORS BELONG THE SPOILS

>>>>>>>>>>>> <<<<<<<<<<<<

After the Dull Knife fight Lieutenant F. D. Baldwin twice attacked Sitting Bull's camp and captured some horses and mules. But already the chief and his braves had determined to take refuge in the Grandmother's Country—the British possessions. They remembered that the Sioux had once belonged to the British. Now they were "going home" to find peace in the land of the Red Coats where there was no war.

Sitting Bull, with about 200 lodges, moved into Canada in 1877. Up there, he found only peaceful Indian tribes and a handful of Red Coats—the Royal Northwest Mounted Police. The Sioux could sleep sound all night then and never have to worry about their women and children or their horses.

For in Canada, they found, there could be no war and, strangely, no treaties for the Sioux—only laws applied with equal firmness and certainty to white men and red. When Sitting Bull's young men ran off a Frenchman's horses, the Red Coats gave the chief his choice between punishing the thieves or having them do it. The chief found that no Indian who committed a crime could find safety in his camp, for one or two Red Coats would come boldly in and get him, take him away, and give him the punishment required by their law. Yet they would hang a white man just as quickly for killing an Indian. The Red Coats were magistrates as well as police.

But what particularly impressed the warriors was the habit the Red Coats had of never firing the first shot. Americans were likely to shoot first and ask questions afterward. But the Red Coats always let the criminal shoot first. Such a display of personal courage was worth ten regiments in keeping the restless Sioux in order.

In Canada Sitting Bull found no such tyranny as the Agency Sioux had to endure on their reservations south of the line. The Red Coats made no effort whatever to force Indians to become like white men, to give up their religion, their customs and their chiefs. Up there every Indian enjoyed the four freedoms. Only two things were required of the tribesmen: they must obey the law, and they must feed themselves. While the buffalo lasted, those were happy hunting grounds.

The Canadian government never admitted Sitting Bull's claim that he and his Sioux were British Indians, though they permitted him to remain north of the boundary so long as he could support himself by hunting and kept the peace. They were continually making representations to Washington urging the American government to take their Indians home. On October 17, 1878, Sitting Bull met with a special commission from the States led by Brigadier General Alfred H. "Star" Terry at Fort Walsh. It was all the Red Coats could do to get Sitting Bull to attend that conference, and he refused flatly to shake hands with the Americans. Terry explained that the Grandfather at Washington was ready to pardon the Sioux and make peace with them, if they surrendered, and would treat them like other Indians at the agencies, take their guns and horses and give them cows in return. He suggested that the Sioux should "march on foot to the reservation," a distance of about 1000 miles. The Army had a fixed aversion to seeing a Sioux on horseback.

Terry appears to have been a mild and well-meaning gentleman and to have supposed that Sitting Bull would willingly accept the amnesty and benefits he offered.

But Sitting Bull's reply was, to say the least, embarrassing to the Americans, playing up as he did the painful contrast between the honesty and efficiency of the Mounted Police and the broken treaties, the corruption of the Indian Office, and the needless bloodshed south of the boundary.

"Sitting Bull: 'For sixty-four years you have kept me and my people and treated us bad. What have we done that you should want us to stop? We have done nothing. It is all the people on your side who started us to making trouble. We could go nowhere else, so we took refuge here. It was on this side of the line that we first learned to shoot, and that's why I came back here again. I would like to know why you came here.

" 'I did not give you my country, but you followed me from place to place, and I had to come here. I was born and raised here with the Red River Mixed-Bloods, and I intend to stay with them. I was raised hand in hand with these people, and that is why I shake their hands (*shaking hands with the Red Coats*). That is the way I was taught. That is the way I intend to go on doing. See how I live with these people.

" 'Look at me. I have ears, I have eyes to see with. If you think me a fool, you are a bigger fool than I am. This house is a medicine-house. You come here to tell us lies, but we do not want to listen to them. I don't wish such language used to me, nor any such lies told to me in my Grandmother's house. Don't say two more words. Go back home where you came from. This country is my country now, and I intend to stay here and raise people up to fill it. I shake hand with these people (*shaking hands again with the Red Coats*). You see me; that's enough. The country that belonged to us, you ran me out of it. I have come here, and here I intend to stay. I want you to go back, and take it easy going back.' " [1]

After other Indians had spoken to the theme, Terry appealed to Sitting Bull again. The report continues:

" 'Shall I say to the President that you refuse the offers that he has made you? Are we to understand from what you have said that you refuse those offers?'

"Sitting Bull: 'I could tell you more, but this is all I have to say. If we told you more—why, you would pay no attention to it. I have no more to say. This side of the boundary does not belong to your people. You belong on the other side; I belong here.' "

After that the Red Coats tried to get Sitting Bull to reconsider his decision. Sitting Bull replied emphatically, " 'We will pay for what we want here: we asked the Americans to give us traders, but instead they gave us fireballs (shells). All of them robbed, cheated, and laughed at us. They never tell the truth. They said they did not wish to fight, but they began it. Everything bad began with them; I have never heard a good word of them. . . . If they liked me, why did they drive me away?' "

All the while Red Coats, traders, scouts from the States, and Indians from the American reservations, as well as missionaries, kept urging the Sioux to surrender and return home. Little by little Sitting Bull's camp dwindled. But the buffalo dwindled even more rapidly and at last, finding that the Red Coats would not feed him or give him a reserve in Canada, the old chief, with many misgivings, agreed to go south and surrender.

He knew well enough what had happened to Dull Knife's people, to Bear Ribs and Crazy Horse and Stirring Bear. He had himself received and helped the Nez Percé Indians who had escaped before Chief Joseph's surrender to join him. He remembered Little Thunder, and Sand Creek. He was thoroughly convinced that all Americans were liars and that they were only waiting to get the Sioux all together to slaughter them. On July 19, 1881, at Fort Buford near the mouth of the

Yellowstone, he and his little band handed over their guns. Ten days later they were put on a steamboat and taken down the Missouri to Fort Randall. There Sitting Bull was held prisoner of war for two years, finally returning to join his people at Standing Rock, May 10, 1883. That was the year of the last great Indian buffalo hunt.

During Sitting Bull's imprisonment at Fort Randall, an agreement had been forced upon the Standing Rock Sioux to sell their lands for a song. The Reverend T. L. Riggs, a man of courage and good sense, who had long served these Indians at the Dakota mission at Oahe, called the attention of the public to that disgraceful business, and so forced an "investigation" of the scandal. This was conducted by a "committee of the Senate sent to investigate the condition of the Indian tribes of Montana and Dakota." The very name of the committee was a whitewash for the scandal. They were sent out to save the face of the administration.

Though many of the chiefs were ready to bootlick the committee, Sitting Bull stood up to it, insisted on his authority as chief, and when the chairman denied his authority and tried to browbeat him, Sitting Bull merely waved his hand and all the Indians left the council in a body.

At a later meeting he made amends and told the ruffled Senators in what respects the government had failed to keep its promises to the Sioux. The committee was discomfited, but from then on the Indian agent, Major McLaughlin, was determined to break Sitting Bull's power.

For Sitting Bull and other Indian patriots were now at a hopeless disadvantage. History shows that whenever a nation has no military power it has no influence. Now that the Plains tribes had been disarmed, set afoot, and were dependent upon the government for the very food they ate, agents of that government were making short work of Indian institutions.

This was as silly as it was unfortunate. For the Plains Indian was no Pueblo, content to shine only in his own village. Never narrowly tribal, he was something of an internationalist, as his highly developed sign language shows. Much as he loved his own kin, he was forever visiting, trading, gambling, dancing, hunting, fighting, and intermarrying with people of other tribes. He might hunt in Canada one summer, and raid in Mexico the next; he might spend one winter in the Rockies and pass the next on the Missouri. He bitterly resented his confinement to a reservation, though it might contain eleven million acres. He was a great joiner, always eager to display his talents before a larger audience; the limited prestige attainable in his own tribe had never been enough for him.

Had our Government made more appeal to this dominant trait by providing the tribesmen with better means of attaining status and prestige in the white man's world, the Plains Indians might have adopted our ways sooner and with less difficulty for all concerned. Instead, everything possible was done to humiliate them.

Their religious ceremonies were suppressed; their hunting economy abolished; their political organization shattered; their marriage customs banned; their doctors forbidden to practice; their children carried away to distant schools where, having no written language, they could not communicate with their anxious parents at home; even their favorite foods were withheld; and they were told that they must become like white men—like their oppressors—*without delay*. This frightful tyranny was the work of idealists who called themselves the Indian's "friends," who only wished to do him good.

It is a curious fact that the only dance the white men permitted the Sioux to keep up was the Victory or Scalp Dance, called by the whites the War Dance.

Within a few years the Indian Bureau destroyed the culture of most of the tribes.

But in the view of the pious humanitarians, the process was

all too slow. Their righteous endeavors to save the Indians from the land grabbers in 1882 had focused their earnest attention upon the Sioux, and they soon discovered that the Sioux were "not co-operative" in the drastic measures taken to turn them into white men overnight. This "forcing process" was regarded as wholly unreasonable by Army men and therefore probably all the more insisted upon by the visionaries, who could not rest until the Indian put on a hat, plowed, and attended church regularly.

It now occurred to certain of these "friends of the Indian" (some of whom were themselves living on dividends from lands of their own) that if the Indian could be pauperized he would have to go to work. The obvious method of reducing him to this necessity was to abolish reservations and put the individual Indian on a farm.

To accomplish this worthy purpose—all for the good of the Indian, of course—it only remained to get his lands away from him. This could soon be accomplished by a system of bribery, intimidation, cutting off of rations, and elaborate legal trickery.

Accordingly, many of the same group which had zealously prevented the land grabbers from stealing the Sioux reservation in 1882 now did an about-face, adopted the very program they had just defeated, and set out to "free" the Sioux from most of their property which the Government had given them in payment under provisions of existing treaties. And so the Indian Bureau now had the backing alike of the Indian Ring, the border settlers, the Army, and the pious visionaries. They even persuaded General George Crook to join the Commission to negotiate the sale of Indian lands.

Thus in spite of all that Sitting Bull and the champions of other Indian tribes could do, millions of acres were quickly transferred from Indian to white ownership in ways of which every honest American can only feel ashamed. In 1889 the great Sioux Reservation was broken up.

By that time, people thought, the Indian must be "thoroughly subdued." True, every trick the white men had tried in handling Indians had failed: pacifism, appeasement, disarmament, isolation, bribery, moral suasion, negotiation, swindling, "extermination." None of these nor all together had been sufficient to tame the Plains tribes. It was the destruction of the buffalo which knocked them out.

In that long bitter struggle men on both sides had butchered noncombatants, scalped the dead, taken hostages, looted and burned the homes of their enemies. Though the wars between the troops and war parties were intermittent, fighting between Indians and white men still went on: there was undeclared war on the Plains for almost forty years. During all that time, when an Indian and a white man met, neither ever had or could have any confidence that the other was friendly, for on neither side was there any competent central authority able to control willful individuals. Sitting Bull complained that the Americans had "too many chiefs." The same thing was true of the Indians. But now, it seemed, all that was over. The white men had triumphed.

But the red men still had one recourse. Their long struggle to maintain themselves was not yet over.

26

THE GHOST DANCE

THE PLAINS INDIANS did not attribute their defeat to any superiority of white men. Indeed, I have never met an old-time Plains Indian who did not take it for granted as an obvious fact that the white man was his inferior physically, morally, and in every other way. As I said in my *New Sources of Indian History*, "That old Indian Bureau was the most un-American institution ever known on the continent. Under its rule liberty was not—neither liberty of person, liberty of property, nor liberty of conscience. Church and State were not separate: the missionaries (who had formerly acted as agents) considered the Red Man their property. Nothing that we call American existed at the agencies. No law—only the orders of the agent. No appeal—for the Bureau's acts were not subject to court review. No freedom of speech—for all news, even personal letters, could be censored by the agent. Self-determination for small peoples had not been heard of, the Civil Service was only beginning to extend to Indian Reservations, and the Rights of Man had been lost somewhere between Thomas Jefferson's study and the cabin of Sitting Bull. How any person could expect an Indian to understand, admire, or adopt American institutions on a Reservation where none of them existed is a puzzle."

The Indian attributed the white man's victory to what we call black magic.

As one old warrior put it to me, "Long ago God made a law. This law was based upon the number four, and under that law the Indians prospered. Then came the white man and broke our medicine by adding one to four, making five. This gave him unfair advantage and brought great evils upon the Indians. Consider all the trouble that comes of money—and the white man's money is based upon the five-cent piece."

In short, the Plains Indians believed that they had been conquered not by the enemy but by the enemy gods.

During the ten years since their surrender they had seen everything they loved abolished, swept away as if it had never been. The white man suppressed their religious ceremonies, forbade their medicine men to practice, destroyed their political organization, "broke" their chiefs—if indeed he did not kill them—disarmed and unhorsed their warriors, carried their children away as hostages to far-off schools or threw bad diseases on them—diphtheria, smallpox, measles—to destroy them. The white man had killed their game, taken away most of their lands, cut down the rations he had promised them, and allowed grafting agents and thieving contractors to rob them of the little that remained. The Indian was being swiftly liquidated. What wonder if he turned at last to counter black magic with what he believed a true religion?

Now Indians, even more than other people, like to be on the winning side. They are practical, and have little heart for lost causes. When I was a boy, I remember the Cheyennes and Arapahoes used to get campaign buttons of both presidential candidates. Then, after the election, all turned out wearing the button of the winner.

For many years Christian missionaries had preached the gospel to the Indians. So now what more natural than that these wretched people should turn from their defeated gods to a new religion—the religion of the victors?

Yet the Indian, hungry and heartbroken, had small desire for Christianity as he saw it practiced by his white neighbors. His heart yearned for the old Indian ways, and whatever religious ideas he might take from the whites must be saturated and surrounded by Indian notions of the good life.

Out in Western Nevada about that time, a Paiute Indian dreamer named Wovoka had a vision, and as a result declared himself the Messiah, the Christ of the Second Coming.

Such Messianic dreamers were not uncommon among Indians, but the cults they set up were usually of local extent and short duration.

But now intertribal peace, rapid communciation through the white man's post office, telegraph and railroad, and the mingling of young men of various tribes in government schools made possible the swift dissemination of new ideas. What happened on one reservation was very shortly known on every other.

Wovoka's doctrine was a simple thing: the Messiah had come back, he taught, but because the whites had denied him and crucified him, he was coming this time as an Indian. But he was not coming alone. With him he would bring from the West whole nations of long-dead Indians brought to life, vast herds of buffalo and fast horses to replenish the starving plains. Before him would roll a wave of new earth to cover the old, submerging all white men by supernatural power. Then all Indians, the quick and the dead, would live forever on the regenerated earth.

Wovoka told his followers that if they wished to be spared and to share in this millennium they must dance the dance he would teach them, holding hands and dancing in a circle toward the left, for four nights once in six weeks.

The prophet instructed both men and women to participate,

and forbade anyone to carry arms in the dance. He came to bring peace. The faithful were told not to fear the earthquake which would precede the Messiah's coming, for the magpie feathers he gave them to wear in their hair would serve as wings to waft them high above the wave of new earth and so preserve them.

The doctrine he taught was explained in short and simple terms: "Do no harm to anyone. Do right always. Do not tell lies. Do not fight. When your friends die, you must not cry."

When the wretched Sioux learned of this new doctrine, they held councils and selected delegates to see the Messiah and investigate. They were gone nearly all winter, and returned in the spring of 1890 to report that the Messiah was coming a year later to save his Indian people. Following this news many, perhaps most, of the Sioux threw away everything the white man had given them, abandoned all his works and ways, zealously to carry out the Messiah's wishes.

Apparently Wovoka knew something of sleight-of-hand, and may have had hypnotic powers. For when he showed one of the Sioux delegates his upturned hat, the Sioux, as he afterward reported, "saw the whole world." Some said that Wovoka had the marks of the nails in his hands and feet.

There was a tremendous religious revival. Dances were held on all the reservations and attended by hundreds of Indians. The white men, who thought of all Indian dances as war dances, were needlessly disturbed, for the music of the Ghost Dance was entirely vocal. No drums thumped as the dancers circled around the pole, singing and praying. As they danced, their leaders by various methods threw those dancers who were susceptible into trances. Naturally enough, those entranced saw visions which confirmed Wovoka's doctrine. When they came to themselves, they told how they had seen and talked with relatives and friends long dead. Some of them brought back souvenirs from the spirit world, or even fresh buffalo meat! What better proof could a Sioux ask than that?

To the Plains Indian, religion was a wholly practical matter. He was entirely tolerant and always ready to try any form of prayer that would get results. In his religion there was no devotion and no faith. He was not one to be damned for the glory of God. But he was reverent and ready for miracles, and never more so than in 1890.

"To the starving, grieving Sioux, the new religion promised the restoration of all they had lost—and they had lost everything. Their nation was only a memory, their own people were plotting against them at the agency. If God also had forsaken them, what had they left but the gaunt scaffolds and the long bundles in the cottonwoods along the river? The white man's road led only to the Indian's grave." [1]

But now, they were told, their dead were coming back again, and there were few families who had not lost a child or some older relative during those long years of increasing hardship, famine, pestilence, war and death. Naturally, all these mourners were pitifully eager to meet their dead again.

Like a prairie fire under a high wind, the new cult swept the Plains. The missionaries illogically maintained that the Ghost Dance was not a Christian religion. But on the face of it, no one can believe in the Second Coming of Christ unless he believes in the First. Wherever Indians were unhappy, they began to dance—in spite of their fear that the white men would attempt to stop it just as they had stopped the Sun Dance.

From time immemorial every Indian warrior had tried to induce a vision so as to gain the favor of some supernatural helper and, if successful, he had been accustomed to protect himself by painting upon his body, his shield, his clothing or his pony the conventional symbol of his helper. And when, in the trances of the Ghost Dance, Indians saw their fathers and grandfathers, they naturally saw them as they remembered them, painted with such designs protective against the bullets and arrows of their enemies.

In their long wars with white men, over and over again they had seen their women and children killed. Indeed, the Custer fight and the Battle of the Rosebud were almost the only conflicts of great importance with white troops in which no women and children were killed—simply because Custer and Crook never got into the Indian camp. The massacre on Sand Creek remained a bitter and terrifying memory.

The Indians knew they stood no chance in a battle with the whites, who outnumbered them in the Dakotas seventeen to one. So, fearful that their families would be massacred again if troops came to suppress their dance, the priests of the cult made all the dancers, young and old, wear dresses or shirts of buckskin or old flour sacks sewed together, on which were painted conventional figures of old Indian helpers and deities, protective designs representing buffalo, eagles, turtles, crows, the sun, the moon, the morning star—and the magpie native to Wovoka's country. These garments, they held, were bulletproof. The whites called them "ghost shirts." Short Bull, a Sioux prophet, told his people, "The guns of the soldiers are the only things we are afraid of. But these belong to our Father. He will see that they do us no harm."

None of the Indian agents on the Plains was alarmed by the new cult. Few white men paid it any heed. They said, "Cold weather will stop it. Let them dance themselves out." But the winter was mild and the dancing went on without letup.

In those days the Spoils System ruled the Indian Bureau, and when in 1888 the Republican landslide swept away the Democrats, many experienced Indian agents were displaced. Green hands took over their jobs, many of them new men who had never seen an Indian before and knew nothing of agency politics. Following the system which had brought them to power, they promptly removed all the progressive Indians who had backed up the previous agents appointed by the Democratic party and filled their places at the agency with chiefs and warriors from the stubborn gang of reactionaries and die-hard hostiles.

Pine Ridge was one of the largest and toughest assignments in the service. For years Dr. V. T. McGillycuddy had handled Red Cloud and his hard-bitten Oglala without once calling in troops. He had done this by backing to the limit every Indian who would work for the civilization of the Sioux. Now the new agent, Royer, found himself at the mercy of thousands of Sioux, all itching to follow the lead of Red Cloud, that indefatigable trouble-maker. The Sioux sized him up very quickly. They called Royer "Young-Man-Afraid-of-the-Indians." Before long he telegraphed frantically for soldiers. General John R. Brooke led the troops. He knew even less of Indians than Royer.

When the troops reached Pine Ridge on November 19, 1890, the Ghost Dancers took fright and stampeded westward into the Badlands. Though some of them burned their own homes and haystacks before leaving, they committed no depredations whatever on the whites. But all the papers in the country had sent newshawks to cover the Ghost Dance War and the journalists had to send in copy to justify that expense. No Indian war was ever covered half so well. In truth, the facts were almost completely covered up.

Major James McLaughlin, agent at Standing Rock, had found Sitting Bull a thorn in his flesh. He was totally undisturbed by the Ghost Dance and scoffed at any danger from the Sioux. In reply to an inquiry from the Indian Office, McLaughlin reported that the Sioux "will not be the aggressors in any overt act against white settlers." He added, "If justice is only done them, no uneasiness need be entertained." On November 27 McLaughlin's right-hand man among the

Indians, Jack Carignan, reported in writing, "No trouble need be apprehended from Sitting Bull and his followers, unless they are forced to defend themselves, and I think it would be advisable to keep all strangers, other than employes who have business amongst the Indians, away." He also declared, "The Indians have been told that soldiers are coming down here, and are badly frightened."

But McLaughlin used his report to the Bureau to recommend that Sitting Bull be arrested. Yet, since the agent was unable to offer any valid reason why "Old Bull" should be arrested, the Indian Bureau ignored the suggestion.

But now the Army saw a chance to take a hand in Indian affairs. Buffalo Bill, in whose Wild West Show Sitting Bull had starred for a whole season, saw his opportunity to get free publicity and pose as a hero once more. He and Sitting Bull had got on famously together, and Cody had no fear of the chief. Meeting General Miles at a banquet, Buffalo Bill persuaded the General to give him authority to arrest the chief. The General scribbled the order for arrest on the back of his visiting card.

When Cody, leading a squad of newspapermen, presented his authority to the agent at Standing Rock, McLaughlin was caught flat-footed. But he was not easily bested. Like all Bureau men, he resented any attempt by the Army to poke its nose into Indian affairs: if any arrests were to be made, he would make them. The officers at Fort Yates also resented the interference of a civilian scout like Buffalo Bill in Army business. He was, in their opinion, "just a beef contractor turned showman." And so McLaughlin easily persuaded the officers at Fort Yates to co-operate in foiling Buffalo Bill. All that night, in relays, they entertained Cody at the Officers' Club, vainly attempting to put the famous scout under the table. Next morning Cody, fresh as a daisy, set off to bring Sitting Bull in. But McLaughlin, by sending him a false message as to Sitting Bull's whereabouts, was able to delay Cody until he could get the order of General Miles rescinded. Indignantly Cody left Standing Rock.

Although McLaughlin was rid of Cody, he could not so easily keep the Army out. Soon after, the commanding officer at Fort Yates received orders to arrest Sitting Bull. However, McLaughlin was able to persuade him to let a force of forty Indian policemen go first and make the actual arrest. The troops were to follow in support. Early on the morning of December 15, 1890, in the darkness before a cold drizzling dawn, Lieutenant Bullhead led his policemen into Sitting Bull's camp. Swiftly they entered the chief's log cabin, struck a light, and dragged him naked from his bed.

The police were on a dangerous mission. Few of them were members of Sitting Bull's own tribe of Sioux, and several were personal enemies of the chief. They well knew that every warrior in his camp would bitterly resent their coming to carry him off. Yet they were brave, and hurried him into his clothes as quickly as might be. But by the time his horse was saddled they found the cabin and their little force surrounded by a threatening swarm of old-time warriors.

Catch-the-Bear, leader of Sitting Bull's bodyguard, hated Lieutenant Bullhead, chief of the Indian police. As soon as he could find him in the dim light he shot Bullhead down, mortally wounded.

As Bullhead fell, he fired into Sitting Bull's body. At the same moment Red Tomahawk shot the chief in the head from behind. Sitting Bull was dead before he hit the ground.

Then began a fierce hand-to-hand fight, Sioux against Sioux, in a fog of powder smoke. Within a few minutes twelve were dead and three others badly wounded, two of these mortally. Four of the twelve dead Indians were policemen. But for the timely arrival of the troops, probably no policeman would have escaped alive.

The killing of Sitting Bull terrified all the Indians up and down Grand River. They offered no resistance to the troops, but hurried southwest to the camps of their relatives on the Cheyenne River Reservation. Some were stopped and encouraged to return, but thirty-eight frightened, weary, half-starved refugees finally reached the camp of Chief Big Foot, more than a hundred miles away. Big Foot made them welcome and fed them from his scanty rations. Later he defended his conduct in these words: "No one with a heart could have done any less."

Meanwhile the Army was moving to round up all the bands and principal chiefs on the Sioux reservations, and already an order had come through to arrest Big Foot and send him as a prisoner to Fort Meade. At that time Big Foot's people were heading for the agency to draw their rations, and the officers with the troops decided not to make the arrest until the Indians reached the agency.

However, the weather grew so cold that the women and children became reluctant to travel. When Colonel E. V. Sumner sent word that they *must* go, his messenger was too emphatic and threatening, telling the Indians that soldiers would come in the morning to get them and "to shoot them if they refused to go." At the same time the frightened Sioux learned of another force moving in their direction from Fort Bennett. That night Big Foot's band, taking only their ponies and tipis, hightailed it toward the Badlands along White River.

The news that Sitting Bull had been killed "without cause" scared Indians on several reservations into a new stampede toward the Badlands. But their flight had no military purpose. As the Commissioner of Indian affairs reported, "No signal fires were built, no warlike demonstrations were made, no violence was done to any white settler, nor was there cohesion or organization among the Indians themselves. Many of them were friendly Indians who had never participated in the Ghost

Dance, but had fled . . . from fear of soldiers . . . or through the overpersuasion of friends. The military gradually began to close in around them and they offered no resistance, so that a speedy and quiet capitulation of all was confidently expected."

27

WOUNDED KNEE

THE SIOUX INDIAN reservations were strung along the Missouri River almost continuously from Standing Rock in North Dakota to the Rosebud Reservation, which extended to the northern boundary of Nebraska. Directly west of Rosebud lay the Pine Ridge Reservation of the Oglala Sioux, in South Dakota, for the most part south and east of White River. The Pine Ridge agency stood close to the Nebraska line in the southwest corner of the reservation on White Clay Creek.

Northwest of the agency, some fifty miles beyond White River, yet within the reservation, lay the desolate Badlands, a rugged, broken and confused country, strange and colorful, containing a level plateau or mesa of considerable extent. A number of small streams flowed northwest from these Badlands into Cheyenne River. Such wild and broken country offered the only refuge for the frightened "hostiles."

On Christmas Day there was a clash between the Cheyenne government scouts on Battle Creek, north of the Badlands, and a party of Sioux led by Kicking Bear, one of the leaders of the Ghost Dance. The cause of this fracas is not clear, but it was certainly not an attack on the whites.

Three days later Big Foot was overtaken with 106 warriors and 250 women and children, a total of 356 souls. They immediately surrendered without any resistance whatever, and moved on with the troops to Wounded Knee Creek, twenty miles northeast of the Pine Ridge agency. All together there were eight troops of the Seventh Cavalry, with four Hotchkiss guns, and one company of scouts, a total of 470 fighting men to guard Big Foot's frightened handful.

Indeed the disproportion was even greater, since some of Big Foot's warriors consented to act as scouts and went out looking for Kicking Bear's camp, hoping to bring it peacefully in to the agency. By that time all the Indians had left the Badlands and were streaming back to the agency. Big Foot himself was in no condition to make trouble, even had he had any wish to do so. He was in bed with pneumonia.

Soldiers surrounded the camp, and next morning the warriors were ordered out of the tents. It was just two weeks after Sitting Bull had been disarmed and then shot down by men in blue coats. The four Hotchkiss guns, on a nearby rise, were trained on the Indian camp. A shallow dry ravine ran down to the creek near the Indian tents.

It was cold. Warriors came out muffled in their blankets and sat down in a line facing the soldiers. It was clear that the Indians had no desire for a fight, and certainly the white officers seem not to have expected one. There had never been any trouble on the Cheyenne River Reservation, and Big Foot's band had committed no depredations whatever.

But they knew that orders had been issued to disarm them and take them to the railroad. For all they knew, they were going to be sent off to a Florida prison like their allies, the Southern Cheyennes. Perhaps they might be shot down after they were disarmed, like Sitting Bull. In any case it was humiliating to give up their weapons, and they had also heard that all their horses would be taken from them.

They had been hungry and frightened: that was their only

offense. They well knew that resistance meant death. Yet some may have felt that "it would be better to die all together."

The warriors were sent into their tents to bring out their guns. They brought out a few—so few that soldiers were sent in to make a search. These drove the frightened women and children from the tents. It was not easy for the warriors to sit there and listen and wonder what might be going on in their tipis.

Not finding many weapons in the tents, the troops came out and prepared to search the warriors. Now, laying hands upon a wild Indian was a dangerous undertaking, and as General Nelson A. Miles reported to the Commissioner of Indian Affairs, when the troops closed in to search the Indians, "a scuffle occurred between one warrior, who had a rifle in his hand and two soldiers. The rifle was discharged."

One of the warriors lost his head and fired at the troops. Standing only one or two paces distant, so near that the guns of the two parties were almost touching, the soldiers fired a volley, mowing down nearly half the warriors.

Then began a terrible struggle hand-to-hand, all the more desperate and bloody because the warriors were armed for the most part only with knives, clubs, or revolvers.

Meanwhile the Hotchkiss guns, already trained on the tents where the women and children stood watching, poured their explosive shells down the slope, making terrible havoc there.

Within a few minutes some 200 Indians, men, women and children, and sixty soldiers lay dead or wounded on the frozen ground. The tipis were knocked over by the shells or stood burning above the helpless wounded, while a handful of Indians, mostly women and children, some of them wounded, fled in wild panic down the dry ravine, pursued by hundreds of maddened soldiers and raked by merciless fire from the Hotchkiss guns.

In blind rage the infuriated soldiers pursued the fugitives

so far that some bodies were later found fully two miles from the spot where the fight began. This massacre was the less excusable, inasmuch as Colonel J. W. Forsyth had separated the women and children from the men before the fight began.

The soldiers manning the Hotchkiss guns must have known they were firing on women and children, since they could not fire on the warriors because of the proximity of their own troops. If, as is claimed, an Indian fired the first shot, the troops were certainly justified in defending themselves and killing the warriors, and it is possible that some of the soldiers were unable to distinguish an Indian man, with his long hair, from an Indian woman. But the wholesale butchery of so many helpless noncombatants made the so-called Battle of Wounded Knee a massacre.

The Indians at the Pine Ridge agency had just been induced to come back from the Badlands. When they heard the firing at Wounded Knee and later saw the terrified and bleeding survivors at their camp, they hardly knew whether to fight or run. Some rode quickly off to the battlefield where the soldiers, two hours later, were still going over the field hunting down survivors and gathering up their dead and wounded. The outraged Sioux drove the soldiers back and forced them to dig in.

Meanwhile Two Strike and his Brûlé warriors attacked the agency. General Brooke sent fifty Indian police to defend it. They loyally fought off their own relatives and prevented Two Strike from burning the agency. Meanwhile the big camp moved away from the agency to White Clay Creek.

On the 30th the Sioux attacked a detachment of the Ninth Cavalry, a Negro outfit, on their way in from the Badlands. Soon after, a messenger came to report an attack being made on the Catholic mission. Brooke sent Forsyth and eight troops of the Seventh Cavalry to drive off the hostiles. They found the mission unharmed, for the Indians were not killing noncombatants. But the warriors swarmed round Forsyth, pressing him so hard that three times he sent for reinforcements.

That day—for the second time—the Sioux were too much for the Seventh. But the Ninth Cavalry, which had already ridden ninety miles and fought one engagement within twenty-four hours, rode out and rescued Forsyth.

The weather had turned bitter cold. There was a heavy snow, and after that a blizzard. Yet it was not until New Year's Day that anyone thought of going out to bring in the Indian wounded. Some women and children, including four babies whom their dying mothers had wrapped in their own blankets, were found still alive. All the wounded were also frozen. Several survived, however. The white men stripped the dead to get the ghost shirts for souvenirs and then tossed the naked frozen bodies helter-skelter into a trench. One who saw that said, "It was a thing to melt the heart of a man, if it was of stone, to see those little children, with their bodies shot to pieces, thrown naked into the pit." But none of the missionaries went out to read the burial service.

There were a few skirmishes early in January; then the "Ghost Dance War" was over.

During all this while the government Indian scouts—Cheyenne, Crow and Sioux—were faithful to a man and earned the warmest commendation of their officers.

After the massacre there was a last frantic spasm of passing the buck between the Indian Bureau and the War Department, and for a time Army officers served as agents in Sioux country. But now, ever since the forty years of fighting ended, Plains Indians have been left entirely to the tender mercies of the Indian Bureau.

Dr. McGillycuddy wrote on January 15, 1891, "Up to date there has been neither a Sioux outbreak or war. No citizen in Nebraska or Dakota has been killed, molested, or can show the scratch of a pin, and no property has been destroyed off the reservation." The trouble lasted all of thirty-two days, but only one white noncombatant was killed—a herder named Miller, on the reservation. Lieutenant E. W. Casey, in charge of Cheyenne scouts, was shot while spying on the hostile camp. But his killer, Plenty Horses, was acquitted by the Federal Court on the grounds that the Sioux were then at war.

Off the reservation three white men attacked an old Indian and his family, bringing a load of meat home from a hunt in the Black Hills. They killed the old man, Few Tails, and shot down his wife too. She, however, survived and managed to get home, hiding in the daytime and traveling by night.

When General Miles called upon Young-Man-Afraid-of-His-Horses to surrender the slayers of Casey and the herder, the old chief replied indignantly, "No; I will not surrender them. But if you will bring the white men who killed Few Tails, I will bring in the Indians who killed the white soldier and the herder; and right out here in front of your tipi I will have my young men shoot the Indians and you have your soldiers shoot the white men, and then we will have done with the whole business."

General Miles persuaded the chiefs to bring in their warriors, hand over their guns, and surrender the leaders of the Ghost Dance cult. These conditions were promptly complied with, Kicking Bear and Short Bull voluntarily giving themselves up. Miles issued rations to the Indians, and that night they enjoyed the first full meal they had known in several weeks.

If we include the fight in which Sitting Bull died, the Ghost Dance campaign cost the lives of forty-nine men on the side of the Government and of some 300 Indians. The total expense for this thirty days of unnecessary bloodshed was somewhat more than a million dollars. In addition, one church, two schoolhouses, a bridge and fifty-three Indian cabins were burned, to say nothing of haystacks, farm machinery, and government cattle destroyed.

Meanwhile, far south among the Kiowa, in Oklahoma, Wooden Lance was mourning the death of a favorite child. Brooding over his loss, he determined to visit the Messiah in person, in the hope of being able to talk again with the spirit of his child. The Kiowa chiefs forthwith appointed him a delegate for the tribe. It was a long journey to Nevada, but Wooden Lance kept on, moving from one reservation to another, until he came at last to the wickiup of Wovoka in Mason Valley. There he had to wait one day before being admitted.

When he entered he saw a man lying down, his face covered with a blanket, singing to himself.[1] When he had finished his song, the Messiah uncovered his face and asked Wooden Lance—through an interpreter—what he wanted. As the reverent Kiowa had supposed that the Messiah knew all things and had the gift of tongues, he was amazed and disconcerted at such a question. However, Wooden Lance identified himself, told why he had come so far, and begged to see his dead.

Wovoka declared this impossible.

"There are no spirits here," he said.

At this cruel disappointment, Wooden Lance began to look for further evidence that the Messiah was genuine. Many Indians had claimed that Wovoka was the Christ and bore the marks of the nails upon his hands and feet. Wooden Lance, not seeing any such scars, inquired whether Wovoka was in truth the Messiah.

Wovoka then declared there was but one Messiah, himself. Then he went on to say, "I taught the Indians a new dance. But the Sioux twisted things and have made so much trouble that now you had better go home and tell the Kiowa to drop the whole business."

Sick at heart, Wooden Lance left the false prophet's wickiup, returned home, and reported to his people. That ended the Ghost Dance on the Southern Plains.

There was no longer any hope of escape into the past. But the old-time Plains Indian was a practical man. The Ghost Dance had not worked, it was "no good." There was no use whining over that. . . .

Early one morning a wrinkled old warrior, with his blanket around him, walked about the Cheyenne camp and in the high-pitched voice of a herald harangued his people:

"Hoo-oo! My children, my children. In days behind, many times I called you to travel the hunting trail or to follow the war trail. Now those trails are choked with sand; they are covered with grass, the young men cannot find them.

"My children, today I call you to travel a new trail, the only trail now open—the White Man's Road."

Appendix

>>>><<<<

ACKNOWLEDGMENTS

>>>><<<<

DURING some forty years the Plains Indians, their history and ways, have been my favorite study. I visited most of the tribes of importance on the Plains in this country and in Canada, and listened to all their old men who were willing to talk. And I have seldom missed a chance to talk with any old-timer—soldier, official, cowboy, missionary, historian or scientist—who could instruct me. It is therefore quite impossible to remember and record the manifold assistance I have received in preparing this book. I can mention only a few individuals here who have been especially helpful:

I. *Indians:* Cheyennes: Bob Tail Horse, George Bent, Comes-in-Sight, Edmond Guerrier, Hump, Roman Nose Thunder, Willis Rowland, Young Two Moon. Sioux: Circling Hawk, Robert P. Higheagle, Old Bull, Chief One Bull, Weasel Bear, Chief White Bull.

II. *White Persons:* Miss Ina T. Aulls, the late General W. C. Brown, Dr. E. E. Dale, Dr. Clyde Fisher, Professor Percy Fritz, Mr. T. J. Gatchell, the late George Bird Grinnell, Mr. L. R. Hafen, Mr. Reese Kincaide, Professor H. G. Merriam, Captain Luther North, Mr. J. L. Rader, Dr. C. C. Rister, Mr. Will G. Robinson, Mr. Martin F. Schmitt, the late John Homer Seger, Mr. W. M. Stirling, Mr. Howard Van Zandt, Mr. Paul I. Wellman, Dr. Clark Wissler, Mr. L. B. Wood, Mr. Frank Zahn, Mrs. Frances Franks, my secretary, and Mr. Guy M. Steele, Jr., who prepared the maps for the book.

It is also a pleasure to express my debt to all those in charge of the files of the National Archives, the Army War College (Historical Section), the Department of State, the War Department, the Office of the Commissioner of Indian Affairs, the Bureau of American Ethnology, the American Museum of Natural History, the Order of Indian Wars, the Western History Department of the Denver Public Library, the Phillips Collection in the University of Oklahoma Library, and the historical societies of all the States in the Plains area. My grateful acknowledgments are due to those in charge of the Canadian Public Archives, the files of the Royal Canadian Mounted Police, and the Provincial Legislative Library at Regina, Saskatchewan.

I am also happy to express my gratitude to the publishers and authors listed below for their gracious permission to reprint passages from their books, as follows:

To the American Museum of Natural History for quotations from *North American Indians of the Plains*, by Dr. Clark Wissler.

To the Bureau of American Ethnology, Smithsonian Institution, for passages quoted from *Calendar History of the Kiowa Indians* and *The Ghost Dance Religion and the Sioux Outbreak of 1890*, both by James Mooney.

To *The Frontier* for the passage quoted from that periodical in Chapter IV.

To the Houghton Mifflin Company for passages quoted from my *Sitting Bull, Champion of the Sioux* and my *The Old Santa Fe Trail*.

To Alfred A. Knopf, Inc., for the passage quoted from *Crazy Horse, the Strange Man of the Oglalas*, by Mari Sandoz.

To Paul I. Wellman for the passage quoted from *Death on the Prairie*, by Paul I. Wellman.

To Charles Scribner's Sons for passages quoted from *The Fighting Cheyennes*, by George Bird Grinnell, and for the use of two maps from that book.

To the South Dakota Historical Society for the passage quoted from their *Collections*, Vol. I.

To the University of Oklahoma Press for the passages quoted from: *Border Command*, by Carl Coke Rister; *General George Crook: His Autobiography*, edited and annotated by Martin F. Schmitt; *Carbine and Lance: The Story of Old Fort Sill*, by Captain W. S. Nye; *Red Cloud's Folk, A History of the Oglala Sioux Indians*, by George E. Hyde; *New Sources of Indian History 1850–1891. The Ghost Dance—The Prairie Sioux: A Miscellany*, by Stanley Vestal; and for permission to use the map of the Battle of the Washita in *Border Command: General Phil Sheridan in the West*, by Carl Coke Rister.

As indicated above, I have quoted certain pertinent passages from other books of mine. For, when once I have cast an idea into the best phrasing I can find, I should think myself unfaithful to my readers if I melted it down again into a soupy paraphrase merely for the sake of novel verbiage. There are few synonymous words in English—and no synonymous paragraphs.

➤➤➤➤◄◄◄◄

NOTES

➤➤➤➤◄◄◄◄

Chapter 1

1. *Five Years a Dragoon ('49-'54) and other Adventures on the Great Plains*, by Percival G. Lowe, pp. 82 and 83.

2. THE PLAINS INDIANS.

A. *True Plains Tribes:* These nomads lived on the prairies, hunted buffalo, dwelt in skin tipis, rode horses, were governed by warrior or "soldier" societies, and held an annual Sun Dance. (Names of the principal tribes are in capital letters.)

I.   The Northern Tribes

a. ASSINIBOINE
b. BLACKFOOT
c. CROW
d. GROS VENTRES OF THE
   PRAIRIE (Atsina)

e. Plains-Cree
f. Plains-Ojibway
g. Sarsi
h. TETON-DAKOTA
   (Prairie Sioux)

II.   The Southern Tribes

a. ARAPAHO
b. CHEYENNE

c. COMANCHE
d. KIOWA

e. Kiowa-Apache

B. *Marginal (Sedentary) Tribes:* Most of these dwelt in the forests or mountains, farmed, and lived part of the year in permanent houses of earth, grass, or bark. But they hunted on the Plains and warred with the Plains Indians.

III. The Village, or Eastern Tribes

a. Arikara (Rickaree, or Ree)
b. Hidatsa (Minnitaree, or Gros Ventres of the Village)
c. Iowa
d. Kansas (Kaw)
e. Mandan
f. Missouri

g. Wichita
h. Omaha
i. Osage
j. Oto
k. Pawnee
l. Ponca
m. Santee-Dakota

IV. The Plateau, or Western Tribes

a. Bannock
b. Nez Percé
c. Wind River Shoshone (Snake)

d. Northern Shoshone
e. Ute

I have added some explanatory material to the table above, quoted by permission from *North American Indians of the Plains*, by Clark Wissler, American Museum of Natural History, New York, 1912, p. 17.

3. Percival G. Lowe, *op. cit.*

Chapter 3

1. *The Fighting Cheyennes*, by George Bird Grinnell, p. 101. Charles Scribner's Sons.

Chapter 4

1. Stanley Vestal, in *The Frontier*, Vol. XII, No. 3, p. 269, March, 1932, "Sitting Bull's Maiden Speech." Reprinted by permission, Montana State University.

2. *South Dakota Historical Collections*, Vol. I, pp. 366–368. Reprinted here, with slight changes, by permission, South Dakota Historical Society.

Chapter 5

1. *A History of Minnesota*, by William Watts Fowell, p. 232.
2. *Sitting Bull: Champion of the Sioux*, by Stanley Vestal, pp. 55–56.

Chapter 6

1. *Personal Narratives of the Battles of the Rebellion*, No. 5.
2. *Carbine and Lance, The Story of Old Fort Sill*, by Captain W. S. Nye, p. 47, University of Oklahoma Press.

Chapter 7

1. See *Condition of the Indian Tribes*, Report of the Joint Special Committee under Joint Resolution of March 3, 1865, pp. 26–98.
2. *The Indian Campaign of Winter of 1864–65*, written in 1877 by Maj. Gen. Grenville M. Dodge and read to the Colorado Commandery of the Loyal Legion of the United States at Denver, April 21, 1907, pp. 16–17.
3. See *The Kearney Herald*, January 6, 1866; also *Jim Bridger*, by Stanley Vestal, pp. 244–245.

Chapter 8

1. *Sitting Bull*, by Stanley Vestal, p. 72, Houghton Mifflin Company.

Chapter 9

1. Unpublished notebook of George A. Boehmer, No. 2066 in the files of the Bureau of American Ethnology, Washington, D. C.
2. George Bird Grinnell, *op. cit.*, p. 225.
3. *Ibid.*, pp. 234–235.

Chapter 12

1. See Photograph No. 3678 in the Indian files of the Bureau of American Ethnology, Washington, D. C. The name "Roman Nose," in Cheyenne "Hooked Nose" or "Aquiline Nose," was

common in the tribe. The photograph (No. 345, Bureau of American Ethnology, taken in 1899) generally published as that of the famous warrior is of a different Indian, Henry Roman Nose, who wears a hat and store clothes. Roman Nose Canyon, near Watonga, Oklahoma, was named for yet another Cheyenne of the same name.

2. George Bird Grinnell, *op. cit.*, pp. 272–273.

3. The making of this bonnet, its powers and care, are described by George Bird Grinnell in *The Cheyenne Indians*, Vol. II, pp. 119 ff.

4. *The Fighting Cheyennes*, by George Bird Grinnell, pp. 276–277. By permission of the publishers, Charles Scribner's Sons.

Chapter 13

1. Reprinted by permission of the Kansas State Historical Society, from Vol. VI of the *Kansas Historical Collections*.

2. Senate Executive Document No. 18, of the Fortieth Congress, Third Session, pp. 4–5.

Chapter 14

1. Capt. W. S. Nye, *op. cit.*, p. 83.

Chapter 15

1. George Bird Grinnell, *op. cit.*, p. 300. By permission.

Chapter 16

1. Capt. W. S. Nye, *op. cit.*, p. 181. By permission.

2. Bureau of American Ethnology, Seventeenth Annual Report. "Calendar History of the Kiowa Indians," by James Mooney, p. 329.

Chapter 17

1. An excellent, detailed account of all Red Cloud's relations with the government will be found in *Red Cloud's Folk*, by George E. Hyde, University of Oklahoma Press, 1937.

Chapter 19

1. Stanley Vestal, *op. cit.*, p. 142. Reprinted by courtesy of the publishers, Houghton Mifflin Company.
2. *The Life and Adventures of Frank Grouard*, by Joe DeBarthe, p. 193.
3. See *Warpath*, by Stanley Vestal, pp. 180 ff.

Chapter 20

1. This chapter thus far is from *Sitting Bull*, by Stanley Vestal. Quoted by permission of the publishers, Houghton Mifflin Company.
2. *Death on the Prairie*, by Paul I. Wellman, pp. 142–144. By permission.
3. *My Story*, by Brig. Gen. Anson Mills.
4. *Ibid.*
5. Lt. James H. Bradley. See *Memoirs of a White Crow Indian*, by Thomas B. Marquis, p. 249.
6. See Stanley Vestal, *Warpath*, Ch. XIX; also George Bird Grinnell, *op. cit.*, Ch. XXV; also Lewis F. Crawford, *Rekindling Camp-Fires*, Ch. XXVII.

Chapter 21

1. *Sitting Bull*, by Stanley Vestal, pp. 165–166. By permission of the publishers.
2. For another instance of this man's suicidal bravery see *Sitting Bull: Champion of the Sioux*, by Stanley Vestal, pp. 226–228. My information comes from Bob-Tail-Horse himself. See also George Bird Grinnell, *op. cit.*, p. 338.
3. Stanley Vestal, *op. cit.*, pp. 178–179. By permission of the publishers.

Chapter 23

1. George Bird Grinnell, *op. cit.*, p. 360. By permission.
2. See *The Frontier Trail*, by Col. Homer W. Wheeler, Los Angeles, 1923, p. 186. These grisly trophies are described in detail

and illustrated in color in *My Life and Experiences among Our Hostile Indians*, by Gen. O. O. Howard, pp. 542 ff. After High Wolf surrendered, he moved heaven and earth to get this necklace back. S. V.

3. *MacKenzie's Last Fight with the Cheyennes: A Winter Campaign in Wyoming and Montana*, by Capt. John G. Bourke, p. 27.

4. *Ibid.*

5. *Crazy Horse*, by Mari Sandoz, pp. 407–408, Alfred A. Knopf, Inc. Reprinted by permission.

Chapter 24

1. George Bird Grinnell, *op. cit.*, pp. 386–388.

2. *Ibid.*, p. 389.

3. *The Old Santa Fe Trail*, by Stanley Vestal, pp. 167–168, Houghton Mifflin Company. Quoted by permission of the publishers.

Chapter 25

1. See Report of the Commission, appointed by direction of the President of the United States under instructions of the Honorable the Secretary of War and the Secretary of the Interior to meet the Sioux Indian Chief, Sitting Bull, with a view to avert hostile incursions into the territory of the United States from the Dominion of Canada, Washington, 1877, and the Canadian records found in *Sessional Papers*, 3 to 4, No. 4, Vol. XI, No. 5, 41 Victoria A. 1878, Appendix D.

Chapter 26

1. *Sitting Bull: Champion of the Sioux*, by Stanley Vestal, p. 278, Houghton Mifflin Company.

Chapter 27

1. See *The Ghost Dance Religion*, by James Mooney, p. 913, Bureau of American Ethnology.

BIBLIOGRAPHY

>>>>‹‹‹‹

A COMPLETE bibliography on our relations with the Indians of the Plains would rival a telephone directory in bulk. Here, in addition to the sources mentioned in the Notes and Acknowledgments, are listed the most pertinent authorities:

Bent, George, "Forty Years with the Cheyennes" (edited by George Hyde), in *The Frontier*.

Bourke, Captain John G., *MacKenzie's Last Fight with the Cheyennes: A Winter Campaign in Wyoming and Montana*. Governor's Island, N. Y. H., 1890.

——, *On the Border with Crook*. New York, 1891.

Brill, Charles J., *Conquest of the Southern Plains*. Oklahoma City, 1938.

Bureau of American Ethnology, Annual Reports.

Byrne, P. E., *Soldiers of the Plains*. New York, 1926.

Clark, W. P., *The Indian Sign Language*. Philadelphia, 1885.

Commissioner of Indian Affairs, Annual Reports to 1891.

Crawford, Lewis F., *Rekindling Camp-Fires*. Bismarck, 1926.

Crook, George, *General George Crook: His Autobiography*. Edited and annotated by Martin F. Schmitt. University of Oklahoma Press, Norman, 1946.

Custer, Mrs. Elizabeth B., *Boots and Saddles*. New York, 1885.

Custer, General George Armstrong, *My Life on the Plains*. New York, 1874.

DeBarthe, Joe, *Life and Adventures of Frank Grouard*. St. Joseph, Missouri, 1894.

Dixon, Olive K., *The Life of Billy Dixon*. Dallas, 1927.

Dodge, Major General Grenville M., *Indian Campaign of Winter of 1864–65*. Written in 1877 and read to the Colorado Commandery of the Loyal Legion of the United States at Denver, April 21, 1907.

Downey, Fairfax, *Indian-Fighting Army*. New York, 1941.

Dunn, Jacob P., *Massacres of the Mountains*. New York, 1886.

Finerty, John F., *Warpath and Bivouac*. Chicago, 1890.

Folwell, Dr. William Watts, *A History of Minnesota*, published by Minnesota State Historical Society.

Forsyth, Colonel G. A., *Thrilling Days of Army Life*. New York, 1900.

Grinnell, George Bird, *The Fighting Cheyennes*. New York, 1915.

——, *Two Great Scouts and the Pawnee Battalion*. Cleveland, 1928.

Hodge, F. W., *Handbook of American Indians North of Mexico*. 2 vols. Bureau of American Ethnology, Bulletin 30, Washington, D. C., 1907–10.

Hyde, George E., *Red Cloud's Folk*. University of Oklahoma Press, Norman, 1937.

Kappler, Charles J., *Indian Affairs, Laws and Treaties*. 2 vols. Compilation. U. S. Document 319, Fifty-Eighth Congress, Second Session. Washington, D. C., 1904.

Keim, De B. Randolph, *Sheridan's Troopers on the Border: A Winter Campaign on the Plains*. Philadelphia, 1870.

Kelly, Fanny, *Narrative of My Captivity Among the Sioux*. Hartford, 1891.

Lowe, Percival G., *Five Years a Dragoon ('49 to '54) and Other Adventures on the Great Plains*. Kansas City, 1906.

McGillycuddy, Julia B., *McGillycuddy, Agent*. Stanford University Press, Stanford, 1941.

McLaughlin, James, *My Friend the Indian*. Boston, 1910.

Miles, General Nelson A., *Personal Recollections of General Nelson A. Miles*. Chicago, 1897.

Mills, General Anson, *My Story*. Published by the author. Washington, D. C., 1918.

Mooney, James, *The Cheyenne Indians*, Memoirs, American Anthropological Association, Vol. I, Part 6, pp. 357–642. Lancaster, Pa., 1907.

——, *Calendar History of the Kiowa Indians*. Seventeenth Annual Report, Bureau of American Ethnology. Washington, D. C., 1898.

——, *The Ghost Dance Religion and the Sioux Outbreak of 1890*. Fourteenth Annual Report, Bureau of American Ethnology. Part II. Washington, D. C., 1895.

Nye, Captain W. S., *Carbine and Lance: The Story of Old Fort Sill*. University of Oklahoma Press, Norman, 1937.

Palmer, H. E., "History of the Powder River Indian Expedition of 1865." Nebraska State Historical Society *Transactions*, Vol. II. Lincoln, 1887.

Personal Narratives of the Battles of the Rebellion, No. 5. Providence, R. I., 1878.

Proceedings of Council with the Comanches, Kiowas, Arapahoes and Apaches at Medicine Lodge Creek, Kansas. October 19, 1867.

Record of Engagements with Hostile Indians, 1868–1882. Official Compilation.

Rister, Carl Coke, *Border Captives*. University of Oklahoma Press, Norman, 1940.

——, *Border Command: General Phil Sheridan in the West*. University of Oklahoma Press, Norman, 1944.

Rogers, Fred B., *Soldiers of the Overland* (Being Some Account of the Services of General Patrick Edward Connor and his Volunteers in the Old West). San Francisco, 1938.

Sandoz, Mari, *Crazy Horse, the Strange Man of the Oglalas*. New York, 1942.

Satterlee, Marion P., *Outbreak and Massacre by the Dakota Indians in Minnesota in 1862*. Minneapolis, 1923.

Secretary of War, Annual Reports to 1891.

Sheridan, General P. H., *Personal Memoirs*. 2 vols. New York, 1888.

Sherman, William Tecumseh, *Memoirs*. New York, 1891.

Stanley, Henry M., *My Early Travels and Adventures*. 2 vols. New York, 1895.

United States Congress, Joint Special Committee, *Condition of the Indian Tribes*. Washington, D. C., 1867. Also published as Senate Report 156, Thirty-Ninth Congress, Second Session.

Van de Water, Frederic F., *Glory-Hunter*. Indianapolis, 1934.

Vestal, Stanley, *Jim Bridger*. New York, 1946.

——, *New Sources of Indian History*. University of Oklahoma Press, Norman, 1934.

——, *The Old Santa Fe Trail*. Boston, 1939.

——, *Sitting Bull, Champion of the Sioux*. Boston, 1932.

——, *Warpath, The True Story of the Sioux Wars, Told in a Biography of Chief White Bull*. Boston, 1934.

Warren, G. K., *Exploration in the Dacota Country*. Senate Document 76, Thirty-Fourth Congress, First Session. Washington, D. C., 1856.

Wellman, Paul I., *Death on the Prairie*. New York, 1934.

Wheeler, Colonel Homer W., *Buffalo Days*. Brooklyn, 1923.

Windolph, Charles, *I Fought with Custer: The Story of Sergeant Charles Windolph*. As told to Frazier and Robert Hunt. New York, 1947.

Wissler, Dr. Clark, *North American Indians of the Plains*. New York, 1912.

THE AUTHOR

Stanley Vestal in private life is Professor Walter Stanley Campbell of the University of Oklahoma. He is an outstanding authority on American frontier history, particularly that of the Indians and has written a formidable list of books, both scholarly and popular, on the subject.

Born in Kansas and educated at Western universities, he was a Rhodes Scholar in Merton College, Oxford, from 1908-1911, taking his Master's Degree and his Doctorate in Literature in studies in the English language. He was a Fellow of the Guggenheim Memorial Foundation in 1930-1931, and served as a Captain in the Army in 1917-1918. Throughout his life Professor Campbell has made American frontier history his special interest; in addition to his academic work in that field he has spent much time visiting the scenes of battles and campaigns, and getting the first-hand recollections of survivors who participated in the events. He is a member of Phi Beta Kappa and is at present Professor of English at the University of Oklahoma.

Among his books are:

Kit Carson

Sitting Bull

King of the Fur Traders

The Old Santa Fe Trail

Mountain Men

Revolt on the Border

The Missouri

Jim Bridger

SOUTHERN
AREA